"Dabashi's book is both a panoramic critique of,
and a revolt against, dominant forms of knowledge.
It is characteristically lucid and accessible.
A worthwhile read."
WAEL HALLAQ, Columbia University

"Dabashi eloquently articulates the intellectual journey
of a whole generation of postcolonial thinkers:
its findings must be heard."
ELIZABETH SUZANNE KASSAB,
author of *Contemporary Arab Thought*

"*Can Non-Europeans Think?* collects Hamid Dabashi's
important provocations on issues ranging from postcolonialism to democracy. These are pieces to wrestle with,
to think about, to discuss and debate. Reading Dabashi is
like going for an extended coffee with a very smart friend."
VIJAY PRASHAD, author of *The Poorer Nations:
A Possible History of the Global South*

"Can non-Europeans think? The simple answer
is yes. The more complicated answer is also yes,
but requires that the reader dismantles the very notion
of 'West' and 'European.' This is a fabulous read."
ZILLAH EISENSTEIN, author of *Sexual Decoys*
and *The Audacity of Races and Gender*

ABOUT THE AUTHOR

Hamid Dabashi is the Hagop Kevorkian Professor of Iranian Studies and Comparative Literature at Columbia University. Born in Iran, he received a dual Ph.D. in the sociology of culture and Islamic studies from the University of Pennsylvania, followed by a postdoctoral fellowship at Harvard University. Dabashi has written and edited many books, including *Iran, the Green Movement and the USA* and *The Arab Spring*, as well as numerous chapters, essays, articles and book reviews. He is an internationally renowned cultural critic, whose writings have been translated into numerous languages.

Dabashi has been a columnist for the Egyptian *Al-Ahram Weekly* for over a decade, and is a regular contributor to Al Jazeera and CNN. He has been a committed teacher for nearly three decades and is also a public speaker, a current affairs essayist, a staunch anti-war activist and the founder of Dreams of a Nation. He has four children and lives in New York with his wife, the Iranian-Swedish feminist scholar and photographer Golbarg Bashi.

CAN NON-EUROPEANS THINK?

HAMID DABASHI

With a foreword by Walter Mignolo

ZED

LONDON • NEW YORK • OXFORD • NEW DELHI • SYDNEY

For
Marwan Bishara
who thinks otherwise

Zed Books
Bloomsbury Publishing Plc
50 Bedford Square, London, WC1B 3DP, UK
1385 Broadway, New York, NY 10018, USA
29 Earlsfort Terrace, Dublin 2, Ireland

BLOOMSBURY and Zed Books are trademarks of Bloomsbury Publishing Plc

First published in Great Britain 2015
Reprinted 2021

Designed and typeset in Monotype Dante by illuminati, Grosmont
Index by John Barker

To find out more about our authors and books visit www.bloomsbury.com
and sign up for our newsletters.

Contents

Acknowledgments

This is my third book published by Zed Books, and in a way they constitute a trilogy – let's call them *The Intifada Trilogy*, in honor of the Palestinian national liberation movement. Publication of the three books would not have been possible without the caring competence of two extraordinary editors at Zed with whom I have worked, along with their colleagues, to get the books into their final shape. Tamsine O'Riordan was my editor for *Iran, the Green Movement and the USA: The Fox and the Paradox* (2010) and *The Arab Spring: The End of Postcolonialism* (2012). For this third volume, Kim Walker has been instrumental in carefully crafting a book out of an inordinate amount of submitted material. She saw through it a succession of themes and ideas now visible in her editorial ordering of the book, which is entirely indebted to her editorial skills.

I propose calling the books *The Intifada Trilogy* because at the root of each is the extended logic of the Palestinian intifada as the archetype of all transnational liberations in which the entire spectrum of contemporary liberation geography is evident and invested. The fierce urgency of the unfolding events over the last few years has required a kind of critical thinking that furnishes the appropriate narrative rhyme and rhythm; having found myself in tandem with these events, I have been blessed with two deeply cultivated, caring, and competent editors without whom the three books would never have found their dynamic momentum. I thank Tamsine O'Riordan and Kim Walker for the generosity and grace of their interest and trust in these three books.

Candice Bridget Lukasik was my research assistant when I was working on the initial drafts of this book. I owe her warm gratitude for diligently collecting my writings together from their various sources. My current research assistant Hawa Ansary was equally helpful during the latter part of the project when the book was being prepared for publication. Nasir ("Naz") Yousefzai Khan, my Al Jazeera editor for many years, and many of his colleagues up to my current editor Tanya Goudsouzian, have been instrumental in helping me shape and publish the contours of the material that now make up the book. It was for Naz that I initially wrote the essay "Can Non-Europeans Think?" Without his enthusiasm and untiring support I would not have known the larger context of the issues raised in that essay. Simon Critchley and Peter Catapano for the *New York Times*, Richard Galant of CNN, and Mona Anis and Rasha Saad at *Al-Ahram Weekly* have been key to seeing the material now gathered in this book through to publication in their respective media.

Finally, to my dear friend and colleague Walter Mignolo goes my everlasting gratitude for having graciously agreed to preface this book with his utterly brilliant critical Foreword. Can non-Europeans think? You need not read beyond his Foreword if you really await an answer to that rhetorical question.

Hamid Dabashi, New York, October 2014

FOREWORD

Yes, We Can

La Europa que consideró que su destino, el destino de sus
hombres, era hacer de su humanismo el arquetipo a alcanzar
por todo ente que se le pudiese asemejar; esta Europa, lo mismo
la cristiana que la moderna, al trascender los linderos de su
geografía y tropezar con otros entes que parecían ser hombres,
exigió a éstos que justificasen su supuesta humanidad.

Leopoldo Zea, *La filosofía americana
como filosofía sin más* (1969)

روشنفکر قرن نوزدهم اروپا با کارگری طرف است که اولاً سه قرن از قرون وسطی و دو قرن از
رنسانس را پشت سر گذاشته، ثانیاً در محیطی زندگی می‌کند که روح مذهبی، روح حاکم بر کارگر
نیست، ثالثاً کارگر به مرحله پرولتر صنعتی رسیده، و دیگر اینکه در یک نظام بورژوازی رشدیافته
صنعتی زندگی می‌کند که روابط، روابط صنعتی است و خود کارگر به یک مرحله بالایی از رشد
و خودآگاهی رسیده و از همه مهم‌تر اینکه، مخاطب او، یعنی پرولتاریای صنعتی، یک طبقه را
تشکیل داده، یعنی خودش به صورت یک طبقه مشخص و مستقل در جامعه که فرهنگ خاص
و امتیازات خاص و شکل خاصی در زیر بنای اقتصادی اروپای غربی پیدا کرده، در آمده است.
آن وقت من به عنوان روشنفکری که می‌خواهم حرف‌های روشنفکر قرن نوزدهم را تقلید کنم،
می‌آیم و این حرف‌ها را به کسی می‌زنم که هیچ یک از مشخصات مخاطب روشنفکر قرن نوزدهم
را ندارد. یعنی من در جامعه‌ای زندگی می‌کنم که بورژوازی هنوز در مرحله ابتدایش است و
فقط در شهرهای بزرگ رشد پیدا کرده است، بورژوازی «کمپرادور» (دلال) است و واسطه است،
بورژوازی نظام تولیدی نیست. از این گذشته طبقه‌ای به نام طبقه کارگر هنوز تشکیل نشده است
و در جامعه ما کارگران به صورت گروه‌های کارگری هستند، که گروه‌های کارگری غیر از طبقه
کارگر هستند. گروه‌های کارگری در منحط‌ترین جوامع بدوی و قبایل بدوی هم وجود دارند. مثلاً
در آفریقا، در عربستان سعودی که منابع صنعتی و تولیدی غربی وجود دارد ۱۰۰, ۵۰۰, ۲۰۰۰

کارگر صنعتی حتی در سطح بالا هستند، اما جامعه زیر بنای کارگری ندارد و یک زیر بنای قبایلی یا زراعتی یا فئودالیته دارد. بنابراین در این جامعه، طبقه کارگر تشکیل نشده است و یک کادری از کارگر به وجود آمده. بنابراین مخاطب من، کارگر نمی‌تواند باشد که یک گروه خاصی در یک گوشه مملکت است، مخاطب من کسانی هستند که هنوز به مرحله بورژوازی نرسیده‌اند.

Ali Shari'ati, "Mission of a Free Thinker" (1970–71)

I take this opportunity to continue the conversation started in Al Jazeera a while ago, prompted by Santiago Zabala's essays on Slavoj Žižek, followed by Hamid Dabashi's "Can Non-Europeans Think?", reprinted in this volume. Dabashi picked up in the first paragraph of Zabala's essays on Žižek an unconscious dismissal that has run through the history of the coloniality of power in its epistemic and ontological spheres: the self-assumed Eurocentrism (the world seen, described and mapped from European perspectives and interests).

Dabashi and I are non-European thinkers and intellectuals, perhaps philosophers too, schooled during the hard years of the Cold War. We have been described and classified as being of the Third World. The describers and classifiers hail from the First World. We both left our places of birth to move to Europe and the US, following – I imagine this was also the case for Dabashi – the dreams and the life of the Spirit, only to realize, at some point, that the Spirit was not welcoming of Third World spirits. Our local histories are at variance, however. Persians are indigenous, with their own memories, languages and territoriality, whereas in the diverse countries of South and Central America and some Caribbean islands the population is of European descent, marginal Europeans (to which I belong) displacing the indigenous and Afro-descendants. That is, from the sixteenth century Europeans and their descendants carried with them imperial memories and languages to the colonies and former colonies (e.g. Spanish in Argentina, French in Frantz

Fanon's Martinique; English in C.L.R. James's Trinidad and Tobago).

I title my intervention "Yes, We Can" in response to Dabashi's question "Can Non-Europeans Think?" I address the general issue of colonial epistemic difference without any inclination to mediate the conversation. The title is a discursive anagram. Readers will recognize in it an echo of President Barack Obama's memorable dictum, used in both of his presidential campaigns. Readers will perhaps also recognize the echo of a much commented-upon book title, although one less familiar, especially in academic circles, written by a Singaporean (a non-European of course) thinker, intellectual and perhaps philosopher too: *Can Asians Think?* by Kishore Mahbubani (1998).[1] The issue highlighted by Dabashi is not personal, but rather long-standing, important and enduring, although it is not a continental philosophical concern. And indeed it shouldn't be. European philosophers have their own, and for them more pressing, issues.

The question asked by the non-European intellectuals Dabashi and Mahbubani – one based in the US and involved in Middle Eastern politics, the other in Singapore and involved in high diplomacy – should not be taken lightly. It is not trivial because epistemic racism crosses the lines of social and institutional spheres. Both questions indeed unveil epistemic racism hidden beneath the naturalization of certain ways of thinking and producing knowledge that are given the name Eurocentrism. Racism is not a question of one's blood type (the Christian criterion used in sixteenth-century Spain to distinguish Christians from Moors and Jews in Europe) or the color of one's skin (Africans and the New World civilizations).

---

1. *Can Asians Think? Understanding the Divide between East and West.* Hanover NH: Steerforth Press, 2001 (1998).

Racism consists in devaluing the humanity of certain people by dismissing it or playing it down (even when not intentional) at the same time as highlighting and playing up European philosophy, assuming it to be universal. It may be global, because it piggybacks on imperial expansion, but it certainly cannot be universal. Racism is a classification, and classification is an epistemic maneuver rather than an ontological entity that carries with it the essence of the classification. It is a system of classification enacted by actors, institutions and categories of thought that enjoy the privilege of being hegemonic or dominant, and which imposes itself as ontological truth reinforced by "scientific" research. Decolonially, knowledge is not taken as the mirror of nature that Richard Rorty critiqued, nor as the "grasper" of ontological properties of objects, as Nikolai Hartmann believed.

Mahbubani's book was published in 1998. It reprinted three times in the following years, and saw second and third editions up to 2007. Who was reading the book and debating this issue? I did not find the book quoted in academic publications I read and workshops and conferences I attended. Not only that, when I asked friends and colleagues if they knew or had read Mahbubani's book, they responded blankly before saying no. Since Mahbubani is a diplomat and a public figure in the sphere of international diplomacy, I suspect that his readers belong to that world and that of the media anchors who interview him. I also suspect that scholars would be suspicious of an Asian thinker playing with philosophy and the silences of history and asking such an uncomfortable question.

The question Dabashi and Mahbubani raise is not whether non-Europeans can *do philosophy*, but whether they/we can *think*. Philosophy is a regional and historical endeavor. Whether we can engage in philosophy or not is irrelevant. Now, if we cannot think, that would be serious! Thinking is a common feature of living organisms endowed with nervous systems. That includes humans (and certainly Europeans). What all human beings do is not philosophy, which is not a necessity, but thinking, which is unavoidable. Greek thinkers named their singular way of thinking philosophy, and by so doing were appointed as philosophers – those who do philosophy. This is of course understandable; but it is an aberration to project a regional definition of a regional way of thinking as a universal standard by which to judge and classify.

In consequence, what Dabashi, Mahbubani and I (among others) are doing is delinking from the "disciplinarity" of philosophy, and from disciplinary racial and gender normativity. It is common to be informed that such and such a person was denied tenure because of hidden ethnic or gender reasons. Disciplinary normativity operates on an assumed geopolitics of knowledge. In the 1970s, it was common among Africans and Latin American scholars trained in philosophy to ask whether one could properly talk about philosophy in Africa or in Latin America. A similar problem was faced by Spanish philosopher José Ortega y Gasset at the beginning of the twentieth century. He returned to Spain after studying philology and philosophy in Germany and defined himself as "philosopher *in partibus infidelium.*" He must have had an instinctive understanding of what Hegel meant when he referred to "the heart of Europe." Ortega y Gasset could have joined us in this conversation today, by asking "Can the Spanish think?" His writings are "indisciplinary" in the strict sense that philology and philosophy require. But I would venture that they are "undisciplinary" as well. For he was a thinker engaged in epistemic disobedience, a practice that is growing around the world, including in Western Europe and the US.[2]

The question asked in the 1970s – whether philosophy was a legitimate endeavor in Africa and in Latin America – was left behind. The following generation trained in philosophy took a different attitude. Nigerian philosopher Emmanuel Chukwudi Eze published a groundbreaking article in 1997 titled "The Color of Reason: The Idea of 'Race' in Kant's Anthropology."[3] Eze inverted canonical approaches to Kant's *oeuvre*. Instead of starting from Kant's major works and leaving aside his minor texts (*Anthropology from a Pragmatic Point of View* and *Geography*), Eze saw in Kant's minor works the racial prejudices embedded in his monumental philosophy. Philosophy turned out to be not only a discipline for theoretical thought and argument (and love of wisdom) but also a tool to *dis-qualify* (that is, to disavow in the act of classifying those people who do not conform to Western conceptions of philosophy and its rational expectations).

Racial classification is an epistemic fiction rather than a scientific description of the correlation between "race" and "intelligence." It is not the color of one's skin that matters, but one's deviation from rationality and from the right belief system. This is why we are now asking whether Asians or non-Europeans can think. At its inception, the modern/colonial racial system of classification (in the sixteenth century) was theological and grounded in the belief of purity of blood. Christians on the Iberian peninsula had the epistemic upper hand over

2. "Epistemic Disobedience, Independent Thought and De-Colonial Freedom," *Theory, Culture & Society* (Singapore), vol. 26, no. 7–8, pp. 1–23.
3. Emmanuel Chukwudi Eze, "The Color of Reason: The Idea of 'Race' in Kant's Anthropology," in E.C. Eze, ed., *Postcolonial African Philosophy: A Critical Reader*. Oxford: Blackwell, 1997, pp. 103–31.

Muslims and Jews. This meant that Christians found themselves enjoying the epistemic privilege of classifying without being classified. It was the privilege of managing zero-point epistemology, as Colombian philosopher Santiago Castro-Gómez has convincingly argued.[4] Theological epistemic privilege extended to indigenous Aztec *tlamatinime* and Inca *amautas* (wise men, thinking individuals, in Anahuac and Tawantinsuyu respectively, areas known today as Mesoamerica and the Andes). In the racial hierarchy of knowledge founded in the sixteenth century, colonial epistemic and ontological differences were historically founded. They were remapped in the eighteenth and nineteenth centuries when theology was displaced by secular philosophy (Kant) and the sciences (Darwin).[5]

Christian theology and secular philosophy and sciences constructed a system of classification of people and regions of the world that still govern us and shape all debate on the issue. It also informs the presuppositions that underline all systems of knowledge.[6] The reasons for the emergence of new disciplinary formations in the US in the 1970s are to be found in the liberation from the epistemic racial and sexual classifications of over 500 years of Western epistemic hegemony. People of color and of non-heteronormative sexual preferences were able to think for themselves and were no longer simply the object of study by white heterosexuals. They could also reflect on the fact that they were considered as people to be studied.

4. "The Missing Chapter of Empire," *Cultural Studies*, vol. 21, no. 2–3 (2007), pp. 428–48.
5. Margaret R. Greer, Walter D. Mignolo, and Maureen Quilligan, eds, *Rereading the Black Legend: The Discourses of Religious and Racial Difference in the Renaissance Empires*, Chicago: University of Chicago Press, 2007, pp. 312–24.
6. Anibal Quijano, "Coloniality of Power, Eurocentrism, and Social Classification," in Mabel Moraña, Enrique D. Dussel and Carlos A. Jáuregui, eds, *Coloniality at Large: Latin America and the Postcolonial Debate*, Durham NC: Duke University Press, 2008 (Spanish edn 2000).

Classification is a pernicious tool for it carries the seeds of ranking. Carl Linnaeus (1707–1778) in science and Immanuel Kant (1724–1804) in philosophy were the two architects of the mutation from theological to secular classification. Secular philosophy and science displaced Christian theology as the epistemic normativity. English, French and German thinkers, philosophers and scientists became the gatekeepers (willingly or not) and regulators of thought. It suffices to read chapter 4 of Immanuel Kant's *Observations on the Feeling of the Beautiful and the Sublime* (1764) to experience a trailer for the point I am making. That was the moment in which Asians entered the picture in earnest. And here I mean East Asia, South Asia and West Asia (today's Middle East). *Orientalism* was nothing but that: knowers and thinkers (philosophers) walking hand in hand with philologists "studying" the Orient. The arrogance of epistemic power mutated from Renaissance Christian men of letters and missionaries to secular philologists and philosophers.

Notice how epistemic racism works. It is built on classifications and hierarchies carried out by actors installed in institutions they have themselves created or inherited the right to classify and rank. That is, actors and institutions that legitimize the zero-point of epistemology as the word of God (Christian theology) or the word of Reason (secular philosophy and science). He who does the classifying classifies himself among the classified (the enunciated), but he is the only one who classifies among all those being classified. This is a powerful trick that, like any magic trick, the audience does not see as such but as something that just happens. Those who are classified as less human do not have much say in the classification (except to dissent), while those who classify always place themselves at the top of the classification. Darwin was right to observe that skin color is irrelevant in the *classification* of races. In spite of that, it is a dominant factor in the public sphere. It comes perhaps from Kant's ethno-racial tetragon. Following Linnaeus' classification, which was basically descriptive, Kant added a ranking among them and connected racism with geopolitics: Yellows are in Asia, Blacks in Africa, Reds in America and Whites in Europe.[7] The trick is that the classification is enacted on the basis of the exclusive privilege of the White race, whose actors and institutions were located in Europe, their language and categories of thought derived from Greek and Latin, inscribed in the formation of the six modern/colonial European languages: Italian, Spanish, Portuguese (dominant during the Renaissance), German, English and French (dominant since the Enlightenment).

I feel that Hamid Dabashi reacted not to Zabala's first paragraph in itself but to the many disavowals that the paragraph elicited. My sense is that if the paragraph had been slightly different, Dabashi would not have engaged in the debate, and neither would I. Had Zabala written something like "Žižek is the most important philosopher in Continental Philosophy," Dabashi may not have paid any attention to it. However, *the problem would have persisted.* Because the problem was not the paragraph per se but what it elicited, which of course long preceded and goes far beyond the paragraph. Žižek's reaction to my intervention, "Fuck you, Walter Mignolo," I did not take as a personal insult, but understood rather as a deep malaise he was confronting and had been keeping under the table.

---

7. See Eze, "The Color of Reason."

Let us further elaborate on the long-standing philosophical assumptions of epistemic racism, which are highlighted in Mahbubani's and Dabashi's titles. Frantz Fanon understood it:

> It is clear that what divides this world is first and foremost what species, what race one belongs to. In the colonies the economic infrastructure is also a superstructure. The cause is effect: you are rich because you are white; you are white because you are rich.[8]

One could translate Fanon's unveiling of the hidden principles of racial socio-economic classification into epistemic and ontological ones: "You do philosophy because you are white"; you are white because you do [European] philosophy," where "whiteness" and "doing philosophy" stand for the ontological dimensions of the person. Behind the person is not just a skin color but also a language operating on principles and assumptions of knowledge. That is, there is an epistemology at work that transforms "black skin" into "Negro," and "Negro" is much more than skin color. The same applies to "thinking." Fanon again perceived this in 1952 when he wrote that to speak (and I believe he implied also to write) a language is not just to master a grammar and a vocabulary but to carry the weight of a civilization;[9] that racism was not only a question of the color of one's skin but of language, and therefore of categories of thought.

If according to racial classifications one is epistemically and ontologically inferior (or suspect), one cannot think (that is, one can, but one is not believable), one does not belong to the club of "universal" genealogy grounded in the Greek and Latin languages that mutated into the six modern/colonial European languages. Persian doesn't belong to that genealogy. And Spanish

---

8. *Les damnés de la terre*, Paris: Maspero, 1961, p. 65.
9. *Peau noire, masques blancs*, Paris: Gallimard, 1952.

missed the train of the second era of modernity in the eighteenth century. In addition, Spanish has been further devalued as a Third World language of Spanish America. Therefore, if one wishes to join the club of continental philosophy and one's language is Persian, Latin American Spanish, Urdu, Aymara or Bambara, or even a civilizational language like Mandarin, Russian or Turkish, one must learn the *languages* of secular philosophy (German and French, mainly). At this point we can take the argument a step further: if one speaks and writes in Spanish, one has trouble in aspiring to become a philosopher. That is what motivated Chilean Victor Farías to write his book on Heidegger. As Farías relates in his preface, Heidegger informed him that Spanish was not a language of philosophy, something José Ortega y Gasset understood at the beginning of the twentieth century. Hence Ortega y Gasset's declaration that he was himself a philosopher *in partibus infidelium*.[10] The South of Europe was already, and openly, considered suspect in terms of rationality by Enlightenment philosophers, chiefly Kant and Hegel.

Robert Bernasconi, trained in continental philosophy, has reflected on the challenges that African philosophy poses to continental philosophy:

> Western philosophy traps African philosophy in a double bind: either African philosophy is so similar to Western philosophy that it makes no distinctive contribution and effectively disappears; or it is so different that its credentials to be genuine philosophy will always be in doubt.[11]

10. Victor Farías, *Heidegger and Nazism*, Philadelphia: Temple University Press, 1991. For Ortega y Gasset, see Jesús Ruiz Fernández, "La idea de filosofía en José Ortega y Gasset," Departamento de Filosofía, Universidad Complutense de Madrid, 2009, http://eprints.ucm.es/9522/1/T31067.pdf.

11. Robert Bernasconi, "African Philosophy's Challenge to Continental Philosopy," in Eze, ed., *Postcolonial African Philosophy*, pp. 183–96.

Bernasconi does not ask whether and/or how continental philosophy traps African (and non-Western) philosophies. I am not faulting Bernasconi for not asking that question. The question asked by Dabashi, "Can non-Europeans think?," addresses the silence revealed in Bernasconi's observation in his role as continental philosopher. This may not be the type of question one has to ask in order to be the most important European philosopher. But it is a question some philosophers engaged in continental philosophy do ask; a question that is crucial to non-European thinkers, philosophers or not.

Mahbubani, with no connection to Bernasconi but attuned to Eurocentrism, points towards other possibilities. Imagine, he suggests, that I ask "Can Europeans think?" or "Can Africans think?" These questions he rejects. He could, he says, ask about Asians because he is Asian.[12] Why so? He doesn't answer his own questions, but I imagine that "Can Europeans think?" asked by an Asian would have been taken by Europeans to be a question asked by someone who had lost his mind or as confirmation that Asians really cannot think, for supposedly Europeans are the only ones who can do so. And if he asked "Can Africans think?" most likely Europeans would not dissent, for since Hume's (in)famous dictum, repeated by Kant, Africans cannot think. Kant challenges his readers

> to cite a single example in which a Negro has shown talents, and asserts that among the hundreds of thousands of blacks who are transported elsewhere from their countries *although many of them have even been set free,* still not a single one was ever found who presented anything great in art or science or any other praise-worthy quality, even though among the whites

---

12. Mahbubani, *Can Asians Think?*, p. 21.

some continually rise aloft from the lowest rabble, and through superior gifts earn respect in the world.[13]

Small wonder that philosopher Emmanuel Chukwudi Eze unveiled Kant's epistemic racism. The paragraph quoted might explain also why Slavoj Žižek was not impressed by the non-European philosophers referred to in my article. For they are all on the other side of the fence, picking flowers from the European philosophical garden. Last but not least, it might be understood why Dabashi and Mahbubani phrased the question as they did and why I am here following suit.

Let's go back to Bernasconi's unasked question. What kind of challenges does continental philosophy pose to non-European thinkers, philosophers and non-philosophers alike? In Argentina the challenge was taken up by Rodolfo Kusch (1922–1979), an Argentine of German descent (his parents emigrated to Argentina from Germany, in 1920), and a philosopher – without his having read Bernasconi of course. The most elaborate of his works is *Pensamiento indígena y pensamiento popular en América* (1970). The first chapter is titled "El pensamiento Americano" (translated as "Thinking in América"). In its opening sentences Kusch confronts head-on continental philosophy's challenges to Argentinian (and South American) philosophers.

Kusch points out that in America there is, on the one hand, an official way of proceeding and, on the other, a private way of proceeding. The first, learned at university, consists basically of a European set of problems and issues translated into philosophical language. The second is implicit in the way of life and the thinking on city streets and in the countryside alike, and

---

13. Immanuel Kant, *Beobachtungen über das Gefühl des Schönen und Erhabenen* (1764). English translation: *Observations on the Feeling of the Beautiful and Sublime*, trans. John T. Goldthwait, Berkeley: University of California Press, 1981, p. 11.

at home, and parallels the official way of doing philosophy at university. Kusch stresses that it is a question not of rejecting continental philosophy but of looking for what, a few years later, he called *pensamiento propio*: losing the fear of thinking on one's own, fear instilled by the force of colonial epistemic and ontological differences. The colonized, we know, more often than not assumes him- or herself as belonging to the ontology in which the classifications have placed him or her. Once you "see" the trick, you delink and start walking on your own, rather than translating European problems into the language of philosophy as taught in America (or Asia or Africa).

Kusch means by *pensamiento propio* the freedom "to appropriate" continental philosophy in this case and delink from the official way of studying it. Delinking implies epistemic disobedience. And that was Kusch's response to the challenge of continental philosophy to Third World philosophers. To do what he proposes in response to the challenges of continental philosophy is not an easy task:

> But this is what is so weighty. In order to carry out such a conceptualization, it is necessary not just to know philosophy, but above all – and this is very important – to face reality abiding a degree of distortion few can sustain. To investigate daily life in order to translate it into thinking is a dangerous venture, since it is necessary, particularly here in America, to make the grave mistake of contradicting the frameworks to which we are attached.[14]

Kusch starts with Heidegger's *Dasein* and then departs from it. That is how border epistemology works. He asks what could be the meaning of *Dasein* in America, given that it was a concept

---

14. Rodolfo Kusch, *Pensamiento Indígena y Popular en América* (1970). Translation: *Indigenous and Popular Thinking in América*, trans. María Lugones and Joshua Price, Introduction by Walter Mignolo, Durham NC: Duke University Press, 2010, p. 2.

nourished and propelled by a certain ethos of the German middle class between the two wars. From that question Kusch derived the conviction that thinking may be a universal activity of all living organisms endowed with a nervous system, but that thinking organisms do so in their own niche – memories, languages, and socio-historical tensions and dissatisfactions. Heidegger's experience, which led to his conceiving of *Dasein*, is quite alien to America. Consequently, how could the purported universality of Being be accepted? Kusch realized also that the Argentinian middle class lived in a parallel universe of meaning but in extremely different socio-historical conditions to those experienced by the German middle class. Kusch's intellectual life began in the last years of the first presidency of Juan Domingo Perón, a so-called "populist" leader; he wrote his *Indigenous and Popular Thinking in America* between the fall and the return of Perón.

From his early work in the 1950s (at the time Fanon was fighting his fight in France) Kusch turned his back on his social roots and turned his gaze towards Indigenous culture. It was not Kusch's intention to describe the life of Indigenous people, as anthropologists do, but to understand the logic of their thinking. This was not easy as he had to deal with the baggage of continental philosophy he learned at university. Here one again experiences epistemic colonial difference and is reminded of the question Bernasconi fails to ask: continental philosophers do not have to deal with thinking and rationality beyond the line that connects Ancient Greece and Rome with the heart of Europe. On the contrary, in order to do philosophy in the colonies and ex-colonies one has two options: to join a branch of continental philosophy (science, psychoanalysis, sociology, etc.), which is equivalent to a branch of McDonald's; or to delink and engage in *pensamiento propio.*[15] At that moment one is already engaging border epistemology, on account of one's residing on the borders.

For example, Kusch found that in the Aymara language the word *utcatha* has certain parallels with *Dasein*, a word that Heidegger picked up from popular German. Through *utcatha* Kusch unfolds a complex universe of meaning that allows him to work his understanding of indigenous ways of thinking (philosophy, if you will) into the simultaneous process of delinking from continental philosophy and uncovering what may constitute thinking in America. In this process, the issue is not to *reject* continental philosophy but, on the contrary, to know it in order to *delink* from it. That is, to undermine it and by the same token undermine epistemic classifications that sometimes operate not by empirical description but by unconscious or conscious silences. Kusch finds out first that the Aymara word *utcatha* has several meanings, all of which he finds are associated with the type of experience that Heidegger was exploring through the word *Dasein.* He then connects the meaning of an Aymara word with Indigenous people's expressions of their sense and understanding of themselves. He discovers a "passive" attitude that has been used to justify "white" middle-class perceptions of "Indians'" laziness.

But Kusch saw something else in what was defined as "passiveness" and the refusal to work. What appeared from the perspective of modernity and modernization, the dream of the urban middle class at the time, as passiveness and laziness was for Kusch an "active passiveness" and a refusal to sell one's labour and change one's way of life. Kusch created

15. Walter Mignolo, *Local Histories, Global Designs: Coloniality, Subaltern Knowledges and Border Thinking,* Princeton NJ: Princeton University Press, 2000; 2nd edn 2012.

the concept of *estar siendo*, taking advantage of the distinction between the verbs *ser* and *estar* in Spanish, which has no equivalent in other Western languages: Italian, *essere–essere*; German, *werden–werden*; French, *être–être*; English, to be–to be. Kusch's groundbreaking category *estar siendo* denotes an active passiveness that refuses, rejects, *negates* the expectation to join the storytelling of modernity and modernization. *Estar siendo* is a negation that at the same time affirms what modernity wants to eliminate or incorporate into "development." *Estar siendo* is a negation that affirms indigeneity and prevents it from being absorbed by and into nationality. From the active–passiveness emerged the revolutionary, philosophical and political, idea of "plurinational state" recently inscribed in the constitutions of Bolivia and Ecuador.

To find one's own way one cannot depend on the words of the master; one has to delink and disobey. Delinking and disobeying here means avoiding the traps of colonial differences, and has nothing to do with the rebellious artistic and intellectual acts that we are used to hearing about in European history. In the history of Europe reactions against the past are part of the idea of progress and of dialectical movement. In the non-European world it is a matter of delinking from dialectics and turning to analectics (Dussel); and delinking from progress and seeking equilibrium. These are parallel trajectories coexisting, in the non-European world, with European critical dissenters. But they must not be confused. The latter is the path Dabashi, Mahbubani, Kusch, Eze and I are taking. The former is the path of Zabala reading Žižek, and Žižek responding to Dabashi's and my comments.

Mahbubani, as his positions in government indicate, thinks "from above" – but he thinks radically from above. If you are not interested in the process of thinking from above, whether radical or organic (like Kissinger, Huntington or Brzezinski), you can skip this section.

In the Preface to the second edition of *Can Asians Think?* Mahbubani writes:

> The title chosen for this volume of essays – "Can Asians Think?" – is not accidental. It represents essentially two questions folded into one. The first, addressed to my fellow Asians, reads as "Can you think? If you can, why have Asian societies lost a thousand years and slipped far behind the European societies that they were far ahead of at the turn of the last millennium?"
>
> The second question, addressed primarily to my friends in the West [remember, he is a diplomat – WM], is "Can Asians think for themselves?" We live in an essentially unbalanced world. The flow of ideas, reflecting 500 years of Western domination of the globe, remains a one-way street – from the West to the East. Most Westerners cannot see that they have arrogated to themselves the moral high ground from which they lecture the world. The rest of the world can see this.[16]

Since the term "the West" is often used, let's pause to clarify it. First, north of the Mediterranean Sea the West refers to the area west of Jerusalem, where Western Christians dwell, before that territory became better known as Europe. South of the Mediterranean the word used is "Maghreb," which means west of Mecca and Medina. But of course neither Mahbubani nor I refer to Maghreb when we use the term "the West." Second, by the West neither I nor probably he means Romania, former Yugoslavia, Poland or Latvia. What constitutes the West more than geography is a linguistic family, a belief system and an epistemology. It is constituted by six modern European and

---

16. Mahbubani, *Can Asians Think?*, p. 9.

imperial languages: Italian, Spanish and Portuguese, which
were dominant during the Renaissance, and English, French and
German, which have been dominant since the Enlightenment.
The latter states and languages form the "heart of Europe," in
Hegel's expression, but they are also held by Kant to be the
three states with the highest degree of civilization. Thus "the
West" is shorthand for "Western civilization."

Let's stay with Mahbubani for one more paragraph.[17] He
continues:

> Similarly, Western intellectuals are convinced that their minds
> and cultures are open, self-critical and – in contrast to ossified
> Asian minds and cultures – have no "sacred cows". The most
> shocking discovery of my adult life was the realisation that
> "sacred cows" also exist in the Western mind. During the
> period of Western triumphalism that followed the end of the
> Cold War, a huge bubble of moral pretentiousness enveloped
> the Western intellectual universe.[18]

Coloniality, not just colonization, has a long history. It
began to take shape in the sixteenth century, in the North
and South Atlantic, but led by the North of course. The South
also participated, by force, through the Atlantic slave trade
and the dismantling of the civilizations in Mesoamerica and
the Andes (Aztecs, Mayas, Incas) and the "Indian" genocide. It
was not just brute force that made all of this possible. It was
the control of knowledge that justified the demonization and
dehumanization of people, civilizations, cultures and territories.
People who are ontologically inferior human beings are also
epistemically deficient. The panorama has changed in the past
five hundred years, but only on the surface. The deep feelings

---

17. I recommend one of his earlier articles in this vein, an invited lecture at the BBC in
2000, collected in *Can Asians Think?*, pp. 47–67.
18. Mahbubani, *Can Asians Think?*, p. 9

and logic remain. When in the 1950s Mexican ethno-historian and philosopher Miguel León-Portilla published *La filosofía Náhuatl* (1958), translated as *Aztec Thought and Culture*,[19] he was harshly attacked. How could he dare to think that "Indians" like Aztecs could have philosophy? The critique came not from continental philosophers, who did not care much about these debates in the New World, but from Eurocentric philosophers in Mexico – imperial collaborationists and defenders of philosophical universality (which means universality as interpreted by regional European philosophy).

Let us consider a more recent example of the way epistemic Eurocentrism works within the unconscious of even intelligent European philosophers. Slavoj Žižek was invited to speak at the Seminarios Internacionales de la Vicepresidencia del Estado Plurinacional de Bolivia, led by Álvaro García Linera, in 2011. The title was "¿Es posible pensar un cambio radical hoy?" – "Is it possible to think a radical change today?"[20] At one point[21] Žižek examines the proposal of John Holloway, an Irish-born lawyer and sociologist of Marxist tendency, based in Puebla (Mexico), to "change the world without taking power." By "without taking power" Holloway means without the "taking of the state" by a revolutionary movement. Holloway based his arguments on the Zapatistas' uprising. His interpretation of the Zapatistas' goals and orientation is not necessarily that of the Zapatistas. Žižek starts by discussing and debunking Holloway's proposals, and at this moment brings the Zapatistas and Subcomandante Marcos into the conversation. At this point he introduces one of his frequent jokes. This one he apparently learned from his

---

19. *Aztec Thought and Culture: A Study of the Ancient Nahuatl Mind*, Norman: University of Oklahoma Press, 1990.
20. Žižek in Bolivia: https://www.youtube.com/watch?v=YoQEi4rOVRU.
21. Ibid., minute 46.

friends in Mexico. They told him that they don't use the title Subcomandante Marcos any more but rather Subcomediante Marcos (subcomedian). I surmise that Žižek's Mexican friends were Marxists. Marxists have a problem with Marcos because he had detached himself from Marxism shortly after arriving in Chiapas, in the 1980s, and immersed himself in Indigenous philosophy and politics – or, if you will, political philosophy.[22]

I don't know about you, but I consider the act of debunking one's opponent, in public, with a joke that carries epistemic racial overtones quite uncalled for. Had the joke been made to an audience in Britain or Austria, it might have been uncontroversial. But in Bolivia, a self-proclaimed state promoting "communal socialism," and having the majority of the Indigenous population behind it, telling the joke certainly showed a lack of tact (and perhaps sureness of touch). The reader should know that Subcomandante Marcos refused President Evo Morales's invitation to attend his inauguration. There were laughs in the Bolivian audience, who were not visible – you hear the laughs in the recording but do not see the faces. Far from being a *comediante*, Marcos is an intellectual who converted from Marxism to Indianism (Indigenous people thinking about themselves and the world, much as how Marxism allows people to think about themselves and the world). He joined an already existing Indigenous organization in the Mayan area, Southern Mexico.[23] Certainly Subcomandante Marcos masqueraded in his outfits, watch, pipes, gun, and so on. But this was just a different sort of masquerade to that practiced by current kings and queens, secular presidents and vice presidents, unless we believe that these are not staged and only the public persona

---

22. Walter Mignolo, "The Zapatista's Theoretical Revolution."
23. See ibid.

of Subcomandante Marcos is. An urban Marxist intellectual, Rafael Guillén (trained in philosophy at university), went to the South of Mexico to teach Indians that they were oppressed and had to liberate themselves, only to discover that Indians have known for 500 years, and without reading Marx, that they were oppressed and have not stopped fighting for their survival and a new existence. Far from being a *comediante*, Marcos (now Subcomandante Galeano) has the openness and courage both to perceive the limits of Marxism and to recognize the potential of decoloniality. This is the kind of philosophy and thinking that one finds among non-European thinkers and philosophers.

Žižek's comment on Subcomandante Marcos reminds me of what I have heard on several occasions in different countries from people who attended his talks. These things have been said in private, in the same way I imagine as Žižek heard about Subcomandante Marcos in private conversations with his Mexican friends. Many different people have observed that Žižek is a clown, in French a *buffon*. But I do not recall anyone saying this in public. It has remained in the realm of private conversation until this moment. I am now making it public to undermine Žižek's uncalled-for comment on Subcomandante Marcos.[24] And, parallel to this, to undermine his dictatorial inclination to confront with insults those who doubt or express indifference to his reputation as the most important (European) philosopher alive, even though this status is irrelevant to non-European thinkers who do not worship continental philosophy. The general issue of epistemic colonial differences touches all of us in different ways. We respond to it accordingly.

24. Žižek in Bolivia.

In a sense I am here following Chandra Muzaffar's recommendation regarding *Charlie Hebdo's* freedom-of-expression insults. There is no reason to kill someone who insults you believing that what he or she did was legitimate according to freedom of expression. Someone who insults on the basis of such a belief is a victim of the arrogance of power and the privileges of zero-point epistemology. Muzaffar correctly understood the situation, and recommended that

> One should respond to satirical cartoons with cartoons and other works of art that expose the prejudice and bigotry of the cartoonists and editors of Charlie Hebdo. *One should use the Charlie Hebdo cartoons as a platform to educate and raise the awareness of the French public about what the Quran actually teaches and who the Prophet really was and the sort of noble values that distinguished his life and struggle.*[25]

We (non-European intellectuals, which Muzaffar is) should use racist jokes and insults (to paraphrase Muzaffar) as a platform to educate and raise the awareness of the European public about colonial epistemic differences and decolonial thinking. This is the spirit in which non-European thinkers and philosopher are, and should be, responding to European arrogance from the right and from the left. We are no longer silent, nor asking for recognition; this should be clear by now. As Tariq Ramadan observes, recognition and integration are words that belong to the past. As First Nation intellectuals, thinkers, artists and activists of Canada insist, recognition is to be wholly rejected.[26] What is at stake is affirmation and the re-emergence

---

25. Chandra Muzaffar, www.globalresearch.ca/paris-a-dastardly-act-of-terror-the-case-for-an-independent-investigation/5423889; stress added.
26. Leanne Simpson, *Dancing on our Turtle's Back: Stories of Nishnaabeg Re-Creation, Resurgence and a New Emergence*, Toronto: Arbeiter Ring Publishing, 2011. Simpson observes, in a groundbreaking chapter, that storytelling is "our way of theorizing." Substitute philosophy

of the communal (rather than the commons and the common good). This is one of the paths that we non-European thinkers are following.

In order to flesh out what I have argued so far, starting from the question raised by Dabashi in his title, and elaborated in the book, I shall consider two examples. One is Arabs throwing their shoes; the other is Dabashi's elaboration of the concept of revolution. The concern expressed by Dabashi in his Al Jazeera article finds forceful expression in a different guise in the essay "The Arabs and Their Flying Shoes." Humor is a crucial epistemic dimension here. It is not philosophy that is in question but a certain imaginary, from which philosophy is not exempt. The imputed discourse is that of anthropology and Western television anchors. The line of the argument is how Western anthropologists and news anchors relying on them make sense of an Iraqi throwing a shoe at George W. Bush in Tehran and, later on, an Egyptian enacting the same gesture. However, the target in the latter case is not Bush but Mahmoud Ahmadinejad. The parallel is crucial, for they stood as the two pillars of a world order that is now governed by different actors and slightly different diplomatic styles. Here, the anti-imperial and anti-colonial arguments that Dabashi explores through the book reach their limit. This is not an "anti" (resistance, reaction) gesture. That is not what moves the revolutionary sirocco blowing through all the authoritarian states of North Africa and the Middle East (MENA), steered by the new generation of Muslims, Arabs, Persians and Turks born at the end of the Cold War and detached from the imperial/colonial antagonism

---

for theory and you will get the picture. See also Glen Sean Coulthard, *Red Skin, White Masks: Rejecting the Colonial Politics of Recognition*, Minneapolis: University of Minnesota Press, 2014.

that Dabashi details. How, then, are we to characterize different manifestations of "revolution" in the making? To answer this question, Dabashi explores in "The Arabs and Their Flying Shoes" the epistemic colonial difference in anthropological knowledge and within mainstream journalism.

Through anecdote Dabashi stages a powerful philosophical argument, weaving different scenarios in which, for example, graduate students from some MENA country will be supported by local foundations and universities to conduct research into Western habits relating to shoes. Professors and institutions supporting the graduate student research would endorse publication of the resultant books, and such works could receive recognition within the profession by way of distinguished awards. Billions of Muslims and Arabs would be able to understand the curious behavior and beliefs of Western people through their habits and feelings concerning shoes. It is only a short step from this scenario to the question "Can non-Europeans think?" Non-Europeans do not think – they throw shoes so that Western scholars and social scientists can study them, and philosophers, if they are interested, can reflect on the meaning of the event of flying shoes in the MENA region. This issue was highlighted by more perceptive Western social scientists in the early 1980s. For example, Carl Pletsch published what was to become a celebrated article, albeit not within the social sciences. He explored the scientific distribution of labor across the "three worlds." Of significance here is that the First World has knowledge while the Third World has culture.[27] The flying shoes story perfectly exemplifies Pletsch's argument. In common parlance the dictum would go something like: Africans have

---

27. Carl Pletsch, "The Three Worlds, or the Division of Social Scientifid Labor, circa 1950–1975," *Comparative Studies in Society and History*, vol. 23, no. 4 (1981), pp. 565–87.

experience, Europeans have philosophy; Native Americans have wisdom, Anglo-Americans have science; the Third World has cultures, the First World has science and philosophy. What is at stake in Dabashi's argument? Anthropological and philosophical knowledge is half the story. Anthropologists are in the main Western professionals making sense of the rest of the world for a Western audience. Thus, non-Western people, scholars and intellectuals (that is, people who think, regardless of whether or not they are philosophers or anthropologists in the Western provincial disciplinary sense) are by default left outside, watching. That was the case in the long history of coloniality of knowledge of being – for knowledge molds subjectivities, the subjectivity both of those who "feel" they are working for the Global Secretary of Knowledge and of those who felt, and perhaps still feel, that they should be recognized by the Secretary. If they are not, they do not exist or do not count as thinking human beings.

The point Dabashi highlights in the title of his response to Zabala's essay on Žižek invokes a sensitive issue. This is the issue that prompted me to enter the conversation. It is not new, although it is (understandably, given the procedure outlined above) unknown to or irrelevant for Western philosophy and other disciplinary formations. And of course there is no reason why Western philosophers and scholars should be interested in what Dabashi and I are arguing. European philosophers have their concerns; we non-European thinkers have ours. However, we cannot afford not to know Western philosophy. The splendors and miseries of non-European thinkers come from this double bind; and with it comes the epistemic potential of dwelling and thinking in the borders. That is, engaging in border thinking.

The second example is Dabashi's essay reflecting on the meaning of "revolution" today. The inquiry was motivated by the impact of the Arab Spring.

Starting from Hannah Arendt's study *On Revolution* (1963), Dabashi soon departs from it. He is interested in Tahrir Square and the Arab Spring or intifada in Egypt, and by extension in the succession of uprisings in North Africa. What kind of revolution were they, and do they fit Arendt's conception? To my mind, Dabashi starts with Arendt the sooner to take his leave, on account of the difficulty in matching what the world witnessed and millions of Egyptian experienced in Tahrir Square with the genealogy of the US and French revolutions analyzed by Arendt. So, in which genealogy of revolutions do the Arab Spring/intifadas belong, or are they a new departure?

First of all, Tahrir Square emerged from colonial difference, from the experience of colonial domination, physical and epistemic. Nothing like that had occurred in the US or France. Colonial difference was partially at work in the US Revolution but hardly so in the French Revolution. This was because the Founding Fathers were gaining independence from their rulers in England (similar to the process of decolonization during the Cold War), while at once being their heirs, and at the same time suppressing Native Americans, expropriating their land and exploiting enslaved Africans. In this sense it was the rearticulation of coloniality exercised by the British Crown and other imperial monarchies of the time (France, Holland, Spain, Portugal). In the US, the revolutionaries were discontented Europeans, slave traders and repressors of indigenous cultures. In France, they were European bourgeois confronting the monarchy and the Church. Both were adding to the long history of Western imperialism that started with the Spanish colonial revolution in the sixteenth century. This revolution dismantled existing civilizations and built upon them monuments, institutions, educational, social and economic structures. The Levellers' movement, the so called "American" (US) Revolution, the Haitian Revolution, and the independence of Spanish America that led to a set of new republics were the first peripheral jolts of the modern colonial world, building upon the foundations of the Iberian colonial revolution in the New World. The Levellers' activity and the French Revolution took place in the heart of Europe, not in the periphery of the Americas where Europe set up the first colonies, before England and France extended their tentacles into Asia and Africa.

The era of decolonization, roughly 1945–1979, was the second peripheral jolt of the modern/colonial world system. But the process failed. Almost half a century later, the Arab Spring and intifadas to the south of the Mediterranean brought to prominence what many had long known. The great leaders and thinkers of decolonization and their work (Lumumba, Cabral, Beko) fell into the hands of imperial collaborators to their own benefit. At the same time in the north of the Mediterranean we have the Indignados of the South of Europe, in Greece and Spain. And forgotten at the time by mainstream and independent media were the uprisings in Bolivia and Ecuador that deposed several presidents. What is the genealogy of these revolutions, or are they revolutions without a genealogy?

Uprisings at the beginning of the twenty-first century created the conditions for the election of Evo Morales in Bolivia and, shortly after, Rafael Correa in Ecuador. Although today it is hard to see these governments as "leftist," they are certainly not "right-wing conservative." An important point, which cannot be explored here, is that the kind of revolutions that erupted in Bolivia and Ecuador at the beginning of the twenty-first century bear comparison to the Arab Spring/ intifadas in MENA and to the Indignados/as in the south of Europe. They seem not to fit the model of the US and French revolutions. Indeed they appear to represent a moving away from the trajectory of the eighteenth-century revolutions, the one creating the United States of America and the other paving the way for the modern nation-state. In the south of Europe, two of the consequences of the Indignados/as uprising was the consolidation of Syriza in Greece and the emergence of Podemos in Spain.

The issues and consequences that the Arab Spring/intifada raise reflect domestic and regional history and circumstances; as such they are closer to the uprisings in Ecuador and Bolivia than to events in Greece and Spain. That is, the MENA and Andean countries are part of the legacy of colonialism and coloniality (the underlying logic of any expression of modern colonialism), while the south of Europe emerged from a history of imperial differences between the north and the south of Europe.

Dabashi needs to depart from Arendt because the local histories he is dealing with demand a double critique, which is not a necessity for Arendt. "Double critique" is a concept introduced by another Third World philosopher and storyteller, the Moroccan Abdelkebir Khatibi. The double critique in Dabashi's essays moves between the Muslim Brotherhood and previous Egyptian governments led by elites collaborating with Westernization. In the case of Egypt it was no longer Britain but the US with which leaders collaborated. Coloniality doesn't need colonialism; it needs a collaborator. Here is one quotation from one of Dabashi's essays on revolution that makes clear the nature of his concern:

To begin to think of the rights of that prototypical citizen,
we should not start with the misleading distinction between
"seculars" and "Muslims" but with non-Muslim Egyptians,
with Copts, with Jews, and with any other so-called "religious
minority." The whole notion of "religious minority" must be
categorically dismantled, and in the drafting of the constitution
the rights of citizenship irrespective of religious affiliation
must be written in such sound terms that there is no distinction between a Copt, a Jew, or a Muslim, let alone a so-called
"secular," who is also a Muslim in colonial disguise.[28]

What are the issues at stake in the "revolutions" in North
African and the South American Andes: who revolted and what
are the consequences? First, it cannot be said that the eighteenth-
century revolutions brought into being the pluri-national state.
The European nation-state was mono-national. For in the South
American Andes the revolts were led by the Indigenous rather
than by Latin American whites (generally mestizos/as); the
result being an Aymara president in Bolivia, and a mestizo in
Ecuador who speaks Quichua, the most widely spoken Indigenous language in the country. The second consequence was
the rewriting of both countries' constitutions, wherein each
defined itself as a "plurinational state." "Plurality" of religion
has not been a major issue in the history of the Americas since
1500. Ancient civilizations – Mayas, Incas and Aztecs, and many
other cultures invaded by the Spanish, Portuguese and later on
the French, Dutch and British – were declared peoples without
religion (and without history too, because they did not use the
Latin alphabet – necessary, according to the Spanish, to have
a history). Dabashi's paragraph quoted above points in that
direction, and in so doing undermines the very foundation of
the modern and secular (and bourgeois if you are a Marxist)

28. "To Protect the Revolution, Overcome the False Secular–Islamist Divide."

nation-state. If we look, then, for the genealogy of the Arab Spring, we would trace it to the first revolutions that claimed the formation of a plurinational state. And this is also valid for the emergence of Podemos in Spain. Spain is ready to begin the conversation that will take it in the direction of a plurinational state. I am not sure that this will be a pressing issue in Greece, although globalization has undermined the very assumption that a nation should be mono-national – that is, to one state corresponds one ethnicity (Greek *ethnos*; Latin *nation*).

The nation-states that emerged from the first modern/colonial jolt in the periphery of Europe (the Americas) and in Europe itself have one element in common: the belief that to one state corresponds one nation. Or, put the other way, only one nation corresponds to the state. That myth was sustainable in Europe in the eighteenth and nineteenth centuries (it is no longer the case; in the twenty-first century, migration has destroyed the illusion), and it could be maintained in the Americas because the population of European descent controlled the state, declared themselves the nation and marginalized, from 1500 to 1800, the Indigenous and Afro-descendant population. When the steamboat and the railroad made migration on a massive scale possible, the idea of one nation/one state was consolidated so successfully that it appeared to be reality rather than a fiction.

Let's ask the question again: what are the meanings and the consequences of Indigenous uprisings in the Andes, the Zapatistas twenty years ago in Southern Mexico and Central America, the Indignados in the south of Europe, the intifadas in the MENA region, the Euromaidan revolution, and more recently the Umbrella Revolution in Hong Kong? The meanings are not the same in South America, Southern Mexico,

the MENA countries, Hong Kong or Ukraine. Each region
has its own local history entangled with Westernization. But
these are no longer a series of revolutions led by an emerging
ethno-class in Europe, the bourgeoisie, and their heirs in the
New World, Anglos and French in North America (the US and
Canada); Spanish and Portuguese in South and Central America;
Africans in Haiti, who were not supposed to take the matter of
freedom into their own hands. And the consequences are clear.
Indigenous uprisings, intifadas, Indignados/as, Euromaidan
have been initiated by the world order to come, the ending of
the era of the national state, the coming of plurinational states,
the reaction of the extreme right to the unstoppable forces of
history, and, most likely, the decline of the nation-state in both
its former mono-national and its plurination national versions.
This may be the major consequence of a politicization of civil
society and the emergence of a process that – in spite of revolutions being taken over by reactionary forces, as in Egypt and
Ukraine, resultant chaos in Libya, and the cycle of peripheral
and Southern European jolts of the captured decolonization
of the twentieth century by native collaborationist elites – is
announcing the emergence and re-emergence of a variegated
global political society corresponding to the waning of the eras
introduced by the US and French revolutions. There is no conti-
nuity but only discontinuity here. That is why Dabashi needed
to depart from Arendt. And this is also another consequence
of the way non-European philosophers think, as their/our own
history is of course entangled with European history by the
chains of coloniality.

In conclusion I shall outline some of the philosophical, episte-
mological and political issues that this debate has brought into

the open, an understanding of which is crucial to addressing the question "Can non-Europeans think?" Certainly we can and do, but the point is, what do we think about, and what are the vital concerns for the Third World (up to 1989) and for non-European thinkers of the global South and the eastern hemisphere today?[29]

First, let us consider the question of coloniality, postcoloniality and decoloniality. The term "postcolonial" appears frequently in Dabashi's book. He points to Edward Said, and particularly his *Orientalism* (1978), as a vital anchor of his thinking, but also of his life. He devotes an essay, now a chapter in this book, to his first encounter and subsequent friendship. I would venture to say that Said is for Dabashi what Jacques Lacan is for Žižek, and indeed what Anibal Quijano is for my own thinking.

Regarding "postcoloniality," Said became postcolonialist *après la lettre*. When he published *Orientalism*, in 1978, the words "postcoloniality" and "postcolonialism" were not yet the talk of the town. In the following year François Lyotard published *La condition postmoderne* (translated in 1984 as *The Postmodern Condition*). So arguably postcoloniality emerged piggybacking on postmodernity. Said's *Orientalism* became postcolonial retrospectively. However, relevant to the issues under discussion here is that Said published another important book in the same year, *The Question of Palestine* (1978), that seldom seems to make it onto lists of postcolonial works. Now, while *Orientalism* fits the postcolonial frame as defined in the 1980s, *The Question of Palestine* points in another direction, one that was framed in the 1950s: the decolonial rather than the postcolonial.[30] It parallels

---

29. On the global South and eastern hemisphere, see Walter Mignolo, "The North of the South and the West of the East," *Ibraaz. Contemporary Visual Cultures in North Africa and the Middle East,* November 2014.

30. Gurminder K. Bhambra, "Postcolonial and Decolonial Dialogues," *Postcolonial Studies,*

arguments made by Albert Memmi's *The Colonizer and the Colonized* (1955), Aimé Césaire's *Discourse on Colonialism* (1955) and Frantz Fanon's *The Wretched of the Earth* (1961).

These arguments, and others similar to them, were contemporaneous with the Bandung Conference of 1955, a landmark event for decolonial thinking and acting, in terms of both interstate relations and intersubjective decolonization. Decolonization, Fanon stated,

> is the veritable creation of new men [*sic*]. But this creation owes nothing of its legitimacy to any supernatural power; the "thing" which has been colonized becomes man [*sic*] during the same process by which it frees itself.[31]

In Fanon's decolonization, and in today's decoloniality, there are two interrelated trajectories. One is the sphere of the state, involving both domestic and interstate relations; the other is the intersubjective sphere in each of us, as persons crossed by racial and gender lines. That is, there are colonial epistemic and ontological differences (as exemplified in the question "Can non-Europeans/Asians think?"). The interrelationship between the two spheres is a topic for another occasion. The point here is that while postcoloniality is anchored on postmodernity, decolonization and decoloniality are anchored on the symbolic legacies of the Bandung Conference and the debates of the 1950s, during the hard times of political decolonization. We have moved from Euro-centered to decolonial epistemology.[32]

A second distinction I wish to make is between multipolarity and pluriversality. Multipolarity is a common concept

vol. 17, no. 2 (2014), pp. 115–21.

31. Fanon, *Les damnés*, p. 28.

32. Linda Martín Alcoff, "Mignolo's Epistemology of Coloniality," *New Centennial Review*, vol. 7, no. 3 (2007), pp. 79–101.

in international relations and political theory today. As such, it names the coming world order in which there will no longer be one state self-appointed to lead a *unipolar* world order, but rather – and we are already entering this new age – a *multipolar* global world order. These are processes in the spheres of state and interstate relations that no doubt impinge on intersubjective relations in a multipolar world order.

Consequently, the goal enunciated by Fanon – the coming of a new human being – requires us to free ourselves from the non-human conditions in which racial and sexual lines have been drawn in the making of the unipolar world order. Freeing ourselves from the classification bequeathed to us requires us to break with the "unipolar" idea of knowledge, which in decolonial vocabulary translates into Eurocentric epistemic universality. Decolonial horizons aim at epistemic pluriversality; or, if one wishes to maintain some kind of universality, one might refer to "pluriversality as a universal project," which today is one of the ultimate decolonial horizons. Argentine philosopher Enrique Dussel would describe it as transmodernity.[33]

I hope that my contribution here helps to highlight the relevance of the issues raised by Hamid Dabashi's question. And I trust that it explains my intervention and the assertiveness of the response "Yes, we can" to the question "Can non-Europeans think?" Yes, we can, and we must. And we are doing so.

Walter Mignolo

---

33. Enrique Dussel, "Eurocentrism and Modernity (Introduction to the Frankfurt Lectures)," *Boundary 2*, vol. 20, no. 3 (1993), pp. 65–76.

INTRODUCTION

Can Europeans Read?

"Fuck you, Walter Mignolo!" With those grandiloquent words and the gesture they must have occasioned and accompanied, the distinguished and renowned European philosopher Slavoj Žižek begins his response to a piece that Walter Mignolo wrote in conversation with my essay "Can Non-Europeans Think?" Žižek is quite eloquent and habitually verbose: "Okay, fuck you, who are these bloody much more interesting intellectuals…? Let's say I was not overly impressed."

What was the reason, you might wonder, for the eminent European philosopher's outburst: why so intemperate a reaction? What had Walter Mignolo said to deserve such precise elocutions from a leading European thinker?

A simple question

In January 2013 I published on the Al Jazeera website the playfully titled essay "Can Non-Europeans Think?" The essay soon emerged as one of the most popular pieces I have written in my academic career. It went viral on the Internet, to the degree that a polemical essay on philosophical thinking can go viral. It received more hits than anything I had ever written on that website. It had touched a nerve and people began to read and reflect on it far beyond my own limited reach or expectation when I wrote it. That piece is now the title of this book, which points to a mode of thinking I have marked as beyond the limits of the condition called "postcoloniality." This book comes together, in effect, as a declaration of independence, not just from the condition of postcoloniality, but from the limited and now exhausted epistemics it had historically occasioned. Here you will perhaps have detected a cautious searching for the paths ahead, for a condition and urgency of thinking beyond coloniality, beyond postcoloniality, and thus above all beyond the explicit or implicit presence of a European interlocutor looking over our shoulder as we write.

And there precisely was the rub! Soon after the publication of my essay, Santiago Zabala, a research professor of philosophy at the University of Barcelona, responded to it. He did so in the belief that I had written it in response to a piece of his and thus felt obligated to reciprocate. This response to my essay, though quite welcome, seemed a bit odd to me, for I had not written it in response to his, but rather had just used something he had written earlier as a hook on which to hang my argument. He appeared to have taken offense at my essay, thought I was accusing him (and by extension other European philosophers) of Eurocentrism, and in turn took the fact that I had mentioned the eminent Italian Marxist philosopher Antonio Gramsci as an indication that I was completely out to lunch, accusing him of something with which I was myself afflicted! It was a very bizarre response indeed to a charge I had never made. In general I find the charge of Eurocentrism punishingly boring, have no interest in the inflated argument, and consider the entire diction of Zabala's piece rather juvenile, akin to the schoolyard pissing contest I had left behind in my high school back in Iran decades ago. Of course Europeans are Eurocentric, just as our Molla Nasreddin famously thought (in jest) that where he had nailed the rein of his mule was the center of the universe – and why shouldn't they believe this, the Europeans or Molla Nasreddin? I was not addressing Zabala, or any other European philosopher for that matter. But he thought I was.[1]

Soon a comrade of Zabala, Michael Marder, joined forces with his European brother and wrote another piece against me in Al Jazeera, in which he too read my piece as addressed to Zabala and thought of it as somewhat comical. Marder's objection was that I had ignored the fact that the philosophers Zabala had cited were all "counter-hegemonic" and thus quite radically subversive, and by virtue of which honorific title they were on my side of the false divide.[2] Again, he could read my piece in whatever way he wished, including this outlandishly silly reading, but what greatly amused me was that these young European philosophers were so self-conscious of being "European philosophers" that they felt obligated to come out gang-like and defend themselves against the colored boy who had dared to piss on their territory. My late mother used to remark that as soon as you pick up the stick the cat that has just stolen something runs away. You may not have intended

1. For my original essay, see www.aljazeera.com/indepth/opinion/2013/01/2013114142638 797542.html (15 January 2013). For Zabala's response, see www.aljazeera.com/indepth/opinion/2013/01/2013127122357321377.html (3 February 2013). For Mignolo's response, see www.aljazeera.com/indepth/opinion/2013/02/20132672747320891.html (19 February 2013). For Žižek's response, see http://backdoorbroadcasting.net/2013/02/slavoj-zizek-a-reply-to-my-critics (28 February 2013), and www.critical-theory.com/zizek-responds-to-his-critics.

2. Michael Marder's essay can be found at www.aljazeera.com/indepth/opinion/2013/03/201331411225576I369.html.

to hit anyone, but the cat knew he was a thief. At any rate, I was not adressing Zabala or Marder. I was in fact addressing no European philosopher at all. But whenever something happens anywhere around the world they think it has something to with them. It does not. And that precisely is the point: people like me are no longer interested in whatever it is they fancy to be "hegemonic" or "counter-hegemonic" in Europe and for Europeans. We have been to much greener pastures. Yet these belated defenders of the dead interlocutor they call "the West" were not up to speed with where we were. We (by which I mean we colored boys and girls from their former colonies) were mapping a new topography of the world (our world, the whole planetary disposition of the globe we are now claiming as ours) in our thinking and scholarship; while they were turning their ignorance of this body of work into a critical point of strength for their philosophical arguments – just as their forebears did with our parents' labor, abused and discarded it. They did not know we had told their Žižek to go enjoy himself long before he said to our Mignolo "Fuck you!"

It was at this point that Walter Mignolo wrote his learned piece in direct response to my essay, in which he returned my question as an answer. Mignolo's was the first essay I took seriously, for in it he began to address in earnest the issues I had raised. My essay had occasioned many other responses, among them – and perhaps the most poignant so far as the substance of my argument is concerned – the magnificent piece by Aditya Nigam, "End of Postcolonialism and the Challenge for 'Non-European' Thought."[3] The advantage of Nigam's piece was that he was deeply informed by my work in general, and to

3. http://criticalencounters.net/2013/05/19/end-of-postcolonialism-and-the-challenge-for-non-european-thought.

the degree he engaged with my argument did so from within my work. Nigam's piece made a critical point very clear to me: that folks like Zabala and Marder really have no clue about my or anyone else's work beyond their European nose, for they had no interest or reason to do so. Mignolo, Nigam and I are part of a generation of postcolonial thinkers who grew up compelled to learn the language and culture of our colonial interlocutors. These interlocutors have never had any reason to reciprocate. They had become provincial in their assumptions of universality. We had become universal under the colonial duress that had sought to provincialize us.

It was in direct response to Walter Mignolo's essay that Žižek had started with that superlative opening and then proceeded to make his case as to why he does not take anything non-Europeans say seriously. I will leave Mignolo to fend for himself, for he is more than capable of doing so when dealing with Žižek. My task here is no longer to defend or fortify the arguments in my essay "Can Non-Europeans Think?" For, whatever it is worth, it stands on its own two feet. Instead I am far more interested in the curious question of whether or not European philosophers can actually read something and learn from it – rather than assimilate it back into what they already know. It is in this context that I wish to ponder what it is that brings a European thinker to use such expletives when confronted by something that a Mignolo or a Nigam or a Dabashi might say.

To read forward

Why should Europeans not be able to read, even when we write in the language they understand? They cannot read because they (as "Europeans," caught in the snare of an exhausted but self-nostalgic metaphor) are assimilating what they read back into that snare and into what they already know – and are thus incapable of projecting it forward into something they may not know and yet might be able to learn. Historical conditions are the bedrock of ideas. The world at large, and the Arab and Muslim world in particular, is changing; these changes are the *conditio sine qua non* of new ideas that are yet to be articulated – precisely in the same manner that the myth of "Europe" or "the West" was born and began to generate ideas. My central argument over the last few decades has been that the condition of coloniality has occasioned a mode of knowledge production across the colonial world – from Asia to Africa to Latin America – that today we know and examine in the moment we designate as "postcolonial." In my books on the Arab revolution and the Green Movement in Iran I have argued that, as evidenced in these revolutionary uprisings, the modes of knowledge production in the postcolonial register – militant Islamism, anticolonial nationalism, and Third World socialism – have in fact exhausted themselves. European thinkers like Žižek and Zabala, important and insightful as they are in their own immediate circles, are out of touch with these realities, and to the degree that they are they cannot come to terms with their unfolding particularities in terms immediate to their idiomaticities. For them "Philosophy" is a mental gymnastics performed with the received particulars of European philosophy in its postmodern or poststructuralist registers – exciting and productive to the degree that they can be. But unless and until those defining moments are structurally linked, thematically moved and conceptually compromised, and thus epistemically violated, they will have very little or nothing to say about the world that is unfolding in front of us.

Žižek claims Fanon all to himself by way of dismissing Mignolo:

> Now let's go back to Mignolo, what Mignolo proposes is thus a version of Baudrillard battle cry... "Forget Foucault".... Forget Europe, we have better things to do than deal with European philosophy, better things than endlessly deconstructing. He explicitly includes deconstruction. This is endless narcissistic self-probing, [and] we should simply step out. The irony here is that this battle cry did not hold for Fanon himself, who dealt intensively [with European philosophy] and was proud of it. The first obscenity seems to me how dare he to quote Fanon! Fanon is my hero, that's why I defend him against soft guys like Homi Bhabha, who wrote long texts trying to neutralize, normalize Fanon. No, he didn't really mean it, with killing and violence; he meant some sublime gesture where there is no blood and nobody is really hurt and so on. Let's face it, Fanon dealt extensively with Hegel, psychoanalysis, Sartre, even Lacan. My third reaction would have been: When I read lines like Mignolo's, I reach not for the gun but for Fanon.[4]

Žižek can have his Fanon all to himself. There is plenty of Fanon left for others. But Fanon on himself? Really? What is that supposed to mean? That we dark folks had our Fanon so we had better sit down and be quiet. Fanon was horribly wrong in his essay "Unveiling Algeria" and totally blinded to the nature and function of veiling in Muslim urbanity. So now what? We Muslims had better shut up and be happy that Mr Žižek has read his Fanon. I agree with Žižek's criticism of Bhabha, whose useless bourgeois postmodernism I cannot stand. But why is Professor Žižek acting like a rookie graduate student regurgitating these names? So what if Fanon had read and engaged with Hegel? The entire world seems to have been cathected for Žižek with the name Fanon, where we colonized

---

4. www.critical-theory.com/zizek-responds-to-his-critics.

folks had our say, and so we had better shush – or, as he so eloquently puts it, "Fuck off!"

The point, however, is not to have any exclusive claim on Fanon, or to fetishize him (or any other non-European thinker for that matter) as a frozen talisman for Europeans to cite to prove they are not philosophically racist. The point is not to dismiss but to overcome the myth of "the West" as the measure of truth. Žižek claims:

> I am a man and what I have to recapture is the whole past of the world, I am not responsible only for the slavery involved in Santo Domingo, every time man has contributed to the victory of the dignity of the spirit, every time a man has said no to an attempt to subjugate his fellows, I have felt solidarity with his act. In no way does my basic vocation have to be drawn from the past of peoples of color. In no way do I have to dedicate myself to reviving some black civilization unjustly ignored. I will not make myself the man of any past. My black skin is not a repository for specific values. Haven't I got better things to do on this earth than avenge the blacks of the 17th century?[5]

This is all fine and dandy – for Žižek. He can make any claim he wishes. All power to him. But the point is the singularity of the world, his world: he claims that as a European he is responsible not just for slavery but also for fighting injustice. He is absolutely right. But so is the "black man" he just buried alive and relegated to the seventeenth century. He asserts prophetically that he is "a man." One hopes he means this not just anatomically. But he is not the only man, either in body or as archetype. The "black man," as he puts it, is also a man, a different man, in flogged body and in denied archetype. The black and brown person – male and female – also has a world, a contemporary

5. www.critical-theory.com/the-critical-theory-guide-to-that-time-zizek-pissed-everyone-off-again.

world, the world that Žižek occupies. Žižek is absolutely right that he has a total claim on this world that he occupies, and over which he and his philosophical precursors have presided. But what about a non-European – made "non-European" by virtue of "the European"? Can she also have a claim on this world, and in a philosophical or artistic or revolutionary move claim for herself the colonial and the postcolonial, the European and the non-European, heritage and thereby transcend the world that Žižek claims exclusively for himself, placing herself in some other world, a different worldliness beyond Žižek's European imagination? Of course she can, without waiting for Žižek's permission, acknowledgement, or even recognition. The world we inhabit, planet Earth, has many imaginative geographies; that of Žižek and all his fellow Europeans is only one such geography. The point is that they are utterly blinded to the possibility of these alternative geographies – both historical and contemporary.

Other people are also entitled "to recapture" – as, of course, is Žižek – a world beyond their imagination. Žižek is correct that "In no way does my basic vocation have to be drawn from the past of peoples of color." But those very "people of color" (as he categorizes them, according to his prerogative) do not only have a past; they also have a present, and a future. Žižek is blinded to that present unless he assimilates it backward into his present, and is indifferent to that future unless he gets (singularly) to define it. He is unconditionally correct that "In no way do I have to dedicate myself to reviving some black civilization unjustly ignored." But a "black civilization" unjustly ignored is peopled by other people, by other thinking people, kicking people, people who talk, and talk back, and talk past Žižek. He is entirely entitled to say "I will not make myself the man of any past" – and he should not, as no one should. But the people of color he just buried alive in their past are also living and breathing a present of which he seems to be blissfully ignorant. He is, of course, pulling my colored beard when he says, "My black skin is not a repository for specific values." But mine is, and I am a living repository of not just "values" but universes, emotions, words, sentiments, rebellions that he and all his Horatios have not yet dreamt of in their philosophy.

Žižek and his fellow philosophers are oblivious to those geographies because they cannot read any other script, any other map, than the colonial script and the colonial map with which Europeans have read and navigated the world; conversely they cannot read any other script or map because they are blinded to alternative geographies that resistance to that colonialism had written and navigated. The condition is exacerbated any time people around the world rise up to assert their geography as the ground zero of a world historical event. At these times Žižek and his followers are all up and about trying to read the world back into what they already know. There is a new condition beyond postcoloniality that these Europeans cannot read, hard as they try to assimilate it back into the condition of coloniality. The task is not a mere critique of neo-Orientalism, which always is commensurate with immediate and short-sighted political interests, but to overcome "Europe" as an idea and make it behave as one among any number of other exhausted metaphors, neither less nor more potent, organic, or trustworthy. Europe was "the invention of the Third World," as Fanon fully realized – both in material and normative senses of the term. I have already argued that we need to change the interlocutor with whom we discuss the terms of our emerging worlds. We should no longer address a dead interlocutor. Europe is dead.

Long live Europeans. The Islam they had invented in their Orientalism is dead. Long live Muslims. The Orient they had created, the Third World they had crafted to rule and denigrate, have disappeared. If only those who still see themselves as Orientals would begin to decolonize their minds too.

Young European philosophers like Zabala and Marder, who think that as Europeans they own the world of ideas, feign the authority of their colonial forebears as if anything anyone says anywhere in the world is about them. History has started anew globally – from the Green Movement in Iran to the Arab Spring, to Indignados in Europe, to Occupy Wall Street in the US, to massive protests in Brazil. These uprisings will generate their own regimes of knowledge, not despite the reactionary and counterrevolutionary forces launched against them but precisely because of them. The anthropology of these revolutions is the first discipline that has been torpedoed into nullity. It is the very idea of "Europe" that is today most suspect and dispensable. Europeans as people, too, have reentered history, if European philosophers old and young were to let them go, and let them be, and learn from them new words. From modernity to postmodernity, from structuralism to poststructuralism, from constructivism to deconstructionism, European philosophers chase after their own tails; and what was called 'postcolonialism' in and of itself was the product of a European colonial imagining that wreaked havoc on this earth and finally ran aground. We are no longer postcolonial creatures.

The condition of coloniality that had given intellectual birth to us – from Césaire through Fanon to Said – has run its course. That episteme is no longer producing any meaningful knowledge. We are free, but not aimless; liberated, but not futile. This "we" is no longer we folks in the global South, for some of us

have migrated to the global North chasing after their capital in
search of jobs, as their capital has gone positively transnational
and chases after our cheap labor in the global South. So this
"we" is no longer color-coded or continental and includes all
those disenfranchised by the global operation of capital whether
in the north or south of planet Earth, or deep into cyberspace,
or else flown into outer space, and those richly privileged by the
selfsame operation. In its originary modernity this globalized
capital was made mythically "European." It no longer is. It has
been de-Europeanized, freed from its overreaching fetishes. Rich
Arab, Indian, Russian, Chinese, Latin American, or African
entrepreneurs, mafia states, deep states, garrison states, Israeli
warlords, and mercenary murderers of Isis are part and parcel
of a worldly reality that has for ever dispensed with the myth
of "the West."

Orientalism then and now

In what way have we actually transcended our forebears, colonial and postcolonial, modern and postmodern? Where exactly
is it that we stand and think, and upon what leveled ground
is it that Mignolo, Nigam and I can invite Žižek, Zabala, and
Marder kindly to drop their guards and join us and let us think
and play together?

In a piece I wrote for Al Jazeera in July 2012, I took the *New
York Times* columnist Nicholas Kristof to task for a series of
cliché-ridden pieces he wrote on Iran following a quick visit.[6]
Soon an article appeared in the *Jerusalem Post* taking me to task
for abusing the term "Orientalism" and using it to bully Mr.

---

6. www.aljazeera.com/indepth/opinion/2012/07/201271131925534684.html?utm_content=
automate&utm_campaign=Trial6&utm_source=NewSocialFlow&utm_term=plustweets&
utm_medium=MasterAccount.

Kristof.[7] In this piece, the author, Seth J. Frantzman, asserts that "the term 'orientalism,' or more specifically the accusation that someone is an 'orientalist,' should be deracinated from discourse" – adding that the term has become "nonsensical in its application." He believes that in criticizing Orientalist clichés we in fact are blinding the world: "This is an attempt to make the world ignorant, so that only the Iranian scholar can tell others about Iran, and only the Chinese communist party official can explain China to outsiders. We are supposed to rely on the Islamists of Mali to explain why they are destroying the 'false idols' present in the Sufi tombs of Timbuktu" – thus effectively and not so subtly equating "the Iranian scholar" with the Chinese communist and the Mali Islamist terrorists. (Does that equation ring a bell with a certain mass murderer in Norway?)

One can, of course, experience a certain passing pleasure in making it onto a Zionist's blacklist, as I did long before this *Jerusalem Post* figure knew of my name from the book his soulmate David Horowitz wrote on the *101 Most Dangerous Academics in America*.[8] But so far as this particular "Iranian scholar" is concerned (now that with a keystroke the *Jerusalem Post* columnist has stripped me of my American citizenship altogether – for quite obviously a "Hamid Dabashi" cannot be an American, while a Seth J. Frantzman can at one and the same time be both an "American" citizen and an "Israeli" settler colonist – a racist assumption that of course is not "Orientalism"), in the very same piece in which I criticized Nicholas Kristof I also praised his *New York Times* colleague Roger Cohen's reporting from

7. The *Jerusalem Post* article can be found at www.jpost.com/Arts-and-Culture/Arts/ Terra-Incognita-The-orientalist-shield.
8. See David Horowitz, *The Professors: The 101 Most Dangerous Academics in America*, Regnery Publishing, Washington DC, 2006.

Iran. So I am quite obviously not in the business of silencing anyone, including non-Iranians, from saying anything (sensible or inane) about Iran, or anywhere else for that matter.

Yet, despite its sophomoric tone and flawed logic, Seth J. Frantzman's piece does indeed have a legitimate point, namely the pervasive abuse of the term "Orientalism" in journalistic writings – though, ironically, his own piece fits perfectly within the realm of such dilettante abuses.

Much to Edward Said's chagrin to his dying day, both his book and the concept of "Orientalism" have been not just duly influential but also widely abused – and that abuse continues apace today. Said never tired of trying his best to correct these erroneous readings of his groundbreaking idea. However, the abuse eventually took the form of a fetishized trope. There are people today who think the very term "Arab Spring" is an Orientalist invention, evidently oblivious to the fact that the term "Spring of Nations" was also used for the European revolutions of 1848. A comment marking the non-violent disposition of the Arab Spring when it was initially launched, is enough to provoke accusations of Orientalism, or, worse, of "self-Orientalization." Indeed, believe it or not, there are even bloggers who consider any comparison between the Iranian and Egyptian revolutions a case of Orientalism!

At the root of the problem is the fact that Edward Said's *Orientalism* (1978) has now assumed the status of the proverbial 'classic': a book that everyone cites but scarcely anyone reads. But just because the term "Orientalism" has been systematically misused by its detractors and admirers alike, or in effect turned into a term of abuse people hurl at anyone and everything they don't like, it does not mean that one of the most powerful analytical concepts of the last century ought to be categorically avoided, disregarded, or indeed "deracinated from discourse," as the *Jerusalem Post* columnist instructs us to do. Quite the contrary: precisely on account of such abusive dilettantism, the term needs incessant theoretical re/articulation. Persistent theorization will not prevent people from abusing it in one way or another, of course, but it might help the rest of us avoid the confusion such misuse is bound to generate.

Contrary to Mr. Frantzman's confusion and that of many others – both "Orientals" and "non-Orientals" – the critique of Orientalism was a critique of a mode of knowledge-production, and most certainly not that of any race or people or culture. The mode of knowledge production called "Orientalism" was commensurate with the European imperial project; the fortunate fact that scholars ranging from Abd al-Rahman al-Jabarti to V.G. Kiernan, Bernard S. Cohn, Anwar Abd al-Malik, and Talal Assad had addressed the relationship between empire and knowledge production before Edward Said (or even Michel Foucault) shows that the tradition of this critique has had a much deeper epistemic history, of which both those who abuse the term and those who are incensed by it seem to be blissfully ignorant. Entirely independent of the Said/Foucault trajectory, that history can be traced back, as I have demonstrated in *Post-Orientalism: Knowledge and Power in Time of Terror* (2008), to a vast and variegated tradition in the sociology of knowledge, whose genealogy includes Karl Marx (1818–1883), Max Scheler (1874–1928), and George Herbert Mead (1863–1931). There is more to "Orientalism" – and to the organic relationship between knowledge and power – than can be conceived of by a *New York Times* or a *Jerusalem Post* journalist.

If we unpack the term "Orientalism," and are attentive to Said's dismantling of it in his classic study, the evolving historical symbiosis between knowledge and power becomes clear. This reading helps provide an insight into the terms of the new *regime of knowledge* of which I have been writing since the rise of the Arab revolutions in 2010 – the premiss that may enable Europeans and non-Europeans alike to move onto the same page, and there to overcome the condition of coloniality that has made one unable to think and the other unable to read the idioms of an emerging world.

Knowledge and power

So where do we get together to think through our fragile worldliness, so that "the European" is finally demythologized and stripped of the remnants of colonial and imperial arrogance; so that when he or she philosophizes with me (the Muslim, the Oriental, the Third World intellectual, or any other term used to mark and alienate me), it is no longer as an Obama or a Hillary Clinton, or as NATO sending drones over the primitive Taliban? It is long overdue that Europeans exit the certainty of their mythical self-philosophizing and re-enter history. They must come down off their high horses and fat Humvees and stop philosophizing me, and instead kindly consider philosophizing *with* me. The moment they dismount they will see me, Walter Mignolo, and Aditya Nigam waiting, with laptops open.

But where exactly will be the location of this historic rendez-vous? Let's take a detour.

"Orientalism" has today become a journalistic cliché. The problem with journalistic uses and abuses is that writers tend to fetishize the term without taking the trouble to learn and convey what it means, and how as a concept it may have an organic life and evolve. Towards the end of my *Post-Orientalism* (a book whose existence has yet to be registered by the *Jerusalem Post*)

I argue that the modus operandi of knowledge production we know categorically as "Orientalism," and that was the subject of Edward Said's magisterial critique, has by now dissolved into a degenerative phase I have identified as "endosmosis," or disposable knowledge – knowledge no longer predicated on any enduring episteme. This proposition is predicated on an active historicization of "Orientalism" beyond the immediate theorization of Edward Said, which was primarily a literary-critical take on the crisis of *representation* embedded in the relation between knowledge and power.

As a mode of knowledge-production, I argue, Orientalism is not a fait accompli, a closed and circuited project. It was the product of a particular moment in the history of European colonialism, and as a result changes and falters with the fate of imperialism. Thus I have sought to formulate a historically more nuanced conception of Orientalism. The current, post-9/11, condition I identified as an amorphous mode of knowledge production, or a case of *epistemic endosmosis*, in which the aggressive formation of a field of public knowledge about Muslims is no longer conducive to the reversed formation of a sovereign (European or American) and all-knowing (Kantian) subject.

The transmutation of classical Orientalism to Area Studies and thence into disposable knowledge produced at US and European think tanks, I propose, was coterminous with the rise of an empire without hegemony. This *epistemic endosmosis* – or interested knowledge manufactured in think tanks and percolating into the public domain – is, I suggest, conducive to various modes of *disposable knowledge production*, predicated on no enduring or coherent episteme, but in fact modeled on disposable commodities that provide instant gratification and are then disposed of after one use only.

This is "fast knowledge" produced on the model of "fast food," with plastic cups, plastic knives, plastic forks, bad nutrition, false satisfaction. The US invades Afghanistan and these think tanks produce a knowledge conducive to that project; then the US leads another invasion of Iraq and these think tanks begin producing knowledge about Iraq, with little or no connection with what they had said about Afghanistan, or what they might say about Iran. There is little or no epistemic consistency among the three – for these forms of knowledge are produced under duress (with tight deadlines) and are entirely disposable. You throw them out after one use.

In *Post-Orientalism* I argue that, as an institutional reflection of this transformation, today right-wing think tanks like the Zionist WINEP (Washington Institute for Near Eastern Policy) or the neocon operation the Hoover Institution have by and large replaced universities as the institutional basis of these modes of knowledge production at the immediate service of the Empire. These two institutions – which are perfect examples of the rest – hire native informers with no academic or scholarly qualifications but who are ideologically compatible with their agenda. In a brilliant essay, "Tentacles of Rage: The Republican Propaganda Mill, A Brief History,"[9] Lewis Lapham has provided a detailed map of these institutions, along with the network of American millionaires and right-wing foundations who ever since the Civil Rights and Antiwar movement of the 1960s have aggressively supported them.

My assessment of this self-degenerative disposition of Orientalism was and remains predicated on the proposition that at this late (or, at least, the latest) stage of capitalism – with the

9. http://harpers.org/archive/2004/09/tentacles-of-rage.

scarcity of resources and the even more aggressive militariza-
tion of imperial domination – we are no longer witness to
sustained disciplinary formations of Orientalism at the stage that
Edward Said had best diagnosed it. Thus no master Orientalist on the model we know from the nineteenth century is in
fact anywhere in sight anymore – if we compare the exquisite
scholarship of someone like Ignaz Goldziher (1850–1921), for
example, with the paper-jammed propaganda copy machine
that is known as Bernard Lewis (b. 1916). (One of my principal
tasks in *Post-Orientalism* was to rescue and exonerate Ignaz
Goldziher from much abuse by both his Zionist biographers
and Muslim detractors.)

My clue regarding that proposition was entirely predicated
on Max Weber's last, prophetic, words in *The Protestant Ethic and
the Spirit of Capitalism* (1905). "One of the fundamental elements
of the spirit of modern capitalism," Weber observed, "and not
only of that but of all modern culture: rational conduct on
the basis of the idea of the calling was born ... from the spirit
of Christian asceticism." This singular insight of Weber into
capitalist modernity leads him to the beautiful discernment
that "the Puritan wanted to work in a calling; we are forced
to do so." From this he concludes:

> Since asceticism undertook to remodel the world and to work
> out its ideals in the world, material goods have gained an
> increasing and finally an inexorable power over the lives of men
> as at no previous period in history. Today the spirit of religious
> asceticism ... has escaped from the cage. But victorious capital-
> ism, since it rests on mechanical foundations, needs its support
> no longer.[10]

---

10. Max Weber, *The Protestant Ethic and the Spirit of Capitalism*, Routledge, London 2001,
p. 124.

As for the Enlightenment, Weber resorted to his occasional, but sublime, sense of humor: "The rosy blush of its laughing heir, the Enlightenment, seems also to be irretrievably fading, and the idea of duty in one's calling prowls about in our lives like the ghost of dead religious beliefs."[11] The astute diagnosis of that degenerative spiral then becomes the premiss upon which Weber builds his magisterial insight regarding the fate of our humanity at large, and the spirit of capitalism in particular:

> No one knows who will live in this cage in the future, or whether at the end of this tremendous development entirely new prophets will arise, or there will be a great rebirth of old ideas and ideals, or, if neither, mechanized petrification, embellished with a sort of convulsive self-importance. For of the last stage of this cultural development, it might well be truly said: "Specialists without spirit, sensualists without heart; this nullity imagines that it has attained a level of, civilization never before achieved."[12]

The Orientalism of those epochs that corresponded with that dawning spirit of capitalism and the predatory imperialism it entailed ultimately degenerated to the propaganda machinery of Bernard Lewis, who corresponds with the nullity that Weber aptly characterizes. But were it to be thought that Bernard Lewis was the example par excellence of "Specialists without spirit, sensualists without heart," I invite my readers to take a look at Nicholas Kristof (and at Seth J. Frantzman) on the precious pages of our "Paper of Record," the *Jerusalem Post* as they call it, to see how that Weberian "nullity" keeps degenerating.

Far beyond the limits of such journalistic dilettantism, however, the critique of the vestiges of Orientalism in the public

---

11. Ibid.
12. Ibid.

sphere should no longer be directed against the politics of representation but in precisely the opposite direction at the crisis of ideology, legitimacy, and hegemony that this phase of globalized imperialism faces. This critique is necessary because we in the Muslim world, in particular, are at the cusp of a new liberation geography (discussed in detail in *The Arab Spring: The End of Postcolonialism*[13]), and the democratic uprisings we witness are in need of new metaphors, and a radical transformation of the regime of knowledge that is integral to the Tahrir Square slogan "People demand the overthrow of the regime."

In the absence of that radical reshaping of the regime of knowledge with which we read the Arab and Muslim revolts, we are at the mercy of the all-time *Jerusalem Post* favorite Bernard Lewis, whose favorite trope in reading them is through his casual and aging conception of sex and bordello houses. "You have these vast numbers of young men growing up without the money, either for the brothel or the brideprice," Lewis once told Seth J. Frantzman's colleagues at the *Jerusalem Post* by way of explaining the Arab revolts, "with raging sexual desire. On the one hand, it can lead to the suicide bomber, who is attracted by the virgins of paradise – the only ones available to him. On the other hand, sheer frustration."[14] These are Frantzman's preferred means of understanding the world historical events we are witnessing. Any critique of such gibberish emanating from the tired but evidently still vivid imagination of an aging Orientalist will rub him the wrong way.

The battle lines are thus drawn as much in the streets and squares of our public spheres as they are around the new *régime*

13. Zed Books. London, 2012.
14. This interview can be found here in full: www.jpost.com/Opinion/Columnists/A-mass-expression-of-outrage-against-injustice.

du savoir that we need in order to understand and alter our emerging world. In that direction we need to clear from the table the lingering legacies of old-fashioned Orientalism and its varied transmutations, expose the theoretical illiteracy of those who have fetishized and keep abusing the term, and allow the emerging facts from our public sphere to define the new regime of knowledge that will speak to our will to resist power and help change it to an institutional claim on that sphere.

In that direction, Joel Beinin is correct in his observation that in the aftermath of the Egyptian presidential election we need a new political language.[15] But that language will emerge as much from new political alliances, as Beinin rightly suggests, as from a much larger frame of epistemic references that these revolutions have occasioned. Equally crucial and insightful is Seumas Milne's suggestion that "Egypt's revolution will only be secured by spreading it."[16] But that process of spreading, too, needs the "new political language" that Beinin calls for, right now, before Seth J. Frantzman contacts Homeland Security officials and has us all stripped of our citizenship and shipped to Guantánamo Bay.

Power is power

I took this detour from a critique of post/Orientalism because such militant misreadings are precisely the delusional prism that separates me, Walter Mignolo, and Aditya Nigam from Žižek, Zabala, and Marder. Instead of the habitual *mise-en-scène* within which we talk to them as they talk to themselves, we need to change the whole architectonics of this interlocution

---

15. Joel Beinin's essay can be found at www.jadaliyya.com/pages/index/6207/in-search-of-a-new-political-language.
16. Read Milne's argument here: www.theguardian.com/commentisfree/2012/jun/26/egypt-revolution-secured-by-spreading.

altogether, and address the only interlocutor that has been left to all of us: a fractured and self-destructing world. The European philosophers can only overcome what they consider their "crisis of the subject" by avoiding the Kantian cul-de-sac that defines the knowing subject as the European knowing subject and designates us – the rest of the world – as their knowable realm. We are no longer (if we ever were) knowable to that European knowing subject. Because we no longer exist as they had fathomed in their process of self-centering subjection, so have they ceased to exist as our or any other kind of knowing subject. They don't and cannot know anymore. The European knowing subject, to the degree that it is incarcerated within the dead certainties of being "European" – namely, as Fanon said, "the invention of the Third World" – cannot have a clue who and what we/they are. We must dismantle the fact that we are each other's figment of the imagination. We have now deposited both Kurtz of the *Heart of Darkness* and Mustapha Said of *Season of Migration to the North* in the dustbin of history.

We therefore come together at a new gathering of knowledge and power not to mourn but to dislodge the link. Here the will is not to power; it is to resist power. Once that negative dialectic (Adorno) is posited, we will see alternative worlds emerge beyond "the West and the Rest." Those worlds exist and enable here and now; they are not located back in the seventeenth century. Yet all those worlds are also on the verge of being subsumed into the two poles of cyberspace and outer space connecting the geopolitics that rules our lives to the cyber- and astropolitics that dwarf our very physicality, at the very moment when all the rich people have gone to the heavens to live on a satellite, leaving us, the wretched of the earth, on earth.[17] On this site I wish to teach them Ahmad Shamlou, Nazem Hekmat, Mahmoud Darwish, and Faiz Ahmad Faiz, in gratitude for what I have learned from their Heidegger, Derrida, Badiou, and Rancière. I wish to invite European philosophers to read these poets not through the exoticized lenses of Orientalism or Area Studies, but with the same attitude of critical intimacy that they approach their own philosophers. Thus I wish for them to join me in collapsing the binary between philosophy and poetry, to stand next to me as I show them the poetic philosophy of our poets, teaching them how to reread philosophical poetry from Nietzsche to Blanchot. If they read Shamlou they will understand Heidegger on Rilke better, and if they learn Darwish they will understand Langston Hughes, James Baldwin and C.L.R. James in a wholly different light.

This is not merely a world of my imagining. It is real. Here on earth the depletion of the myth of "the West" has created new alliances. Zionists in Israel think and act precisely like the Islamists in Iran, as a new generation of comprador intellectuals have moved into Europe and North America and collaborate with neocon cohorts to incorporate their homelands into the quagmire of globalized neoliberalism. Notorious Islamophobes like Ayaan Hirsi Ali and Foad Ajami are Muslims from whose company I would happily run to that of Giorgio Agamben, Alain Badiou, Daniel Bensaïd, Wendy Brown, Jean-Luc Nancy, or Jacques Rancière on any given day, and twice at the weekend. On the other side of the divide are those who abuse the charge of "Orientalism" from a position of power.

It is not just those like the *Jerusalem Post* columnist who are incensed by the term "Orientalism." It is also abused by

17. As I argue in my essay on Neill Blomkamp's science-fiction thriller *Elysium* (2013). See www.aljazeera.com/indepth/opinion/2013/09/2013917155618563387.html.

the leading propagandist officers of the Islamic Republic as a scare tactic to silence their opponents.[18] Seth J. Frantzman's counterpart in Iran is Mohammad Marandi. Common to both these forces, represented by Frantzman (Zionist) and Marandi (Islamist), is the most basic insight of the Saidian argument in *Orientalism*: the relation between knowledge and power. Those in power in Israel dislike the term "Orientalism" to the same degree that those in power in the Islamic republic like and abuse it for their own benefit. What Israeli propagandists and their counterparts in the Islamic Republic have in common, then, is that they are both in power. There is no iota of difference between the manner in which Zionists like Frantzman wish to silence the Palestinians and that in which propaganda officers of the Islamic Republic like Marandi wish to stifle the voices of their opponents.

Consider the fact the Islamic Republic funds graduate students from one end of the Islamic world to the other, either to go to Iran and study in Shi'i seminaries or else study in Europe or the United States and receive a degree in "Islamic Studies," and thereafter join forces with the ruling clerical establishment to bolster a militant reading of Shi'ism compatible with the political interests of the ruling ideology. These graduate students – later young faculty – soon see their very livelihood as being contingent upon aiding and abetting the leading propagandist officers of the Islamic Republic to write and generate knowledge from and for the position of power they serve. The operation of this power/knowledge symbiosis is identical to that of Orientalism.

---

18. Here is a perfect example of one such propaganda officer of the Islamic Republic charging "the West" with Orientalism: www.aljazeera.com/indepth/opinion/2014/04/iran-orientalism-western-illusio-2014438363158180.html.

These propagandists call themselves "professors" and operate in the occupied territories of Tehran University, where
generations of principle and uncompromising faculty have been
systematically purged. They dare to write articles and publish
them on Al Jazeera, levelling the charge of Orientalism at "the
West." Furthermore, they enabled ex-CIA agents to write articles
and books denying the legitimacy of the Green Movement. Four
years later the highest military officers of the Islamic Republic
confess in broad daylight that they engineered the election
and violently oppressed the dissidents.[19] It is not just European
Orientalists who abused their positions of power to produce
knowledge at the service of that power. On this issue I stand
firmly against these propagandists who have brutalized a nation
and who preside over its destiny. My being "an Iranian scholar"
is nothing but a red herring.

Is the mother of Sattar Beheshti, whose son was murdered in
the prisons of the Islamic Republic, an Orientalist? Are the mothers of Neda Agha Soltan and Sohrab Arabi, murdered point-blank
by the agents of the security apparatus of the Islamic Republic,
Orientalists? Is Mohammad Nourizad, who has risked his life
to inform the world of the atrocities of the Islamic Republic,
an Orientalist? Are leading political prisoners like Mohsen
Aminzadeh, Mostafa Tajzadeh, Abdollah Ramazanzadeh, Feizol-
lah Arabsorkhi, Moshen Safai Farahani, Mohsen Mirdamadi, and
Behzad Nabavi all Orientalists? Are Mir-Hossein Mousavi, his
wife Zahra Rahnavard, and their fellow presidential candidate
Mehdi Karroubi – all of whom have accused the ruling regime
of fraudulent behavior and abuse of power – also Orientalists?

---

19. Here is a link to the video clip in which Major General Mohammad Ali Jafari, the
commander of the Army of the Guardians of the Islamic Revolution of Iran, publicly
boasts of having both engineered the presidential election of 2008 and swiftly crushed the
demonstrators when they poured onto the streets: www.kaleme.com/1393/03/11/klm-186448.

Lines of alliance and solidarity long ago crossed the false binary of "the West and the Rest."

The fierce urgency of now

The shifting centers of power have become amorphous, and produce equally unstable modes of knowledge. In what I have called "liberation geography," the world at large is now actively engaged in reimagining itself. This book is informed by a feeling for "the fierce urgency of now," as Martin Luther King called key moments, as a form of eyewitness history, from the trenches. This mode of thinking is the material of a future history of our present. Beyond the condition of coloniality was the reactive moment of postcoloniality. The combined effects of the Green Moment in Iran and the Arab revolutions have put an end to that – epistemically, far more than politically. Politically the battles rage not just in Egypt and Syria, but also in the trenches of ideas that can no longer afford to be bored with banal bifurcations such as "Islam and the West," and "the West and the Rest."

In my essay "Can Non-Europeans Think?" I asked a very simple question. A couple of young European philosophers thought I was addressing them, even though a quick look at the title alone clearly indicates that the target was non-Europeans. I have concluded from their response that there is a structural flaw in the make-up of the European philosophical mind, at least in the version that these two philosophers practice: they cannot read other people's thoughts, even when they have crossed the linguistic divide and write in one of their languages, one of those they have colonially imposed upon the world at large; consequently they are blinded to these other realms, do not reads their scripts, cannot fathom their universes, and systematically and habitually assimilate whatever they read back into what they already know and have epistemically pasted upon the world. This is doubtless natural for them, but is quite a nuisance for the world at large, for the inhabitants of other worlds, those that European imperialism has ravaged and left in ruins, and whose inhabitants might indeed one day fathom things out for themselves.

These philosophers cannot comprehend the notion of the moment when a thinker might actually not be talking *to* them, but rather be standing right *next to them*, neither under nor over them, nor indeed up *there*. They are blinded to the world in which other people think their unthinkable thoughts. When their anthropologists and area specialists read the world for them, they assimilate this reading into what they already know; and what they know is how to rule, how to own, how to possess, and how to map the world in defiance of its inhabitants' will, wishes, and resistance against their will to know. This will to know has made them the knowing subject since the pages of Immanuel Kant; the very same pages that state that we colored folks cannot think because we are colored, and consequently we are part of the knowable world. Another map more familiar to others will drive them mad, so they consider those who have created those maps and who live by them to be mad. Orientalism is about knowledge and power; it is not just about European power and the knowledge it needed to rule the world. All empires have produced knowledge that is compatible with their imperial interests – witness the Arabs, Persians, Mongols, Romans, and so on.

Europeans as Europeans (the saturated sign of a self-raising, other-lowering ruse) will be unable to read unless and until they join the rest of humanity in their common quest for a level remapping of the world. The relations of knowledge and power are multiple and varied. Thus the Islamic Republic of Iran can mimic, ape, and even up the ante on the model of imperial notions of soft power by revising it through asymmetric warfare. We thus need to change the interlocutor, for we are no longer talking to the dead interlocutor code-named "Europe," or "the West." For "the West" was (as Fanon said) the invention of the Third World; since the Third World has imploded and gone in search of its own future beyond the European imagination, so has "the West." And since where the colonial world once was is now an empty echo chamber awaiting future philosophers, European thinkers like Zabala and Marder need to stop playing with their philosophical drones. Otherwise, when their favorite guru screams "Fuck you, Walter Mignolo!" all he hears back is the echo of his own words, and in his own voice: "Fuck you..."

ONE

Can Non-Europeans Think?

In a lovely little panegyric for the distinguished European philosopher Slavoj Žižek, published recently on Al Jazeera, we read:

> There are many important and active philosophers today: Judith Butler in the United States, Simon Critchley in England, Victoria Camps in Spain, Jean-Luc Nancy in France, Chantal Mouffe in Belgium, Gianni Vattimo in Italy, Peter Sloterdijk in Germany and in Slovenia, Slavoj Žižek, not to mention others working in Brazil, Australia and China.

What immediately strikes the reader when seeing this opening paragraph is the unabashedly European character and disposition of the thing the author calls "philosophy today" – thus laying a claim on both the subject and time that is peculiar, and in fact an exclusive property of Europe.

Even Judith Butler, who is cited as an example from the United States, is decidedly a product of European philosophical genealogy, thinking somewhere between Derrida and Foucault, brought to bear on our understanding of gender and sexuality.

To be sure, China and Brazil (and Australia, which is also a European extension) are cited as the location of other philosophers worthy of the designation, but none of them evidently merits a specific name to be sitting next to these eminent European philosophers.

The question, of course, is not the globality of philosophical visions that all these prominent European (and by extension certain American) philosophers indeed share and from which people from the deepest corners of Africa to the remotest villages of India, China, Latin America, and the Arab and Muslim world ("deep and far," that is, from a fictive European center) can indeed learn and better understand their lives.

That goes without saying, for without that confidence and self-consciousness these philosophers and the philosophical traditions they represent can scarce lay any universal claim on our epistemic credulities; nor would they be able to put pen to paper or finger to keyboard and write a sentence.

Thinkers outside Europe

These are indeed not only eminent philosophers. The philosophy they practice has the globality of certain degrees of self-conscious confidence without which no thinking can presume universality.

The question is rather something else: what about other thinkers who operate outside this European philosophical pedigree, whether they practice their thinking in the European languages they have colonially inherited or else in their own mother tongues – be it in Asia, in Africa, in Latin America – thinkers who have actually earned the dignity of a name, and perhaps even the pedigree of "public intellectual," not dissimilar to Hannah Arendt, Jean-Paul Sartre, and Michel

Foucault, who in the Al Jazeera piece on Žižek are offered as his predecessors?

   What about thinkers outside the purview of these European philosophers; how are we to name and designate and honour them with the epithet of "public intellectual," and learn from them, in the age of globalized media?

   Do the constellation of thinkers from South Asia, exemplified by leading figures like Ashis Nandy, Partha Chatterjee, Gayatri Spivak, Ranajit Guha, Sudipta Kaviraj, Dipesh Chakrabarty, Homi Bhabha, Aijaz Ahmad, Pankaj Mishra, and Akeel Bilgrami, come together to form a nucleus of thinking that is conscious of itself? Would that constellation perhaps merit the word "thinking" in a manner that would qualify one of them – as a South Asian – to the term "philosopher" or "public intellectual"?

   Are they "South Asian thinkers" or "thinkers," in the way these European thinkers are? Why is it that a Mozart sneeze is "music" (and I am quite sure the great genius even sneezed melodiously) but the most sophisticated Indian music ragas are the subject of "ethnomusicology"?

   Is that "ethnos" not also applicable to the philosophical thinking that Indian philosophers practice – so much so that their thinking is more the subject of Western European and North American anthropological fieldwork and investigation?

   We can turn around and look at Africa. What about thinkers like Henry Odera Oruka, Ngũgĩ wa Thiong'o, Wole Soyinka, Chinua Achebe, Okot p'Bitek, Taban Lo Liyong, Achille Mbembe, Emmanuel Chukwudi Eze, Souleymane Bachir Diagne, V.Y. Mudimbe: would they qualify for the term "philosopher," or "public intellectual" perhaps, or is that also "ethnophilosophy"?

   Why is European philosophy "philosophy," but African philosophy ethnophilosophy, in the the same way that Indian music is ethnomusic. This logic is based on the very same reasoning that decrees that when one visits the New York Museum of Natural History (popularized in Shawn Levy's *Night at the Museum* of 2006), one sees only animals and non-white peoples and their cultures featured inside glass cages, with no cage in sight for white people and their cultures – they just get to stroll through the aisles and enjoy the power of looking at taxidermic Yaks, cave dwellers, elephants, Eskimos, buffalo, Native Americans, and so on, all in a single winding row.

The same ethnographic gaze is evident in the encounter with the intellectual disposition of the Arab or Muslim world: Azmi Bishara, Sadiq Jalal al-Azm, Fawwaz Traboulsi, Abdallah Laroui, Michel Kilo, Abdolkarim Soroush. The list of prominent thinkers is endless.

In Japan, Kojin Karatani; in Cuba, Roberto Fernandez Retamar; and even, in the United States, people like Cornel West, whose thinking is not entirely in the European continental tradition – what about them? Where do they fit in? Can they think – is what they do also thinking, philosophical, pertinent, or is it also suitable for ethnographic examinations?

The question of Eurocentrism is now entirely blasé. Of course Europeans are Eurocentric and see the world from their vantage point, and why should they not? They are the inheritors of multiple (now defunct) empires, and they still carry within them the phantom hubris of those empires; they believe their particular philosophy is "philosophy" and their particular thinking is "thinking," while everything else is – as the great European philosopher Emmanuel Levinas was wont to say – "dancing."

The question is rather the manner in which non-European thinking can reach self-consciousness and evident universality, not at the cost of whatever European philosophers may think of themselves for the world at large, but for the purpose of offering alternative (complementary or contradictory) visions of reality more rooted in the lived experiences of people in Africa, Asia, Latin America – countries and climes once under the spell of that which calls itself "the West," but happily no more.

The trajectory of contemporary thinking around the globe is not spontaneously conditioned in our own immediate time and disparate locations, but has a much deeper and wider spectrum that goes back to earlier generations of thinkers, ranging from José Martí to Jamal al-Din al-Afghani, to Aime Cesaire, W.E.B. DuBois, Liang Qichao, Frantz Fanon, Rabindranath Tagore, Mahatma Gandhi, and others.

So the question remains, why not the dignity of "philosophy" and whence the anthropological curiosity of "ethnophilosophy"?

Let's seek the answer from Europe itself – but from the subaltern of Europe.

The intellectuals as a cosmopolitan stratum

In his *Prison Notebooks*, Antonio Gramsci has a short discussion of Kant's famous phrase in *Groundwork of the Metaphysic of Morals* (1785) that is quite critical in our understanding of what it takes for a philosopher to become universally self-conscious, to think of himself as the measure and yardstick of globality. Gramsci's stipulation is all-important here. This is how he begins:

> Kant's maxim "act in such a way that your conduct can become a norm for all men in similar conditions" is less simple and obvious than it appears at first sight. What is meant by 'similar conditions'?

To be sure, and as Quintin Hoare and Geoffrey Nowell-Smith (the editors and translators of the English translation of

Gramsci's *Prison Notebooks*) note, Gramsci here in fact misquotes Kant: that "similar conditions" does not appear in the original text; rather, the German philosopher states: "I am never to act otherwise than so that I could also will that my maxim should become a universal law." This principle, called "the categorical imperative," is in fact the very foundation of Kantian ethics. So, where Kant writes "universal law," Gramsci writes "a norm for all men," and then adds "similar conditions," which is not in the German original.

> The world at large, and the Arab and Muslim world in particular, is going through world historic changes – these changes have produced thinkers, poets, artists, and public intellectuals at the centre of their moral and political imagination.

This misquotation is quite critical here. Gramsci's conclusion is that the reason Kant can state what he states and offer his own behaviour as the measure of universal ethics is that "Kant's maxim presupposes a single culture, a single religion, a 'world-wide' conformism ... Kant's maxim is connected with his time, with the cosmopolitan enlightenment and the critical conception of the author. In brief, it is linked to the philosophy of the intellectuals as a cosmopolitan stratum."

What in effect Gramsci discovers, as a Southern Italian suffering in the dungeons of European fascism, is what in Brooklyn we call chutzpah – to think yourself the center of the universe, a self-assuredness that gives the philosopher that certain panache and authority to think in absolutist and grand narrative terms.

Therefore the agent is the bearer of the "similar conditions" and indeed their creator. That is, he "must" act according to a "model" which he would like to see diffused among all mankind, according to a type of civilization for whose coming he is working – or for whose preservation he is "resisting" the forces that threaten its disintegration.

It is precisely that self-confidence, that self-consciousness, that audacity to think oneself the agent of history that enables a thinker to believe his particular thinking is "Thinking" in universal terms, and his philosophy "Philosophy," and his city square "The Public Space," and thus himself to be a globally recognized Public Intellectual.

There is thus a direct and unmediated structural link between an empire, or an imperial frame of reference, and the presumed universality of a thinker thinking in the bosom of that empire.

As with all other people, Europeans are perfectly entitled to their own self-centrism.

The imperial hubris that once enabled that Eurocentricism and still produces the infomercials of the sort we read in Al Jazeera for Žižek are the phantom memories of the time that "the West" had assured confidence and a sense of its own universalism and globality, or, as Gramsci put it, "to a type of civilization for whose coming he is working."

But that globality is no more. People from every clime and continent are up and about claiming their own cosmopolitan worldliness, and with it their innate ability to think beyond the confinements of Eurocentricism, which to be sure is still entitled to its phantom pleasure of thinking itself the center of the universe. The Gramscian superimposed "similar conditions" are now emerging in multiple sites of liberated humanity.

The world at large, and the Arab and Muslim world in particular, is going through world historic changes. These changes have produced, at the center of their moral and political imagination, thinkers, poets, artists, and public intellectuals – all thinking and acting in terms at once domestic to their immediate geography and yet global in their consequences.

Compared to those liberating tsunamis now turning the world upside down, cliché-ridden assumptions about Europe and its increasingly provincialized philosophical pedigree are a tempest in a teacup. Reduced to its own fair share of humanity at large, and like all other continents and climes, Europe has much to teach the world. But this will now take place on a far more level and democratic playing field, where its philosophy is European philosophy not "Philosophy," its music European music not "Music," and no infomercial is necessary to sell its public intellectuals as "Public Intellectuals."

Originally published in Al Jazeera, January 2013

Found in Translation

Though it is common to lament the shortcomings of reading an important work in any language other than the original and the "impossibility" of translation, I am convinced that works of philosophy (or literature for that matter – are they different?) in fact gain far more than they lose.

Consider Heidegger. Had it not been for his French translators and commentators, German philosophy of his time would have remained an obscure metaphysical thicket. And it was not until Derrida's own take on Heidegger found an English readership in the United States and Britain that the whole Heideggerian–Derridian undermining of metaphysics began to shake the foundations of the Greek philosophical heritage. One can in fact argue that much of contemporary Continental philosophy originates in German with significant French and

Italian glosses before it is globalized in the dominant American English and assumes a whole new global readership and reality. This has nothing to do with the philosophical wherewithal of German, French, or English. It is entirely a function of the imperial power and reach of one language as opposed to others.

The mother tongue

At various points in history, one language or another – Latin, Persian, Arabic – was the lingua franca of philosophical thinking. Now it is English. For all we know, it might again turn around and become Chinese.

In eleventh-century Iran, the influential philosopher Avicenna wrote most of his work in Arabic. One day his patron prince, who did not read Arabic, asked whether Avicenna would mind writing his works in Persian instead, so that he could understand them. Avicenna obliged and wrote an entire encyclopedia on philosophy for the prince and named it after him, *Danesh-nameh Ala'i*.

Avicenna was, of course, not the only one who had opted to write his philosophical work in Arabic. So did al-Ghazali (*c.* 1058–1111) and Shihab al-Din Yahya al-Suhrawardi (*c.* 1155–1208) – who were both perfectly capable of writing in their mother tongue of Persian and had in fact occasionally done so, notably al-Ghazali in his *Kimiya-ye Sa'adat* (a book on moral philosophy) and as-Suhrawardi in his magnificent short allegorical treatises. But in Avicenna's time, Arabic was so solidly established in its rich and triumphant philosophical vocabulary that no serious philosopher would opt to write his major works in any other language. Persian philosophical prose had to wait for a couple of generations after Avicenna. With the magnificent work of Afdal al-din Kashani (d. *c.* 1214) and that of Avicenna's follower Khwajah Muhammad ibn Muhammad ibn Hasan al-Tusi (1201–1274) – particularly *Asas al-Iqtibas* – Persian philosophical prose achieved its zenith.

Today the term "Persian philosophy" is not easily separated from "Islamic philosophy," much of which is in Arabic. This was the case even in the sixteenth century, when Mulla Sadra wrote almost his entire major opus in Arabic. Although some major philosophers in the nineteenth and twentieth centuries did write occasionally in Persian, it was not until Allameh Muhammad Iqbal (1877–1938) opted to write his major philosophical works in the language that Persian philosophical prose resumed serious significance in the larger Muslim context. (Iqbal also wrote major treatises on Persian philosophy in English.)

It is Amir Hossein Aryanpour's magnificent Persian translation of Muhammad Iqbal's *The Development of Metaphysics in Persia* (1908), which he rendered as *Seyr-e Falsafeh dar Iran* (The Course of Philosophy in Iran, 1968), that now stands in my mind as the paramount example of excellence in Persian philosophical prose and testimony to how philosophical translation is a key component of our contemporary intellectual history. If there were a world for philosophy, or if philosophy were to be worldly, these two men, philosopher and translator, having graced two adjacent philosophical realms, would be among its most honored citizens.

Two teachers

It is impossible to exaggerate the enduring debt of gratitude that my generation of Iranians have to Aryanpour (1925–2001), one of the most influential social theorists, literary critics, philosophers and translators of his time, and for us a wide and inviting window to the rich and emancipatory world of

critical thinking in my homeland. He is today remembered
for the generations of students he taught at Tehran University
and beyond, and for the rich array of path-breaking books he
wrote or translated, which enabled us to develop a broader
philosophical imagination.

Having been exposed to both scholastic and modern educational systems, as well as widely and deeply educated in
Iran (Tehran University), Lebanon (American University in
Beirut), Britain (Cambridge) and the United States (Princeton),
Aryanpour was a cosmopolitan thinker and a pioneering figure
who promoted a dialectical (*jadali*) disposition between the
material world and the world of ideas. Today, more than forty
years after I arrived in Tehran from my hometown of Ahvaz
in late summer 1970 to attend college, I still feel under my skin
the excitement and joy of finding out how much there was to
learn from a man whose name was synonymous with critical
thinking, the theorizing of social movements and, above all,
the discipline of sociology.

Aryanpour was the product of many factors: Reza Shah's
heavy-handed, state-sponsored "modernization"; the brief
post-World War II intellectual flowering; travels and higher
education in Iran, the Arab world, Europe and the United
States; the McCarthy witch-hunts of the 1950s; and finally the
CIA-sponsored coup of 1953, after which university campuses
in his homeland became the primary site of his intellectual
leadership of a whole new generation. He was a thorn in the
side of both the Pahlavi monarchy and the Islamic Republic
that succeeded it, making him at times dogmatic in his own
positions, but always path-breaking in a mode of dialectical
thinking that became the staple of his students, both those
who were fortunate enough to have known and worked with

him directly and the millions of others (like me) who benefited from his work from a distance.

Aryanpour was sacked from his teaching position in the theology faculty in 1976. He retired in 1980. Just before his death on July 30, 2001, one of his last public acts was to sign a letter denouncing censorship in the Islamic Republic.

Aryanpour's legendary translation of and expanded critical commentary on Iqbal's *Development of Metaphysics in Persia* not only became the first and foremost text of my generation's encounter with a learned history of philosophy in our homeland, but also brought about a far broader and more expansive awareness of the world of philosophy. It is impossible to overstate the effect of the beautiful, overwhelming, exciting and liberating first reading of that magnificent text on a wide-eyed provincial boy who had come to the capital of his moral and intellectual imagination.

Iqbal was born and raised in Punjab, British India (Pakistan today), to a devout Muslim family, educated by Muslim teachers and at the Scotch Mission College in Sialkot, growing up multilingual and polycultural. After an unhappy marriage and subsequent divorce, Iqbal studied philosophy, English, Arabic and Persian literatures at the Government College in Lahore, where he was deeply influenced by Thomas Arnold, who became a conduit for his exposure to European thought, an exposure that ultimately resulted in his traveling to Europe for further study.

While in England, Iqbal received a Bachelor's degree from Trinity College, Cambridge, in 1907, around the time his first Persian poems began to surface. As he became increasingly attracted to politics, he managed to write his doctoral thesis on "The Development of Metaphysics in Persia," with Friedrich

Hommel. Reading *Seyr-e Falsafeh dar Iran*, Aryanpour's Persian translation of Iqbal's seminal work, became a rite of passage for my generation of college students, eager to discover our philosophical heritage.

We grew up and matured into a much wider circle of learning about Islamic philosophy and the place of Iranians in that tradition. There were greener pastures, more learned philosophers who beckoned to our minds and souls. We learned of the majestic writings of Seyyed Jalal Ashtiani, chief among many other philosophical sages of our time, who began to guide our way into the thicket of Persian and Arabic philosophical thinking. But the decidedly different disposition of Allameh Iqbal in Aryanpour's translation was summoned precisely in the fact that it had not reached us through conventional scholastic routes and was deeply informed by the worldly disposition of our own defiant time. In this text we were reading superlative Persian prose from a Pakistani philosopher who had come to fruition in both colonial subcontinent and postcolonial cosmopolis. There was a palpable worldliness in that philosophical prose that became definitive for my generation.

Beyond East and West

When today I read a vacuous phrase like "the Western mind" – or "the Iranian mind," "the Arab Mind," "the Muslim Mind," for that matter – I cringe. I wonder what "the Western mind" can mean when reading the Persian version of a Pakistani philosopher's English prose composed in Germany on an aspect of Islamic philosophy that was particular to Iran. Look at the itinerary of a philosopher like Allameh Iqbal; think about a vastly learned and deeply caring intellect like Amir Hossein Aryanpour. Where is "the Western mind" in those variegated geographies of learning, and where is "the Eastern mind"? What could the terms possibly mean?

The case of *Seyr-e Falsafeh dar Iran* was prototypical of my generation's philosophical education – we read left, right and center, then north and south from the Indian subcontinent to Western Europe and North America, Latin America and postcolonial Africa, with a voracious worldliness that had no patience for the East or West of any colonial geography. We were philosophically "in the world," and our world was made philosophical by an imaginative geography that knew neither East nor West.

Works of philosophy – and their readers – gain in translation not just because their authors begin to breathe in a new language but because the text signals a world alien to its initial composition. Above all they gain because these authors and their texts have to face a new audience. Plato and Aristotle have had a life in Arabic and Persian entirely alien to the colonial codification of "Western philosophy." The only effective way to make the foreign echoes of that idea familiar is to make the familiar tropes of "Western philosophy" foreign.

Originally published in *New York Times*, July 2013

TWO

The Moment of Myth
Edward Said, 1935–2003

Close proximity to a majestic mountain is a mixed blessing –
one is at once graced by the magnanimity of its pastures and
the bounty of its slopes, and yet one can never see where one
is sitting, under the shadow of what greatness, the embracing comfort of what assurance. The splendor of mountains
– Himalayas, Rockies, Alborz – can only be seen from afar,
from the safe distance of only a visual, perceptive, appreciative,
awe-inspiring grasp of their whereabouts.

A very happy few – now desolate and broken – have had the
rare privilege of calling Edward Said a friend, fewer a colleague,
even fewer a comrade, only a handful a neighbor. The closer
you came to Edward Said the more his intimate humanity,
ordinary simplicity, the sweet, endearing, disarmingly embracing character – his being a husband, a father, a father-in-law, an
uncle, a cousin – clouded and colored the majesty that he was.
Our emails and voicemails are still full of his precious words,
his timely consolations, anecdotal humor, trivial questions,
priceless advice – all too dear to delete, too intimate to share.

We were all like birds flying around the generosity of his roof, tiny dandelions joyous in the shade of his backyard, minuscule creatures pasturing on the bounteous slopes of the mountain that he was. The prince of our cause, the mighty warrior, the Salah al-Din of our reasoning with mad adversaries, source of our sanity in despair, solace in our sorrow, hope in our own humanity, is now no more.

In his absence now it is possible to remember the time when you existed and he was not part of your critical consciousness, your creative disposition, your presence in the world – when he did not look over your shoulder watching every single word you wrote. If remembering the time that you existed, but he was not integral to you, is not to be an exercise in archeological futility, then it has to account for the distance, the discrepancy, between the bashful scholasticism of the learning that my generation of immigrant intellectuals received and the confidence and courage with which we can stand up today in face of outrageous fortune – hand in hand with our brothers and sisters across races and nations, creeds and chaos – and say, "NO!"

Today, there is a solidarity of purpose among a band of rebels and mutineers – gentiles are among us and Jews, Christians and pagans, Hindus and Muslims, atheists we are and agnostics, natives and immigrants – who speak truth to power with the voice of Edward Said the echo of our chorus. How we came here – where we are, hearing with his ears, seeing with his eyes, talking with his tongue – is a question not for making a historical record but for taking moral courage.

Now, in the moment of his myth, when Edward Said has left us to our own devices and joined the pantheon of mythic monuments, is precisely the time to have, as he once said, a Gramscian inventory of our whereabouts – once with and now without him. Today the world is at once poorer in his absence and yet richer through his memory – and precisely in that paradox dwell the seeds of our dissent, the promise of our future, the solemnity of our oath at the sacred site of his casket.

I come from a generation of immigrant intellectuals who mark the origin and disposition of their critical intelligence from the publication of Edward Said's *Orientalism* (1978). The shape of our critical character, the voice of our dissent, the texture of our politics, and the very disposition of our courage, are all rooted in every nook and cranny of that revelatory text. It was in the year of the Iranian Revolution, 1979, less than a season after the publication of *Orientalism*, that Samuel Klausner, who taught us theory and method, first introduced me to Edward Said's spectacular achievement in an utterly prosaic manner. I was a graduate student at the University of Pennsylvania, finishing a dual degree in Sociology of Culture and Islamic Studies. By the time I read *Orientalism* (inhaled it, rather, in one deep, satisfying swoop – drank it like a glass of freshly squeezed lemonade on a hot summer's day), I had already read Karl Marx, Max Scheler, Max Weber, and George Herbert Mead on the sociology of knowledge. What Said had argued in *Orientalism* was presented straight from a sociology-of-knowledge angle, and yet with a globality of vision, a daring, defiant imagination, and such assured audacity that I remember I could not believe my eyes – that I was reading these words in that particular succession of reason and rhetoric.

By the mid-1970s, my generation of sociologists at Penn had already started reading Michel Foucault in a systematic and rather unusual curriculum, given that the discipline of sociology was then being rapidly sold out to federally funded policy research and demography – a downward spiral from which a once groundbreaking discipline never recovered. But at that time at Penn, Philip Rieff, Digby Baltzell, Samuel Klausner, Harold Bershady, Victor Lidz, and Fred Block were serious theorists with a relatively universal approach to their sociological concerns. I wrote my doctoral dissertation with Philip Rieff advising me on the sociological aspect of my work and with the late George Makdisi on the Islamic aspect. But the seed that *Orientalism* had planted in my critical consciousness never left my thoughts after that fateful fall semester of 1979 when we read it with Samuel Klausner in that dimly lit, tiny room on the fifth floor of the McNeal Building off Locust Walk on the Penn campus – smack in the middle of the hostage crisis in Iran, when I could hear a chorus of Penn undergraduates shouting in unison, "Nuke Iran, Maim Iranians!"

Take *Orientalism* out of that curriculum, Edward Said out of our consciousness, and my generation of immigrant intellectuals would be a bunch of dispirited souls susceptible to chronic melancholy, or else, *horribile dictu*, would pathetically mutate into native informers of one sort or another – selling their souls to soulless sultans in DC or else to senile patriarchs in Princeton.

I had no clue regarding Edward Said's work in literary criticism prior to *Orientalism*, and for years after my graduation I remained entirely oblivious to it. It was *Orientalism* that would not let go of the way I thought and wrote about modern or medieval Islamic or Iranian intellectual history. From then on, I embarked on a journey, at once professional and personal, moral and intellectual, that brought me literally to his doorstep on the campus of Columbia University – where I now teach. To my dying day, I will cherish the precise spot next to Miller Theater on the corner of 116th and Broadway where I met Edward for the first time and went up to him and introduced myself – the gratitude of a liberated voice in my greetings.

I discovered Edward Said first from *Orientalism*, then his writings on Palestine, from there to his liberating reflections on the Iranian Revolution. I then began an almost Jesuit training in every book he ever wrote, along with the majority of his essays and articles, reading and rereading them like a dutiful student preparing for a doctoral exam, long after I was myself conducting doctoral examinations.

Today, of the myriad things I have learned from Edward Said, nothing matters to me more than the rhapsodic eloquence of his voice – the majesty, confidence, courage, audacity, and poise of his diction, without which my generation of immigrant intellectuals would have been at the mercy of the mercenary academics and embedded journalists who have now flooded the gutters of the mass media – uttering their pathologies with thick Arabic, Persian, or South Asian accents and yet speaking with a nauseating "we" that sides with the bankrupt architects of this predatory empire. In the presence of Edward Said's voice, in his princely posture and magisterial air of confidence, the fragile tone of our almost silent objections and the frailty of our say in the matter would suddenly rise to the occasion.

Through Edward Said we suddenly found comrades we never knew we had, friends and families we never suspected in our own neighborhood – Asia, Africa, and Latin America suddenly became the extension of our home away from home. José Martí I discovered through Edward Said, as I did Kojin Karatani, Chinua Achebe, Eqbal Ahmad, Tariq Ali, Ranajit Guha, Gayatri Spivak, Seamus Deane, Masao Miyoshi, Ngũgĩ wa Thiong'o. Everyone else we thought we knew he made new sense of for us – Aimé Césaire, Frantz Fanon, Mahatma Gandhi,

Mahmoud Darwish, Nazim Hikmat, Vladimir Mayakovsky,
Faiz Ahmad Faiz.

As the color of our skin began to confuse the color line
drawn tyrannically between blacks and whites in the United
States – segregated in the respective corners of their misplaced
confidence about their races – we Asians and Latinos, Arabs,
Turks, Africans, Iranians, Armenians, Kurds, Afghans, and
South Asians were instantly brought together beyond the un-
common denominator of our origin and toward the solidarity
of our emerging purpose, the nobility of our handshake with
Edward Said.

For years after I had come to Columbia, I could not quite
reconcile the public, mythic, iconic Edward Said, and the immediate Edward of my increasing acquaintance and friendship,
camaraderie, and solidarity. It was as if there was an Edward
Said the Magnificent for the rest of the world and then another
Edward for a happy few. The two were not exactly irreconcilable; they posited a question, a distance in need of traversing
– how could a mortal so fragile, frail, and accessible cut a global
figure so monumental, metaphoric, parabolic?

When an infamous charlatan slandered me in a New York
tabloid and created a scandalous website to malign my public
stand against the criminal atrocities he supports, my voicemail
was flooded with racist, obscene, and threatening messages
by the lunatic fringe he had let loose. Smack in the middle of
these obscenities, as if miraculously, there was a message from
Edward – a breath of fresh air, refreshing, joyous, reassuring,
life-affirming: "Hamid, my dear, this is Edward..." Life was so
amazingly beautiful. I kept listening to those obscenities just for
the joy of coming to Edward's message. There was something
providential in his voice – it restored hope in humanity. Today at

Edward's funeral, the heartbroken few who could look over the shoulder of the pallbearers of Edward's coffin were witness to yet another sublime restoration of hope when Daniel Barenboim played Bach's Prelude in E-flat from *The Well-Tempered Clavier* as a musical tribute to his deceased friend. Those in the vicinity of this miracle saw and heard that the Maestro's loving farewell was no longer just a virtuoso pianist playing a beautiful piece of music – they were privy to Daniel Barenboim speaking with Edward Said for the very last time, in the common language of their choice, privilege, and transcendence.

Edward Said was the walking embodiment of hope – one extraordinary incident that sought and detected an extraordinary sparkle in otherwise very ordinary people who happened on his watch. Many years ago, when I had open heart surgery and my dear, now departed, friend and colleague Magda al-Nowaihi had just been diagnosed with ovarian cancer, Edward was extraordinary in his support: calling on us regularly, sending us his new books and articles, reading our manuscripts, making fun of what he called our postmodernisms. He was the sound of our laughter, the color of our joy, the shape of our hope. Magda fought her malignant cancer for years until her young children became teenagers; I defied my congenital fate and lived – Edward, the model of our endurance, the measures of our truth, the meaning of our daring to walk into a classroom.

The closer I became to Edward, the more impossible it seemed to tell what exactly it was that went into the making of his heroic character in such mythic measure – by now I was too close to the mountain, embraced by its grace, oblivious to its majesty. But, even in public, the account of his life that Edward Said published is no different. One reads his *Out of Place* (1999) in vain looking for a clue, a succession of historical or psychological causes and traits, as to what great or consequential events make for a monumentally moral life. Everything about Edward Said was rather ordinary, and yet an extraordinary adventure was made of the prosaic occurrences of this life.

Born in Palestine in 1935, named Edward after the Prince of Wales, he lived a life of exile like millions of other Palestinians in the Arab world. Sent to Mount Hermon High School in New England, and subsequently attending Princeton and Harvard for his higher education, Edward Said reports of no extraordinary event that one can identify, analyze, theorize as the defining moment of the mythic figure that he cut at the time of his untimely death. Edward was an ordinary man. Edward Said was a giant. The distance was covered by nothing other than the glory of his daring imagination.

Knowing Edward Said personally was a study in how heroes are made from the flesh and blood of the most ordinary and perishable realities. A Palestinian, an exile, an academic intellectual, a teacher, a scholar, a husband, a father, a friend: none of this common and abundant evidence of a disjointed world can account for the sum total of Edward Said as a towering figure measuring the very definition of a moral life.

"Did you know Professor Said," I asked Chaplain Davis here at Columbia, when looking for a place for Miriam Said to receive the flood of visitors who wanted to pay their respects last Friday. "I never met him," she said, "but I know he was a warrior," and then she looked at me with a bright set of shining eyes and added "for justice." "It was just like a light going off on campus," another colleague said of Edward's death.

If one is to begin anywhere to place the particulars of Edward Said's moral and intellectual life together it is not in the prosaics of his exilic life that he shares with millions of others,

Palestinian or otherwise, but in the poetics of his creative defiance of his fate – where he was able repeatedly to give birth to himself. At his death, Edward Said was the moral mandate, the volcanic outburst of a life otherwise wasted in and by accidents that accumulate to form nothing. Exile was his fate and he triumphantly turned it into the fruit of his life – the gift he gave to a world now permanently cast into an exilic departure from itself.

We can find few instances in *Out of Place* that reveal the creative concatenation of such moments better than the concluding paragraph of the book. Like his life, Said's autobiography has to be read from its endings and not from its beginnings. "Sleeplessness for me," he says, "is a cherished state to be desired at almost any cost." He stayed awake when the world went to sleep – the insomniac conscience of the world, conversant with Minerva, observant with his eyes wide awake, like a wise owl, all-seeing, all-hearing, vigilant. "There is nothing for me as invigorating as immediately shedding the shadowy half-consciousness of a night's loss, than the early morning, reacquainting myself with or resuming what I might have lost completely a few hours earlier."

It is here, in the twilight borderline of repeated promises of a dawning light against the assured persistence of darkness, when it appears that the darker moments of our despair must yield to brighter hopes, that we always find Edward Said waiting for the rest of us to awake, to arrive. "With so many dissonances in my life I have learned actually to prefer being not quite right and out of place." Right here, I believe, Edward Said has rested his case and left his indelible mark on the rest of us, trying, as we are, to learn from him how to complement fatefully while remaining humanly incomplete. That, in my judgment, is the principal reason why such a multitude of people ordinarily at political and ideological odds with each other deeply loved Edward without contradicting themselves or him. His was a spontaneous soul – he generated and sustained goodwill and moral purpose on the impulses of the premiss he was given, not on the projected idealism of some metaphysical certainty.

What was paramount about Edward Said was that in his utter solitude he was never alone. He always spoke for an otherwise muted possibility of living a moral life against all odds, a graceful David swinging his sling and launching his stones against the Goliath of a world so mercilessly cast in the logic of its own madness – to be the moral voice of a people, and to turn the tragic fate of that people into the tragedy of a global predicament in which we have all become homeless Palestinians. His virtue was to turn the vices of his time into momentous occasions for a more universal good that went beyond the specificity of one wrong or another.

There was a catholicity to his liberating knowledge, a generosity to his moral rectitude, that easily transgressed boundaries and put to shame all territorial claims to authenticity. He was, as he rightly said, always slightly out of place, but that only brought out what was wrong with that place that could not completely accommodate him in the entirety of his character and culture.

In his legacy, Said has made a universal virtue out of the particular predicament that the world handed him at birth. Born in Palestine but denied his ancestral claims on that land, raised in Egypt but schooled with a British colonial education, dispatched to the United States by way of his father's claiming a more permanent part of his American dream but constantly driven to speak the truth of that lie to the powers that hold it, Said turned the inevitability of his fate into the defining moment of his stature as the iconic figure of an entire generation of hope – against a whole culture of despair.

Edward Said's life has its most immediate bearing as an eloquent testimonial of a people much maligned and brutalized in history. His life and legacy cannot and must not be robbed of that immediacy. It is first and foremost as a Palestinian – a disenfranchised, dispossessed, disinherited Palestinian – that Edward Said spoke. The ordinariness of his story – particularly in those moments when he spoke openly, frankly, innocently of his early youth, adolescence, sibling rivalries, sexual maturity, and so on – is precisely what restores dignity to a people demonized by a succession of purposeful propaganda, dehumanized to be robbed of their homeland in the broad daylight of history. No assessment of his multifaceted achievements as a teacher, a critic, and a scholar, no laudatory endorsement of his universal humanism, no perfectly deserving appreciation of him as a musician, an essayist, a subaltern theorist, a political activist – nothing should ever detract from his paramount significance as a Palestinian deeply wounded by the fate of what he repeatedly and wholeheartedly called "my people."

But Edward Said was not just a Palestinian, though a Palestinian he proudly was. Edward Said also became an icon, a moral paragon in a time when taking desperate measures have cast doubt on the very possibility of a moral voice, and here the ordinariness of his life makes the extraordinary voice that he was even more enduring. Said was not just a Palestinian. But he made every one else look like a Palestinian: made homeless by the mad logic of a brutal game of power that has robbed the whole world of any semblance of permanence.

How to remain an incessantly moral voice in a morally impermanent world, how to transfigure the disfigured mutations of the world into a well-mannered measure of truth, how to dismantle the power that false knowledge projects, and yet to insist that the just is right and the truth is beautiful: that is the legacy of Edward Said, right from the mountain top of his majestic peak visible from afar, down to the slopes of his bountiful pastures which few fortunate souls were blessed to call home.

Originally published in *Asia Society*, September 2003

The Name that Enables:
Remembering Edward Said

Stop all the clocks ... let the mourners come.
W.H. Auden

The common leitmotif of writing on the milestone anniversary of a friend's passing is a strong element of nostalgia – how wonderful things were when he was alive and how sad that he is no more. This element of nostalgia becomes even stronger when the fallen friend is a towering intellectual figure whose voice and vision were definitive to an age that now seems almost irreversibly altered. When the site of that dramatic alteration is the home and habitat of that colleague, with Palestine as its epicenter and the larger Arab and Muslim world all gathering momentum around it, the act of remembrance becomes positively allegorical.

This September, we mark the tenth anniversary of Edward Said's passing, at a time when the entire Arab world is in turmoil and Palestine is being stolen even more savagely by the hour. We as a community of his friends, comrades, and colleagues actively remember his voice, his vision, and his steadfast determination to lead our causes around the globe. But how is it exactly that he still shows the way a decade after his silencing?

The fact is that when today I think of Edward Said, and the more than a decade that I was fortunate to know him personally as a friend and a colleague here at Columbia, my paramount feeling is not a sense of loss, but a sense of suspension. Some people, it seems to me, never die for those whose moral and political imagination is organically rooted in their living memory. For me at least, the temporal timber of our politics has frozen ever since that fateful morning of September 24, 2003, when Joseph Massad called me to say Edward had taken his last breath. I had just received the news of my own younger brother Aziz having passed away, so the sense of loss of a brother, of two brothers, a younger and an older brother, is frozen in time for me, framed as it were on a mantelpiece that defines the focal point of where I can call home.

I have written a few pieces specifically on Edward Said's passing, my immediate thoughts and feelings when he passed away, and then my travelogue from Palestine, from which trip I brought back a fistful of dust from a sanctified cemetery of the Prophet's companion cemetery in Jerusalem near the Dome of the Rock, to take to Brummana in Lebanon and place it on Edward's last resting place. I then wrote another piece that his widow Mariam Said had requested for a small-circulation volume to mark a memorial for Edward at Columbia in March 2004.

But none of those pieces has been able to put anything resembling a full stop at the end of my moral, imaginative, political, and scholarly engagements with Said. They are far less about who Edward Said was than what he enabled me to become. I now read them more like various punctuation marks in my evolving conversations with his enduring memory. After Philip Rieff and George Makdisi, the two towering intellectual figures whose gracing shadows bends over every sentence I write, Edward Said is sitting next to my laptop, as always dashingly well-dressed, inquisitive, playful and determined all at the same time, wondering what I am cooking.

Citing Said

Much has happened since Said's passing – and on too many occasions we have all thought, what would he have said if he were with us today, particularly when the Arab revolutions started? What would he have said of the carnage in Syria, of the coup in Egypt, of the NATO bombing of Libya, of the revolution in Tunisia – and above all of the continued barefaced armed robbery of Palestine?

Though Said is no longer here to share his thoughts, he has done enough to enable us to think with him. Certain towering intellectuals become integral to the very alphabet of our moral and political imagination. They no longer need to be here physically for one to know what they might have thought or said or written. They live in those who read and think them through – and thus they become indexical, proverbial, to our thinking.

Said lived so fully, so consciously, so critically through the thick and thin of our times that he is definitive to our critical thinking, just like Marx, or Freud, or Fanon, or DuBois, or Malcolm X are. They are the sound with which we sing, the sight with which we see, the aroma of the things we smell, definitive to the intuition of our transcendence.

On many occasions I would run into Said on our campus while I was having a conversation with him in my mind, at which point I just continued with that mental conversation out loud. And he seemed to do the same: he would just abruptly say something, as if we had started a conversation long before we had seen each other on campus. That sense of suspended and continued conversation is still very much alive. Perhaps it is a state of denial, perhaps it is due to the fact that thinkers like Said are epistemic to our thinking, a time-lapsed process that keeps unpacking itself.

I don't think I can mourn Edward Said as long as I live, if mourning is a ritual of reconciliation with a loss, for I don't believe my kind of conversation with him is ever over. I still live in the same block where he and his family lived for decades. I still run into his widow Mariam once in a while, in almost exactly the same spots where I used to run into him.

I still read Edward's books and essays with his voice in my ear, and am still moved by the joy and anger of his principles on the bone marrow of my own politics. I have travelled quite a distance from where Edward Said was in terms of literary and historical theories, for we started from different vantage points. But I think him in my own thoughts, feel him in my own sentiments, and echo him in my own politics. I feel at home with him in almost exactly the same way that he was at home anywhere, slightly out of place, having come to similar (but not identical) conclusions as he did, but from different points of embarkation and looking at adjacent shores. He was an enabler, not a guru. He did not replicate himself. His friends became more of themselves by his virtue.

Towering intellects like Said or Fanon or Césaire enable you in your own voice – making sure you never repeat but rather extend them, expostulate their logic, navigate uncharted territories with their compass but not their itinerary. To me, it is impossible to be a Saidian or a Fanonite, for they were so particular in their universalities that one could not but trigger one's own particularities in awaiting their own intuition of transcendence.

A new intellectual organicity

With the death of Edward Said we immigrant intellectuals ceased to be immigrant and became native to a new organicity. We are the fulfillments of his battles. He theorized himself to be out of place in so timely a way and so punctiliously that after him we are no longer out of place, at home whereever we can hang our hat and say no to power.

After Said there are no native, no national, no international, no First, Second, or Third World intellectuals. Battlefields of ideas are site specific and global. One cannot wage any battle at any local level without simultaneously registering it globally. If one is not global one is not local, and if one is not local one is not global. The most boring and irrelevant intellectuals are those who think the US, Iran, India, or the North Pole are the center of the universe. The universe has no center, no periphery. We are all free-floating. Said was very site-specific about Palestine – and thereby he made the Palestinian predicament a metaphysical allegory, grounding it in the physical agony and heroism of his people.

It is meaningless after Said to speak of "exilic intellectuals," precisely because he so thoroughly theorized the category for his own age. There is no home from which to be exiled. The capital and the empire that wishes but fails to micromanage it are everywhere. There is no exit from this world, and home and exile are illusions that late capital and the condition of empire have dismantled.

The new intellectual organicity that Said enabled requires that one rolls up one's sleeves, gets down and dirty, so that in the midst of chaos one can seek solace, of darkness, light, of despair, hope.

Missing Said

There are times that I do not even miss Said, for, in an enduring sense, he has never left us. One thinks one's phone will ring and it is he calling to chat about one thing or another, or one runs into him on campus, or his name appears in one's Inbox. I don't miss him because I think I am still not quite done talking, arguing, agreeing, disagreeing, confiding in him. He is always there – there in the midst of a haze of happiness and despair that agitates and endears all his writings.

And then there are times, especially in the heart of the very early morning darkness when I habitually get up and start reading and writing only a few buildings away from where he used to live and do the same, that I suddenly sense the weight of his absence, the hollowed presence of his absence, the aura and audibility of his voice, the inquisitive frivolity of his gaze, his always speaking with you directly, pointedly, specifically, and yet from the rested assurances of distantly assured seashores he had seen. It is the accidentality of those encounters, just as I turn the corner of 116th and Broadway, that I suddenly see him coming – "You and your postmodernity," he would tease me, and, as I was about to protest, "Don't you worry, I invented the vocabulary!"

Edward loved to add an entirely superfluous *shadda* to the middle of my last name and pronounce it not just with two but, it seems, five or six extra "ds." "He is not even an Arab," he would say tongue in cheek, when praising me to his friends and family. Countless memories, voicemails, emails, casual encounters, planned collaborations, formal academic occasions connect my life at Columbia to Edward Said, and I live them all in my mind and play with them happily in my soul every single day of my life, and will do so for as long as I live, for as long as I am able to think, to remember, recollect, rethink him in my own thought.

I have a mental picture of Edward Said that is increasingly fading in my mind, and the more it fades the more actively I remember it. It was April 28, 2003. We were all in Swarthmore College in Pennsylvania to celebrate the poetry of Mahmoud Darwish, who had just received the Lannan Cultural Freedom Prize. At the end of the ceremony, Darwish, Said, Massad, and I went to pay a visit to our friend and colleague Magda al-Nowaihi, who was on her deathbed and would soon die of cancer. Magda was lying on her bed, a shimmering shadow of herself, but her paradisiac smile still mapped her beautiful face. I cannot recall a word that was said by anyone around that bed, only a mental picture, frozen, freezing, a fresco carved on the deepest wall of my memories, and upon it the three faces of Magda, Edward, and Mahmoud now shine more brightly.

"Perhaps," Levinas once wrote, "the names of persons whose *saying* signifies a face – proper names, in the middle of all these common names and commonplaces – can resist the dissolution of meaning and help us to speak." It is in that sense that the name, the persona, and the memory we call "Edward Said" is definitive to the sense and purpose of the moment when I sign my name over or under this homage and call myself by a proper name.

Originally published in Al Jazeera in September 2013

THREE

The Middle East is Changed Forever

> Take up the White Man's burden –
> Send forth the best ye breed –
> Go bind your sons to exile
> To serve your captives' need;
> To wait in heavy harness,
> On fluttered folk and wild –
> Your new-caught, sullen peoples,
> Half-devil and half-child.
>
> Rudyard Kipling,
> "The White Man's Burden" (1899)

Thinking beyond the US invasion of Iran

Once again the drums of war are roaring in Washington DC. Once again the signs and signals of a pending US/Israeli attack on yet another country, this time Iran, are heard louder than ever. The build-up to an anxiety-provoking crescendo has already started to gain momentum. Direct threats, indirect allusions, guarded remarks, provocative bluffs – no one knows exactly what the Bush administration has in mind – and *that*

precisely seems to be the point: generating and sustaining a
general condition of suspenseful uncertainty, an atmosphere of
amorphous fear and intimidation, and a perpetual state of war.

The practice of anti-war activism throughout the world has
hitherto been a periodic and scattered mobilization against
one war or other that the US/Israel has launched – very much
chasing after the evolving military designs of the neoconservatives in the US, and the reinvigorated Zionists in Israel, and
simply reacting to their proactive acts of global terrorism. As
we are waiting for the Iran war to happen (or not to happen),
it is now perhaps time to step back and take stock of what this
transcontinental axis of global terrorism – the United States
of America and the Jewish state of Israel – is up to and thus
rethink the civic manners of opposing and resisting it. When
the US launched its wrath on Afghanistan in October 2001, even
such progressive and astute American observers as Richard Falk
(seconded by the editorial staff of *The Nation*) thought that it
was a "just war." This argument was no mere act of historical
folly. It was a singular sign of political naivety.

We are now way beyond those perhaps innocent yet angry
misreadings of what has fast come upon us. After the mayhem of
Iraq, instead of constantly waiting for the other shoe to drop and
wonder if the US/Israel will or will not attack Iran, will or will
not bomb Syria, will or will not completely take over Somalia,
will or will not militarily engage North Korea, will or will not try
for yet another coup in Venezuela, we need to think beyond such
probabilities, and reach into the heart of *the state of war* that this
very waiting game entails. As all indications testify, a Democratic
US Congress will not make any significant difference in this state
of war. Looking at the emerging patterns of this state of war, it
is now safe to suggest, for example, that what the US is *perhaps*

(and such conjectural phrases are the symptoms of this very state of war) planning to do in Iran is modeled on what Israel did to Lebanon last July – hence the necessity of no longer treating these two imperial and colonial nexus of warmongering in the world as two separate political propositions and state entities, but in fact collapse them into a singular axis of state terrorism aimed at undisputed global domination.

For that drive toward global domination to be politically effective and psychologically enduring, *the state of war* is far more important than the actual act of war, and the threat of violence politically far more destabilizing than the act of violence itself. For the state of war and the threat of violence change the very political culture in which we receive and interpret any particular act of war, or occurrence of violence, so much so that the enormity of the human cost, infrastructural damages, and environmental catastrophes, for example, contingent on any act of war, gradually begin to dwindle and dissipate in the miasmic emergence of the omnipresent state of war. For more than five years now, the US/Israel and its European allies have been systematically at it, inflaming acts of "shock and awe," as the former US secretary of defense Donald Rumsfeld called it, in one place or another, so that now the law of diminishing returns has set in, and the staggering acts of violence in Iraq under the US-led occupation, or the barefaced barbarity of Israel in Palestine and Lebanon, cease to register their enormous weight and unfathomable consequences. In other words, the state of war numbs the human consciousness, and thus we fail to respond (for we lack any meaningful language) to the fundamental acts of moral depravity that we witness on a daily basis in Palestine and Iraq in anything remotely resembling a corresponding calibre.

So, as US/Israeli military and intelligence agencies, think-tanks, and, above all, mass media (all integral to the same militarized state of mind) are engaged in discussions on how to deal with "terrorism," the world, as well, needs to reverse the order, return the gaze, and begin to wonder how to deal with these two terrorist states and save humanity from their mutual, complementary, and strategically integrated acts of terrorizing the world. These two galvanized military machineries masquerading as nation-states are today the most violent source of militarized madness on our planet (and beyond). The Iraq War, in particular, competing with Israeli atrocities in Palestine, has long since ceased to be a singular crime against humanity. Initiated and sustained as it is by the US-led colonial occupation of a sovereign nation-state, the world needs to invent new terms to name, and grasp, it.

For this military machinery to work best, the threat of violence or state of war is a more effective tool for creating fear and sustaining hegemony than is the actual fact of violence or event of war, which is effectively the neutralizing moment of its catharsis. The key to sustaining the state of war, the warmongers in Washington DC seem to have learned, is to constantly keep alive an immanent specter of the enemy, as the Nazi theorist of political power Carl Schmitt and his philosophical shadow Leo Strauss both fully realized. Both Carl Schmitt (in theological terms) and Leo Strauss (in philosophical conviction) believed that the absence of this enemy and the neutralizing effect of liberal democracies will be tantamount to the death of the state as the modus operandi of moral virtues. A pending war, predicated on the ghostly apparition of a monstrous Muslim goblin about to leap from the darkness and swallow the earth, is thus politically far more expeditious than is the actual event of war. In this psychopathology of power, the American neoconservatives have learned their lessons as much from the advocacy of the German Nazi Carl Schmitt as from the guru of American neoconservatism Leo Strauss – and then perfected their theory with widespread practice.

Crafting a chronology

As the world waits to see if US/Israel will or will not attack Iran, we can begin to think through the state of war that this waiting game has generated and sustained. The laundry list of the US/Israel litany against the Islamic Republic is long and tiresome: they sponsor terrorism, they do not support the Arab–Israeli peace process (never mind that Israelis are murdering Palestinians in Gaza on an hourly basis), they are fomenting trouble in Iraq, Lebanon, and Palestine, and on top of it they intend to develop nuclear arms. But how this old and banal list is revamped and brought to a crescendo is the way that the state of war – while both Afghanistan and Iraq are burning and the US is heavily engaged in Somalia – is moving apace.

In December 2006, Iran hosted a provocative conference on the Jewish Holocaust, rightly attracting global condemnation. The conference, along with outlandish comments by President Ahmadinejad, was evidently meant to cover up the humiliating defeat of the Iranian president's faction during the City Council and the Assembly of Expert elections in the same month. At the same time, the UN Security Council voted to impose sanctions on Iran and its trade in sensitive nuclear materials and technology. The US/Israeli reaction to the Holocaust conference was swift, angry, and overdetermined. "Iranians" are insensitive to Jewish suffering. Their president has said he wants to wipe Israel off the map. They now intend to develop a nuclear arsenal. So two plus two equals let's bomb the living daylight out of Iran. The Security Council resolution, meanwhile, failed to silence Ahmadinejad's bellicosity.

The new Christian year began on similarly ominous notes. According to a January 7 article in the British *Sunday Times*, two Israeli air force squadrons were "training to blow up an Iranian [nuclear] facility using low-yield nuclear 'bunker-busters." Quoting "several Israeli military sources," the *Sunday Times* reported: "as soon as the green light is given, it will be one mission, one strike and the Iranian nuclear project will be demolished." Moreover, "Israeli and American officials have met several times to consider military action. Military analysts said the disclosure of the plans could be intended to put pressure on Tehran to halt [uranium] enrichment, cajole America into action or soften up world opinion in advance of an Israeli attack." The Israelis denied that this report was in any way accurate. The net effect was an evident increase in the state of war – a war that may or may not happen.

Soon after this *Sunday Times* report, in a speech on January 11, 2007, President Bush announced a new strategy in which additional US troops were to be dispatched to Iraq. Many observers read this troop increase as being more a sign of preparation for a military engagement with Iran than an attempt to bolster security in Iraq – a seemingly impossible task for this administration. The day after President Bush's speech, US forces accompanied by military helicopters stormed the Iranian consulate in the Kurdish city of Arbil, arresting five employees. The US, the common wisdom suggested, was provoking Iran into some sort of rash military action, so it could use it as an excuse to attack Iran. But this was all in the realm of speculation – precisely what the state of war (not the actual war) demands and exacts.

Soon after that provocative act in Arbil, on January 14, US vice president Dick Cheney upped the ante and declared that Iran was "fishing in troubled waters." About a week after the Arbil incident, on January 20, a US defense official (speaking to the press on condition of anonymity) blamed Iran for the kidnapping and killing of a number of American soldiers in Karbala. This incident, suspicion and speculation had it, was in retaliation for the arrest of five Iranians by US troops in Arbil. But all of these events were matters of doubt, suspicion, innuendo, anonymity and, above all, denial. There can of course be no doubt that the Islamic Republic will do anything that it can to affect developments in neighboring Iraq, in a manner compatible with its interests. Nor is there any question that the Islamic Republic must not interfere in the internal affairs of Iraq. But is US/Israel in a moral position to point the finger at the Islamic Republic? How could anyone blame the Islamic Republic for having five agents in Iraq, if that indeed is true, when US/Israel and its European allies have mobilized the army of Attila the Hun from halfway around the globe and, officially, illegally, immorally, and murderously occupied Iraq against the will of its people. If five Iranians have been identified as interfering in Iraqi affairs, how many tens of thousands of Americans (Israelis?) and British share that shameful identification?

Echoing Vice President Cheney's threatening remarks and confirming these suspicions, a Kuwait-based newspaper *Arab Times* reported that the US might launch a military strike against Iran before April 2007. The report cited "a reliable source" and predicted that the attack would be launched from the sea, while Patriot missiles would guard all Arab countries in the Gulf. The news was brought home to the ayatollahs in Qom and Tehran by their next-door neighbor. But why would the Kuwaitis know something that others did not? The question remained on the borderline of un/certainty, where the state of war is habitually intensified.

Such speculations and haphazard guesses were rampant until President Bush's State of the Union address delivered on January 23, when, as the BBC World Affairs correspondent Paul Reynolds put it, "one of the notable features ... was its hostile attitude towards Iran. He accused the 'regime' in Iran of arming 'terrorists like Hizbullah' and of directing 'Shia extremists' in Iraq." Again: no particular declaration of war was evident. But the suggestion was as tall and thick as is the Israeli apartheid wall. You could not possibly overlook its threatening shadow.

Public knowledge as psyop

The following particular reference of President Bush in his State of the Union Address was quite noteworthy:

> If American forces step back before Baghdad is secure, the Iraqi government would be overrun by extremists on all sides. We could expect an epic battle between Shia extremists backed by Iran, and Sunni extremists aided by al-Qaeda and supporters of the old regime. A contagion of violence could spill out across the country – and in time the entire region could be drawn into the conflict.

How did that happen? When did President Bush learn about the difference between Sunnis and Shias? This particular presidential pronouncement on Shia–Sunni hostilities seems to have been the handiwork of a certain Seyyed Vali Reza Nasr, who teaches American military personnel about matters Islamic (and thus *ipso facto* dangerous and detrimental to American national security) at the Department of National Security Affairs of the Naval Postgraduate School. This, according to its website, "is an academic institution whose emphasis is on study and research programs relevant to the Navy's interests, as well as to the interests of other arms of the Department of Defense. The programs are designed to accommodate the unique requirements of the military."

In his recently published book, *The Shia Revival: How Conflicts within Islam Will Shape the Future* (2006), Seyyed Vali Reza Nasr reported to his students at the Naval Postgraduate School and whoever else wishes to learn about Islam and Shiism that Americans had better watch out because there is a new chimerical creature called the "Shia Crescent." Stretching its venomous posture all the way from Pakistan, through Iran and Iraq, and then down to Syria and Lebanon, this creature is about to gobble up the region in its "epic" hostility with Sunnism. With this, it threatens moderate US allies and interests, for the protection of which Professor Seyyed Vali Reza Nasr has been hired by the US military, in his current position at the School. It is precisely this presumed threat that appears in President Bush's State of the Union address.

To be sure, there are observers such as Michael Hirsh of *Newsweek* who believe that this particular attention of President Bush to the Shia–Sunni divide in the Muslim world is due to the presumed resurrection of Henry Kissinger in the US president's post-catastrophe strategy in Iraq. "In an extraordinary series of moves," Michael Hirsh reports in *Newsweek* on 1 February 2007, "Secretary of State Condoleezza Rice and other US officials have been seeking to create a united front of Sunni Arab regimes and Israel against Shia Iran as part of an aggressive new approach to Tehran." But whereas Henry Kissinger's "fingerprints," to use Michael Hirsh's word, can be gleaned in his classical line of negotiating from a position of power, Seyyed Vali Reza Nasr's "fingerprints" are reflected in a more substantial and circumstantial stipulation. His significant imprint is reflected in the manner in which the state of war is not just sustained, but also put on automatic pilot. If the role of Osama bin Laden was to give US global imperialism (aka "the war on terror") a generically *Islamic* disposition, then the function of Seyyed Vali Reza Nasr's book (perhaps, as Michael Hirsh suggests, circumstantially commensurate with Henry Kissinger's strategies) is to give that cosmic battle with "Islamic terrorism" an innately *Islamic* disposition. In other words, if Afghanistan is in a state of utter desolation and the Taliban are about to take over, or if almost four years into the US-led invasion of Iraq the country is from one end to another suffering total devastation, with hundreds of thousands of Iraqis maimed, murdered, tortured, raped, incarcerated and made into refugees in their own homeland, then the United States has really nothing to do with any of this. It is really this "epic battle," as President Bush puts it, "between Shia extremists backed by Iran and Sunni extremists aided by al-Qaeda" that is to blame. The circumstantial appearance of Seyyed Vali Reza Nasr's argument, Henry Kissinger's strategic council, and President Bush's renewed strategy of aggressive domination in Iraq, and the potential invasion of Iran are all integral to sustaining a state of war that is now almost entirely self-propelling, and on automatic pilot because the US is dragged into an epic (cosmic and pre-eternal) battle. This is not due to its own will or volition, but is in fact entirely despite itself, and against its best intentions.

As a major ideological intervention in aiding and abetting the US/Israel "war on terror," Seyyed Vali Reza Nasr's book on *The Shia Revival*, published while he is employed by the US military, opens a whole new chapter on the politics and power of knowledge production. In the entire gamut of the sociology of knowledge, and in the deepest layers of Michel Foucault's theorization of the relationship between knowledge and power, no one ever imagined a day when the military apparatus of a globalized empire, as Chalmers Johnson's groundbreaking *Blowback* trilogy has convincingly demonstrated, will itself begin to generate its own homegrown knowledge about its enemy, and start disseminating it to the public at large. For this reason *The Shia Revival* is best read as a piece of military psyop meant to prepare the public at large for an even more prolonged state of war against "Islamic terrorism." The latter is ostensibly a terrorism that is, because of "the epic battle" between Sunnis and Shias, actually entirely independent of US good intentions, and squarely laid at the feet of medieval ("epic") hostilities between two factions of Muslims. President Bush was offering Muslims peace and prosperity on behalf of the Americans; however, the Muslims' own tribal barbarism prevents them from deserving such a splendid gift.

Sustaining a source of menace

The catastrophe that faces the whole world – Americans included – is not limited to this level of psyop chicanery. Something far more serious is the matter with the world. For every one to two years, George W. Bush perceived a new source of menace in the world, and launched a massive new war against Arabs and Muslims while telling them that really he is shooting at them in order to save them from their own evil. The normative vacuity of these identical terms of fear and warmongering has reached incomprehensible proportions, to the point that, except for the lives of yet another few hundred thousand waiting to be annihilated in the region, if the US/Israel attacks Iran, it no longer makes any difference if the axis will or will not actually do so. What matters, and what remains a corrosive force in the soul of an entire nation, is the state of war in which US/Israeli ideologues are determined to keep themselves and the world, which they systematically endanger.

More than being at war, what works best for the US/Israeli warlords is being in "a state of war" – for the fear of war is the condition in which they want to keep the world. Come March, April, May or whenever, US/Israel may or may not invade Iran. If the war indeed happens, no one will count the Iranian dead, for counting them will not amount to moral outrage loud enough to match what is happening to the world. CNN will count the US soldiers' casualties, but even this, too, will dissipate into a vacuous pomposity that could not care less about the poor and disenfranchised Americans who are grabbed by the throat of their poverty, and catapulted halfway around the globe to maim, murder, torture, and rape their own brothers and sisters. For every one US casualty (which is one too many) there will be anywhere between one and two hundred Iranian casualties, if we take the Iraqi case as our measure. No one will hold anyone responsible. The Iranian neocon contingency will have made their career and lucrative contracts, and still appear on television. Just like Fouad Ajami, they will tell Americans that these Iranians, just like the Iraqis, did not deserve the gift of freedom and democracy that the Americans were offering them (as he proposes in his book *The Foreigner's Gift: The Americans, the Arabs, and the Iraqis in Iraq*). The rest of the world will have gotten even more used to the state of war that US/Israel is imposing on the globe. The invasion of Iran will add yet another front to the US/Israeli global flexing of its military prowess. And if they – the US government and the Jewish state (the two most violent states on planet Earth) – don't invade Iran, it still makes no difference. All it takes is a comment here by President Bush, or a suggestion there by Vice President Cheney, or yet another confession by Israel that it indeed has a massive nuclear capacity – or else the planting of a news story that Israel may attack Iran. The actual context of such news – that the US/Israel may or may not attack Iran – is entirely irrelevant to the reality of positing these threats. It is this that keeps the world on the edge of its seat, making fear and warmongering the paramount condition of our lives.

In his groundbreaking work on the "state of exception," the distinguished Italian philosopher Giorgio Agamben has begun the uncanny task of theorizing what has hitherto been delegated to the realm of *necessities legem non habet* (necessity has no law). Defying this dictum, Agamben has taken Carl Schmitt's famous pronouncement in his *Political Theology* that the sovereign is "he who decides on the state of exception" quite seriously and sought to theorize that state of exception. In Agamben's own project, what he calls the "no-man's land between public law and political fact, and between the juridical order and life," remains paramount. But adjacent to that effectively juridical project, there remains a widespread culture of catastrophe that must systematically generate and sustain that state of exception, which here and now in the United States, and the world it ruthlessly rules, amounts to a perpetual state of war. It is to that state, and not merely its potential and actual evidence, that we must learn how to respond.

Originally published in *Al-Ahram Weekly*, February 8–14, 2007

Iran's Democratic Upsurge

A messianic apocalyptic cult...

Israeli prime minister Binyamin Netanyahu
on Iran and Iranians

By design or serendipity, the Israeli claim to be "the only democracy in the Middle East" has suddenly been globally exposed for the ludicrous joke that it is.

The June 2009 parliamentary elections in Lebanon will go down in history as a major advance for the cause of democracy in that small but vital country. The victory of the March 14 coalition of Saad Al-Hariri, by which they now hold 71 seats in the 128-member parliament, has left the remaining 58 seats to the Hizbullah-led coalition. Israel and its American allies have been quick to paint this result as a victory for "pro-Western" elements and thus a defeat for Hizbullah. This is not the case. Victory of the March 14 coalition is the victory of democracy in Lebanon – a victory Hizbullah shared.

Because Israel is a racist apartheid state, it cannot see the world except through its own tribal lens. The victory of the March 14 coalition in Lebanon is the victory of the electoral process, which now solidly includes Hizbullah and its parliamentary allies. Hizbullah is now not only part of Lebanon's civil society, but also its political apparatus and institutionalized democratic process, and Hizbullah achieved this without abandoning its status as a national liberation army that will defend its homeland against any and every Israeli barbarity that may come its way.

As the Arab and Muslim worlds celebrate this democratic victory, it is imperative to see it as having nothing to do with Obama's presidency, or his speech in Cairo, lecturing Muslims in

the region on democracy while his army is illegally occupying
Iraq and slaughtering Afghans.

On the heels of the Lebanese elections, the cause and the
march of democracy took an even bolder leap in Iran, and that
leap is not because of US promotion of democracy, but despite
and against it. At the time of writing, millions of Iranians inside
and out of their homeland are angry and heartbroken with the
official results. Some go so far as to consider what happened a
coup d'état. There are perfectly legitimate reasons to question
the validity of the official results that have declared Mahmoud
Ahmadinejad the clear winner. The only point of which Iranians
can be sure and proud is the extraordinary manifestation of their
collective will to participate in their politics. This unprecedented
participation neither lends legitimacy to the illegitimate apparatus of the Islamic Republic and its manifestly undemocratic
organs nor should be abused by bankrupt oppositional forces
outside Iran to denounce and denigrate a glorious page in
modern Iranian history.

Every four years, during presidential elections followed by
parliamentary elections, the paradox of the democratic theocracy
of the Islamic Republic of Iran fascinates and baffles the world.
During this presidential campaign, Iranians boisterously joined
rallies and then stood in long queues to vote under the extended
shadow of Israeli warlords threatening a military strike. The
propaganda machinery at the disposal of Israel will have the
world believe that a populist demagogue like Ahmadinejad is
"the dictator" of Iran, as one of their spokesmen in New York,
Columbia University president Lee Bollinger, once put it. And
thus on the model of an Oriental despot he represents a backward people whose fate deserves to be determined by others (the
US/Israel, of course). As that prominent Israeli scholar of Iran

Haggai Ram, one of a handful of courageous Israeli dissidents, has aptly demonstrated in his *Iranophobia*, Israel's fixation with Iran has now reached pathological proportions and is a case study of self-delusional hysteria feeding on itself.

The reality of the Iranian polity, as the world has once again witnessed, is vastly different to the picture US/Israel propaganda is feeding the world. A vibrant and restless society is defying all mandated limitations on its will and demanding and exacting its democratic rights. The undemocratic institutions of the Islamic Republic – beginning with the idea of *velayat-e faqih*, rule of the cleric, down to the unelected body of the Guardian Council – are not obstacles to democracy in Iran but invitations to democratic assault. What the Iranian electorate, young and old, men and women, seem to be doing is far more important than a mere head-on collision with aging and arcane institutions. They are pushing the limits of their democratic exercises in unfathomable and unstoppable directions. The Internet has connected Iran's youth to the global context, and they have in turn become the catalyst of discursive and institutional changes beyond the control of the clerical clique in Qom and Tehran.

This is more than anything a battle between generations. Iranian society is changing and fast. The aging custodians of the Islamic Republic wish to limit what can be said or expected. But the globally geared youth, more than 60 percent of the electorate, is now radically altering the contours of those limits. They are not merely defying them, but are sublimating them. The red line in Iran is thinning by the hour, for facing it are skillful players exercising their political muscles. It was quite evident in the course of the US presidential election of 2008 that an Internet-savvy Obama outmaneuvered McCain's arcane operation. The same is true of Mir-Hossein Mousavi and

Mehdi Karroubi's campaigns, the two reformist candidates, on the one side, and Ahmadinejad's, on the other, with Mohsen Rezaei in between. The social basis of Mousavi's platform is the urban middle class, the youth, and women. The economic basis of Ahmadinejad's demagoguery is the rural and urban poor. They are both campaigners skillful at reaching out to their respective constituencies.

The rising demographic tide is against the old revolutionaries. Iranian children born after the revolution in the late 1970s have no active memory of its hopes and furies and could not care less about those who do. Every four years since the end of the Iran–Iraq war in 1988, and the death of Ayatollah Khomeini in 1989, the Iranian electorate has been upping the ante. They voted for Rafsanjani in 1989 and for eight years he rebuilt the economic infrastructure of the country after the war, creating a class of nouveau riche. Then in 1997 they voted for Moham-mad Khatami, who gave them a modicum of civil society and opened up the vista of wide-ranging social reform, and yet did nothing – or very little – to alleviate the poor masses Rafsanjani had left behind. In 2005, those disenfranchised by Rafsanjani's economic project and indifferent to Khatami's social and cultural agenda pushed power into the hands of Ahmadinejad. And now, in 2009, a major segment of disaffected voters, in their millions, are investing trust in Mousavi, a former prime minister with impeccable revolutionary credentials, a war hero, and a socialist in terms of economic projects.

Again, the scene is overwhelmed by the massive participation of the youth, students, and above all women, on both sides of the political divide. This new generation is Internet-aware, versatile with Facebook, YouTube, and Twitter. It is globally wired. The presence of Zahra Rahnavard, Mousavi's distinguished wife, is an added aspect of this campaign. A prominent public intellectual and a former university chancellor; a poet, painter, and sculptor; and a staunch advocate of women's rights, Rahnavard is dubbed by some foreign journalists as the Michelle Obama of Iran. "No," retorted one of her Iranian admirers in response, "Michelle Obama could have aspired to become the Zahra Rahnavard of the United States."

This election has also been extraordinary on account of live televised debates that exposed skeletons collected for thirty years in the closets of the aging elders of the republic. Ahmadinejad, bastard son of the Islamic Revolution, is fast devouring, in his populist demagoguery, the idealism and aspirations of that revolution. Opposing Ahmadinejad are the architects of Iran's creative imagination. More than ever Iranian artists and filmmakers have been active in this election. They have published open letters, produced video clips, and joined others in rallies. From Paris, Mohsen Makhmalbaf wrote an open letter supporting Mousavi and encouraging everyone to vote for him while dispatching his youngest daughter Hana to Iran to make a documentary about the elections. When Mousavi challenged the official results, Makhmalbaf became a conduit of his campaign with international news outlets, using his connections with foreign journalists.

Majid Majidi, another prominent Iranian filmmaker, directed Mousavi's campaign commercials. Other Iranian directors, actors, and producers have similarly exerted their efforts. Student organizations, labor unions, professional associations, and women's rights organizations – all have been engaged, on the streets, on the Internet sites, writing fiery essays, shooting movies, and producing video clips. Rahnavard, a painter with a talent for color symbolism, chose green for her husband's campaign (neither red for violence nor white for martyrdom, the other two colors in the Iranian flag). And when Khatami went to Isfahan to campaign for Mousavi, upwards of 100,000 people came together in the historic Meydan-e Naqsh-e Jahan to cheer him and support the reformist candidate. This is democracy from below; democracy not by virtue of institutions, but by collective and defiant insistence. Israeli warlords should think twice before behaving aggressively toward the Iranians.

Disappointed by this democratic flourishing are not just Israeli and American Zionists who spent time and money portraying Iran as a diabolic dictatorship deserving to be bombed. Equally scandalized by this election are the colorful band of lipstick jihadi Hirsi Ali wannabes who are writing one erotic fantasy after another about Iranian "women," oversexualizing Iranian politics as they opt for "love and danger" during their "honeymoon in Tehran." The representation of Iranian women in the flea market of the US publishing industry began under President Bush with Azar Nafisi's *Reading Lolita in Tehran* and has now reached a new depth of depravity in Pardis Mahdavi's *Passionate Uprisings: Iran's Sexual Revolution.* Between a harem full of Lolitas and a bathhouse of nymphomaniacs is where Nafisi and Mahdavi have Iranian women, marching in despair, awaiting liberation by US marines and Israeli bombers. What a contrast to the real work of women, as testified to in this election, and now on the street in defense of the collective will of the nation.

On two sides of Iran lie in waste Iraq and Afghanistan, liberated for democracy by George W. Bush and now Barack Obama. In the middle, millions of Iranians who would have been maimed or murdered by a similar "liberation" peacefully poured into streets and jubilantly marched to polling stations to vote, in a grassroots march towards democracy, albeit limited and flawed, but nevertheless promising and beautiful. And now that they think their votes have been stolen from them they are more than capable of demanding them back.

Whoever the final winner of Iran's election may be, fanatical Zionists in Israel and the US, power-mongering mullahs in Tehran and Qom, comprador intellectuals and career opportunists from Washington DC to California, are its sorest losers. The winners are the indomitable Iranian people. We are witness, regardless of controversy, to a triumph of democratic pluralism, from Lebanon to Iran – a nightmare for the Jewish state that wants the whole region remade in its delusional, racist, apartheid image where sects and factions fight each other to the dogged end. "A messianic apocalyptic cult" can only describe the country of the man who pronounced it.

Mr. Prime Minister, thou dost protest too much.

Originally published in *Al-Ahram Weekly*, June 18–24, 2009

People Power

Khonak an qomarbazi keh bebakht har cheh budash,
Benamand hichash ella havas e qomar e digar

(Lucky that gambler who lost all he had,
Left with nothing but the urge for yet another game)

Rumi

The Iranian presidential election of June 2009 will go down in history as one of the most magnificent manifestations of a people's indomitable will to achieve enduring democratic institutions. The beleaguered custodians of the Islamic Republic, thoroughly aware of their own lack of legitimacy, were quick to use the occasion as a vindication of their illegitimate rule. They are wrong. This was not a vote *for* their legitimacy. It was a vote *against* it – albeit within the mediaeval juridical fortress they have built around the notions and principles of citizenry in a free and democratic republic. The feeble "opposition" to the clerics abroad also rushed to admonish those who participated in the election, insisting on regime change, at a time when upward of 80 percent of eligible voters willingly participated in the election. Both of these desperate, hasty, and banal readings of the election, predicated on bankrupt positions, are false.

Let's begin with the losers of this presidential campaign. The single most important loser of the Iranian presidential campaign of June 2009 is Ali Khamenei, the supreme guide, and the *velayet-e faqih*. If this election – the *process* of the election, not its fraudulent result – showed anything, it would be that the nation is not *safih* (indigent) enough to need a supreme *faqih* (most learned) to shepherd it. The election revealed the political maturity of a nation that can now be allowed to return to its own devices, with the obscenity of the notion of a *velayet-e faqih* wiped off its body politic. The very office of the supreme guide is an insult to the democratic intelligence and the collective will of this nation. If Ali Khamenei had an iota of decency left in him, at the autumn of his patriarchy, he would dismantle this obscene office forever, convene a constitutional assembly and disband the three other undemocratic institutions of the republic – the Assembly of Experts of Leadership, the Guardian Council of the Constitution, and the Expediency Council of the Regime. These are the enduring vestiges of a theocratic legacy that have no room in a democratic republic. The vast majority of Iranians are Muslim. However, there are millions of Iranians who are not Muslim, or not believing or practising Muslims – which should not matter in terms of their privileges and duties as citizens of a republic. As he witnesses the erosion of every single iota of legitimacy that the Islamic Revolution claimed over the nation, the soon-to-be 70-year-old Ali Khamenei can leave a legitimate legacy for himself by seeing to it that this medieval banality is wiped from Iranian democratic aspirations. It is simply unseemly to see grown-up people, Mahmoud Ahmadinejad or Mir-Hossein Mousavi, appear so obsequious and sycophantic toward another man. What is the difference between a shah and a supreme guide? Nothing.

An equally important loser in this campaign, though declared its winner, is the populist buffoonery of that unsurpassed charlatan Ahmadinejad, the bastard son of the Islamist revolution. In his demagoguery and fanaticism he represents the most fascistic tendencies of the Islamic Revolution and Republic. All revolutions have a dose or two of populism and demagoguery mixed with their idealism and high aspirations. What has happened in the Islamic Revolution is that its innate populism has now been personified in one demagogue who seeks to stay in power by manipulating the poor and disenfranchised segments of his constituency by fraudulent economic policies that give people fish instead of teaching them how to fish, governmental subsidies and handouts instead of generating jobs. The economic policies of Ahmadinejad have been catastrophic and institutionally damaging, causing double-digit inflation and endemic unemployment in an oil-based economy at the mercy of global market fluctuation far beyond Ahmadinejad's control or comprehension. His religious populism and ludicrous claims to divine dispensation are a cruel joke at the expense of signs and symbols people hold sacred.

The next loser was Mousavi's poorly run presidential campaign – ill-advised, ill-prepared, sentimental; full of the necessary color symbolism but lacking in substance, a clearly articulated platform, economic detail, political programming and an attempt to reach out to a wider spectrum of his constituency. His campaign was too elitist, tied in its visual paraphernalia to a northern Tehran sensibility and lacking appeal across an oil-based economy. His delay in entering the race, his to-ing and fro-ing with Mohammad Khatami, suggested a poor degree of preparation, as did his debate with Ahmadinejad. While Ahmadinejad had come with charts and graphs and dossiers, flaunting his lumpen demeanor, thinking himself "a man of the people," Mousavi had nothing except his gentility to offer. He rambled along, read from written statements in a barely audible voice, ran out of things to say before his time was over. The problem with the Iranian democratic movement is not that it is unable to produce an Obama – if he is the model. Mousavi could have very well been an Iranian Obama. The problem was there was no David Axelrod or David Plouffe, what the Mousavi campaign desperately needed and sorely lacked. A band of self-indulgent Muslim yuppies surround him with not an idea of how to reach his multiple constituencies. If Mousavi did reach these constituencies it was for having saved the integrity of the country during the Iran–Iraq war (1980–88). But he faced a new Iran, a new generation, an entirely different constituency that loved and admired him and his wife Zahra Rahnavard at face value. But you never win a campaign on goodwill. This is not to suggest that the election was not rigged – it may or may not have been. But there are rudimentary strategies for reaching out to diverse constituencies which his campaign ignored.

The next big loser in this Iranian election was the legacy of

George W. Bush – that is, the Bush–Wolfowitz doctrine. Look at Iraq, Pakistan, and Afghanistan, on two sides of Iran, and then consider Iran on June 12, 2009: millions of Iranians in a peaceful, orderly, joyous, and enthusiastic march to the ballot box. The second they thought their votes were stolen they poured onto the streets – what Americans should have done in 2000. Along with the Bush–Wolfowitz doctrine, the losers include the US Congress, and its headquarters at AIPAC. The US Congress can scarcely be imagined as behaving in a more transparently hypo-critical way. On the night before the Iranian election, on June 12, AIPAC pushed a button and its stooges in the US Congress began pushing for a resolution imposing more severe economic sanctions on Iran, knowing only too well that the following day the news would increase the chances of Ahmadinejad, Israel's favored candidate, as its officials have readily admitted.

Losers also include expatriate Iranian monarchists, along with all other politically bankrupt banalities and their native informers and comprador intellectuals, from Washington DC to California, who have established vacuous centres for "dialogue" or to save "democracy" in Iran. What a band of buffoons they were made to look in light of the evident grassroots, native expression of democratic rights.

The sole winner of the presidential election of 2009 was the Iranian people, whomever they voted for – some 40 million of them, out of an eligible voting population of 48 million, upward of 80 per cent. The election showed that the democratic will of Iranians has matured beyond the point of return, no matter how violently the unelected officials of the Islamic Republic may wish to reverse it. It is too late. As was made evident during the presidential election of 2009, Iranians are perfectly capable of organizing themselves around competing views, campaigning

for their preferred candidates, peacefully going to polling stations and casting their vote. It is high time that the Shia clerics
packed their belongings and went back to their seminaries, and
for regime-change charlatans like Paul Wolfowitz to retire in
ignominy, and for career opportunist comprador intellectuals
of one think-tank or another in Washington DC or Stanford
University to go back to the half-decent teaching position they
had before.

Before I close, I must also say that a major loser is Hassan
Nasrallah of Lebanon. Nasrallah must know that the deep and
variegated roots of Iranians' commitment to the Palestinian
cause and the fate of the Shias in Lebanon are in the vast ocean
of their hearts and minds, fed to them with their mother's milk
and not in the deep corners of Ali Khamenei's pocket. Arabs
in general, and Palestinians in particular, ought to know that
Iranians are watching them closely, and wish to hear their
voices. This is the Iranian Intifada. A leading slogan in the streets
of Tehran is *Mardom chera neshestin, Iran shodeh Felestin* (People,
why are you sitting idly by, Iran has become Palestine). Arabs
and Muslims, and their leading public intellectuals, must come
out and take the side of this grassroots and peaceful demand
for a healthy and robust democracy.

The US congressional stooges of AIPAC – the Israeli generals
were all squarely on the side of Ahmadinejad – are in the same
league as Hassan Nasrallah.

All Arab and Muslim potentates ought to know that their
young are watching events in Iran with a keen interest. It is not
only Iranians who are wired to Facebook and Twitter; so are
their brothers and sisters around the globe, throughout the Arab
and Muslim world. Young Arabs and Muslims around the globe
are not immune to the demands young Iranians are exacting

at heavy cost, courageously exposing their bare chests against
the bullets and batons of tyranny. This is a post-ideological
generation. They could not care less about their parents' political hang-ups. They demand, and will exact, human, civil and
women's rights through a grassroots, entirely legitimate uprising, without compromising an inch in the face of the imperial
machinations of the United States or the colonial thuggery of
Israel. The custodians of the Islamic Republic are in violation
of Article 27 of the constitution of the Islamic Republic. To the
best of my knowledge, this is not a revolution to topple the
Islamic Republic. This is a grassroots demand for civil rights.
Iranians being clubbed and shot in the streets of Tehran are not
the stooges of the United States, whereas the Arab and Muslim
medieval potentates suffocating the democratic aspirations of
their people are. Fear the day that young Arabs and Muslims
learn from their Iranian brothers and sisters and demand their
inalienable human rights, freedom of peaceful assembly, freedom
of expression, equal rights for men and women, economic opportunity, respect for human decency and for the rule of law.

Originally published in *Al Ahram Weekly*, June 25–July 1, 2009

Looking in the Wrong Places

In his astute take on the current electoral crisis in Iran,[1] by far
the best in the literature so far, Azmi Bishara lays out a very
concise premiss for our reading of the unfolding event; but,
alas, he reaches a hasty and flawed conclusion. What I write
below is respectfully submitted in a spirit of complete solidarity

---

1. "An alternative reading," *Al-Ahram Weekly*, June 25–July 1, 2009.

with the leading Palestinian intellectual, whom I admire as a guiding light in our critical assessment of where we stand in our contemporary world.

Having carefully outlined the totalitarian disposition of the Islamic Republic, Bishara proceeds to identify two ways in which it differs from other totalitarian regimes: one, it has a democratic component that allows for two opposing camps to compete for elected office, not too dissimilar in their political formations to the Republican and Democratic parties in the US; two, it is religion that constitutes the state ideology and not an alien or imported ideology shared by the political elite but foreign to the rest of society.

Compared to China and the Soviet Union, Bishara rightly concludes that, "looking at Iran from the perspective of its degree of democratic competition, tolerance of criticism and peaceful rotation of authority in accordance with set rules, it is much closer to the pluralistic democracies in the West than to a dictatorial regime." Be that as it may, he is equally aware of the fact that a totalitarian ideology indeed permeates all spheres of private and public life in Iran, not unlike the power of consumer ideologies doing pretty much the same in North American and Western European societies.

These accurate and insightful observations, however, begin to appear on more fragile ground when Bishara observes that

> the criticisms levelled at the regime on the part of a broad swath of youth who have joined the reformists, especially those from middle class backgrounds who are more in contact with the rest of the world, are reminiscent of the grievances aired by the young in Eastern Europe, who held that their regimes deprived them of their individual and personal freedoms, the freedom to choose their way of life and the Western consumer lifestyle.

This careless use of the key term "middle class" soon coagulates into a more solid assertion that is even more seriously flawed: "While not dismissing or belittling such criticism," Bishara observes,

> it is important to bear in mind that these people are not the majority of young people but rather the majority of young people from a particular class [i.e. the middle class] ... Most of the youth from the poor sectors of society support Ahmadinejad.

From this false premiss, Bishara then proceeds to assert that

> the mood among those who think that their votes carry more weight qualitatively than the numerically greater votes of the poor, and who may actually believe that they represent the majority because they form the majority in their own parts of town, even if they are the minority in the country, has an arrogant, classist edge.

The assumption that supporters of Mousavi and/or Karrubi, or indeed that masses of millions of people who have poured into the streets of Tehran and other cities, come from "the middle class" is a common fallacy that Bishara shares with quite a number of others who are watching the Iranian scene from a theoretical distance that conceals more than it reveals. Even a seasoned historian of contemporary Iran like Ervand Abrahamian, a distinguished professor of history in New York, has opined a similar assessment, though with more qualified phrasing. "The core of the support for Mousavi," Abrahamian told Amira Haas of *Haaretz*, "is in fact university graduates and educated people, who can be described as middle class, and who are a clear product of the welfare state and the policy of expanding social services in force since the establishment of the [Islamic] Republic. Ahmadinejad's support base is those I

call 'evangelical' rather than 'fundamentalist'. These are not
the poor, but the religious poor – between 20 and 25 per cent."
Abrahamian's latter point about what he calls the "evangelical
poor" has a number of other serious holes in it, which for now
I will leave alone.

The problem with the false impression about this mysterious
"middle class" is not only that it distorts the reality of what we
are observing in Iranian cities, but that it also inadvertently fuels
the conspiratorial theories among certain segments of the North
American and Western European left that take this observation
one delusional step further and believe that the CIA (on behalf
of neoliberal economics) is behind this "velvet revolution." That
particular pathology needs a separate diagnosis, but the false
premiss of "middle class" support for Mousavi, particularly by
people I deeply admire, needs more urgent attention.

Of a total Iranian population of 72 million, upward of 70
percent are under the age of 30. While the overall rate of
unemployment under Ahmadinejad, predicated on correspond-
ingly high numbers under Khatami's two-term presidency, is 30
percent, this rate, according to Djavad Salehi-Isfahani, the most
reliable Iranian economist around, for young people between
the ages of 15 and 29 (some 35 percent of the total population) is
70 percent. So seven out of every ten people in this age group
can scarce find a job, let alone marry, let alone have children
and form a family. In exactly what phantasmagoric definition
of "the middle class" can they hope to be included?

Let me cite other statistics. You must have noticed the overwhelming presence of women in these demonstrations, right?
Now, 63 percent of university entrants in Iran are women, but
they make up only 12.3 per cent of the workforce. In other words,
one out of every two women university graduates earn their

degrees and then go back to live with their parents, remain a burden on their limited budget, and can only hope to leave their parents' home if they find a husband among those three out of ten young men who may be lucky enough to find a job that would enable them to marry. In what Marxist, Keynesian, or neoliberal definition of this blessed "middle class" would they fit?

Consider another fact. If we were to believe the official tabulation of the presidential election – and I have no way of proving otherwise (though that they are rigged is now a "social fact") – twice as many of these young voters have voted for Ahmadinejad as they did for Mir-Hossein Mousavi, Mehdi Karroubi and Mohsen Rezaei put together. In other words, the official results blow the argument of a pro-Mousavi "middle class" out of the water, for we will end up either with the bizarre proposition that pro-Mousavi Iranians voted for Ahmadinejad, if the results are accurate, or else the perfectly plausible possibility that the unemployed – and thus by definition the poor – voted for Mousavi, if the results are rigged. Either way, the supporters of Mousavi are not the upper-middle-class bourgeois class that thinks its votes are worth more than those of others.

But all these and similar statistics pale in comparison to another statistic that shows the real horror at the heart of the Islamic Republic – for which not just Ahmadinejad but the entire militant disposition of the ruling elite is responsible. In 1997, some 3 million high-school graduates participated in the Iranian national university entrance examination, of which only 240,000 managed to pass through the Seven Tasks of Rostam and enter a university. So the full capacity of the entire Iranian university system is less than 10 percent of total applicants. What happened to that 90 percent plus? Where did they go? Into what job, what opportunity, and what education?

The answer is frightful. A significant portion of this remaining 90 percent is absorbed into various layers of the militarized security apparatus, including the Basij and the Pasdaran. If in fact anyone qualified for that dreaded "middle class" status it is precisely this component of the 15- to 29-year-olds who have not made it into the university system and have joined the security apparatus of the regime, for they have a steady job, can marry, form a family, and have a solid investment in the status quo and be considered "middle class." In other words, instead of spending the national budget on expanding the university system, and then generating jobs, the custodians of the Islamic Republic – not just Ahmadinejad – insecure of their own legitimacy, as they are, would rather spend it on fortifying a security apparatus that keeps their aging banality in power.

Of course Ahmadinejad is not entirely responsible for this sad state of affairs. The Iranian economy is 85 percent oil-based, and an oil-based economy is not labour-intensive, while the Iranian "middle class" has always, since the nineteenth century, been a feeble and shaky proposition. But Bishara's assumption that "Ahmadinejad is less a representative of Iranian conservatives than a rebel against them from within their own establishment," or that "he has lashed out against them, including corrupt clergy, using the principles of the Islamic Revolution as his weapons," is deeply flawed. Of course there was corruption in the two administrations that preceded him, those of Khatami and Rafsanjani, which gave free rein to neoliberal privatization and its catastrophic consequences. But in what particular way has Ahmadinejad corrected that course? The answer: in no way. The battle between Ahmadinejad and Rafsanjani is not a battle between revolutionary purity and aging corruption; it is one between a retiring elite and an emerging, previously lower-ranking, echelon that is asserting its authority. It is romanticism of the most dangerous sort to imagine Ahmadinejad as a man who "wants to restore the revolution to its youthful vigor and gleam." He is so patently transparent that all one has to do is sit through ten minutes of his charlatanism during the televised presidential debates to see through the rampant lumpenism with which he operates. The only way that "he distributes oil revenues among the poor" is by recruiting them into the multilayered and brutal security apparatus of the Basij and the Pasdaran. This, again, is not his invention. He simply adds to the innate insecurity of the regime by overinvesting in security forces.

Bishara pursues a far more accurate course when he rightly observes that "Ahmadinejad's populist rhetoric has come as a boon to racist Western policies towards the Arabs, Muslims and easterners in general. The certificate of exoneration he has handed Europe for the holocaust is catastrophic in every sense." And yet again he overrides his own insight by suggesting that "Ahmadinejad has also shocked the West with a set of correct principles that challenge the colonialist legacy and that are rarely uttered now that everyone has been tamed to the axioms of Western racist arrogance." How so? How could a banal and parochial reiteration of certain truisms about colonialism and imperialism qualify Ahmadinejad for acting according to "correct principles"? Just because the Arab and Muslim world is cluttered with gutless collaborationists in positions of power does not mean that an irresponsible demagogue displays courage or enacts "correct principles." Quite the contrary: Ahmadinejad's imbecilic speech in Geneva in the course of Durban II in April 2009 was chiefly responsible for whitewashing the Israeli massacre of Palestinians in Gaza in December 2008–January 2009.

The cause of Palestinian national liberation has to be rescued from such demagoguery and rewritten into our democratic aspirations in an emerging geopolitics of which these young Iranians, men and women, lower and middle class, demonstrating in the streets of their cities are a vanguard. Democratic institutions and civil liberties ought to be salvaged from the combined banality of neoliberal and neoconservative economic and political chicanery. Israel loves nothing more than its own mirror image in the region – fanatical regimes that make it feel at home in the neighborhood. And it would much rather deal with corrupt collaborationists from one end of the Arab and Muslim world to another, punctuated by populist demagogues.

This is a moment in our history that requires visionary leadership. Consider the case of Hassan Nasrallah. After his initially wise and judicious position, refusing to take sides, he rushed to congratulate Ahmadinejad for his "victory." This was a terrible strategic mistake. He must have known for a fact that the solidarity of Iranians with the noble causes of Palestine and Lebanon is not contingent on Ahmadinejad's victory or defeat. His subsequent statement, that "Iran is under the authority of *velayat-e faqih* and will pass through this crisis," was of course far more astute but was too little too late, coming after Ali Khamenei had authorized the bloody crackdown on the uprising. Why could Nasrallah not show the same judicious poise displayed when Hizbullah lost the recent Lebanese parliamentary elections to the March 14 coalition of Saad Al-Hariri? What is the difference between the cause of democracy in Lebanon and in Iran? But lest my criticism of Nasrallah is abused by people in Tel Aviv and Washington, let me make sure they know that we are more than capable of tolerating the principle of democratic dissent, even in the direst circumstances, without losing sight of what racist colonial settlement is – the single most dangerous threat to democracy in our region.

We are witness to an epistemic shift in our received political culture. We must learn from those who are risking their lives in the streets of Iran and muster courage and imagination to face and read it proactively, rather than collapse back to a structural-functional analysis of the status quo in which we, in effect, say to ourselves, "Listen folks, we are Orientals. Oriental despotism is written into our DNA, and charlatans like Ahmadinejad are the best we can produce," as our false guilt mistakes their lumpenism for their proletarian origins and projects, and then allows for our intellectual reticence to theorize their victory as self-evident. We need, for the sake of posterity, to think better of ourselves.

Originally published in *Al-Ahram Weekly*, July 2–8, 2009

Left is Wrong on Iran

When a political groundswell like the Iranian presidential election of June 2009 and its aftermath happen, the excitement and drama of the moment expose not just our highest hopes but also our deepest fault lines, most troubling moral flaws, and the dangerous political precipice we face.

Over the decades I have learned not to expect much from what passes for "the left" in North America and/or Western Europe when it comes to the politics of what their colonial ancestry has called "the Middle East." But I do expect much more when it comes to our own progressive intellectuals – Arabs, Muslims, South Asians, Africans and Latin Americans. This is not a racial bifurcation, but a regional typology along the colonial divide.

By and large this expectation is apt and more often than not met. The best case in point is the comparison between what Azmi Bishara has offered on the recent uprising in Iran and what Slavoj Žižek has felt obligated to write. Whereas Bishara's piece (aspects of which I have had reason to disagree with) is predicated on a detailed awareness of the Iranian scene, accumulated over the last thirty years of the Islamic Republic and even before, Žižek's (the conclusion of which I completely disagree with) is entirely spontaneous and impressionistic, predicated on as much knowledge about Iran as I have about the mineral composition of the planet Jupiter.

The examples can be multiplied by many, when we add to pieces written by Azmi Bishara those by Mustafa El-Labbad and Galal Nassar, for example, and compare them to the confounded blindness of Paul Craig Roberts, Anthony DiMaggio, Michael Veiluva, James Petras, Jeremy Hammond, Eric Margolis, and many others. While people closest to the Iranian scene write from a position of critical intimacy, and with a healthy dose of disagreement, those farthest from it write with an almost unanimous exposure of their constitutional ignorance, not having the foggiest idea what has happened in that country over the last thirty years, let alone the last 200 years, and then having the barefaced chutzpah to pontificate on one aspect or another – or, worse, to take more than 70 million human beings as stooges of the CIA and puppets of the Saudis.

Let me begin by stating categorically that in principle I share the fundamental political premiss of the left, its weariness of US imperial machinations, of the major North American and Western European media (but by no means all of them) by and large missing the point on what is happening around the globe, or, even worse, seeing things from the vantage point of their governmental cues, which they scarcely question. It has been but a few months since we have emerged from the nightmare of the Bush presidency, the combined chicaneries of Dick Cheney, Donald Rumsfeld, Paul Wolfowitz and John Ashcroft, and the continued calamities of the "war on terror." Iran is still under the threat of a military strike by Israel, or at least more severe economic sanctions, similar to those that during the Clinton administration were responsible for the death of hundreds of thousands of Iraqis. Iraq and Afghanistan are burning, Gaza is in utter desolation, Northern Pakistan is in deep humanitarian crisis, and Israel is stealing more Palestinian lands every day. With all his promises and pomp and ceremony, President Obama is yet to show in any significant and tangible way his change of course in the region from that of the previous administration.

The US Congress, prompted by AIPAC (the American Israel Public Affairs Committee), pro-war vigilantes lurking in the halls of power in Washington DC, and Israeli warlords and their propaganda machinery in the US, are all excited about the events in Iran and are doing their damnedest to turn them to their advantage. The left, indeed, has reason to worry.

But having principled positions on geopolitics is one thing, being blind and deaf to a massive social movement is entirely different, as is being impervious to the flagrant charlatanism of an upstart demagogue like Ahmadinejad. The sign and the task of a progressive and agile intelligence is to hold on to core principles and seek to incorporate mass social uprising into its modus operandi. My concern here is not with that retrograde strand in the North American or Western European left that is siding with Ahmadinejad and against the masses of millions of Iranians daring to confront the draconian security apparatus of the Islamic Republic. They are a lost cause, and frankly no one could care less what they think of the world. What does concern me is when an Arab intellectual like As'ad AbuKhalil opts to go public with his assessment of this movement; what he says so vertiginously smacks of recalcitrant fanaticism, steadfastly insisting on a belligerent ignorance.

Asad AbuKhalil has finally categorically stated, on his website "Angry Arab," that he is "now more convinced than ever that the US and Western governments were far more involved in Iranian affairs during the demonstrations than was assumed by many." He then tries to be cautious and cover his back by qualifying this claim:

> Let us make it clear: the US, Western and Saudi intervention in Iranian affairs does not necessarily implicate the Iranian protesters themselves. And even if some of them were involved in those conspiracies, I do believe that the majority of Iranian protesters were motivated by domestic issues and legitimate grievances against an oppressive government.

This qualification is in fact worse than the categorical statement suggesting that a conspiratorial plot lay behind the movement, for it seeks to deploy fancy speculative footwork to cover up a moral bankruptcy – that a stand not be taken, one way or another. AbuKhalil's final edict: "I was just looking at US and Western media coverage of Honduras, where the situation is rather analogous, and you can't escape the conclusion that the US media were involved with the US government in a conspiracy the details of which will be revealed years from now." In other words, since the US media are not covering the Honduras development as closely as they do (or so AbuKhalil fancies) the Iranian event, then the US media are in cahoots with the US government in fomenting unrest in Iran, and thus this movement is manufactured by US imperial designs with Saudi aid; and though we may not have evidence of this yet, we will learn of its details thirty years from now, when a Stephen Kinzer comes and writes an account of the plot, as he did about the CIA-sponsored coup of 1953.

One simply must have dug oneself deeply and darkly, mummified, inside a forgotten and hollowed grave on another planet not to have seen, heard and felt for millions of human beings risking their brave lives and precious liberties by pouring onto the streets of their cities demanding their constitutional right to peaceful protest. Thousands of them have been arrested and jailed, their loved ones worried sick about their whereabouts; hundreds of their leading public intellectuals, journalists, civil and women's rights activists, rounded up and incarcerated, harassed and even tortured, some put on national television to confess that they are spies for "the enemy." Pregnant women are among those leading reformists arrested, along with such leading intellectuals as Said Hajjarian, paralysed having barely survived an assassination attempt by precisely those in the upper echelons of the Islamic Republic who have yet again put him and his wheelchair in jail. Three prominent reformists, all heroes of the Islamic Revolution – Khatami, Mousavi, and Karroubi: a former president, a former prime minister, and a former speaker of the house to this very Islamic Republic – are leading the opposition, charging fraud, declaring Ahmadinejad illegitimate. The senior Grand Ayatollah of the land, the octogenarian Ayatollah Montazeri, has openly declared Khamenei illegitimate. The Iranian parliament is deeply divided and in turmoil. A massively militarized security apparatus has wreaked havoc on the civilian population: beating, clubbing, tear-gassing, and shooting at them. University dormitories have been savagely raided by plain-clothes vigilantes, and students beaten up with batons, clubs, kicks, and fists by oversize thugs. Millions of Iranians around the globe have taken to the streets, their leading public figures – philosophers like Abdul-Karim Soroush, clerics like Mohsen Kadivar, public intellectuals like Ata Mohajerani, filmmakers like Mohsen Makhmalbaf, pop singers like Shahin Najafi, footballers of the Iranian national team, countless poets, novelists, scholars, scientists, women's rights activists, ad infinitum – coming out to voice their defiance of this barbarity perpetrated against their brothers and sisters.

Not a single sentence, not a single word, that I utter comes from CNN, the *New York Times*, Al-Arabiya or any other source that Asad AbuKhalil loves to hate. None of these people means anything to Mr AbuKhalil. Can he really face these millions of people, their best and brightest, the mothers of those who have been cold-bloodedly murdered, tortured, brutally beaten, paralysed for life, and tell them they are stooges of the CIA and the Saudis, and that CNN and Al-Arabiya have put them up to it? AbuKhalil has every legitimate reason to doubt the veracity of what he sees in US media. But at what point does a legitimate criticism of media representations degenerate into an illegitimate disregard for reality itself; or has a sophomoric reading of postmodernity so completely corrupted our moral standards that there is no reality any more, just representation?

Asad AbuKhalil dismisses a mass social uprising that is unfolding right in front of his eyes as manufactured by Americans and the Saudis. What else does AbuKhalil know about Iran? Anything? Thirty years (predicated on 200 years) of thinking, writing, mobilizing, political and artistic revolts, theological and philosophical debates – does any of it ring a bell for Professor AbuKhalil? Do the names Mahmoud Shabestari, Abdul-Karim Soroush, Mohsen Kadivar, among scores of others, mean anything to him? Has he ever listened to these young Iranians speak, cared to learn the lyrics of their music, watched the films they make, visited a photography exhibition they have put together, seen any of their art work, or perhaps glanced at their newspapers, journals, magazines, weblogs, websites? Are all these stooges of America, manipulated by CIA agents, bought and paid for by the Saudis? What depth of intellectual depravation is this?

In his most recent posting, AbuKhalil has this to say about Iran:

> For the most reliable coverage of the Iran story, I strongly recommend the *New York Times*. I mean, they have Michael Slackman in Cairo and Nazila Fathi in Toronto, and they have "independent observers" in Tehran. What else do you want? If you want more, the station of King Fahd's brother-in-law (Al-Arabiya) has a correspondent in Dubai to cover Iran. And according to a report that just aired, Mousavi received 91 per cent of the vote in "an elite neighborhood". I kid you not. They just said that.

Do the Iranians have no reporters, no journalists, no analysts, no pollsters, no economists, no sociologists, no political scientist, no newspaper editorials, no magazines, no blogs, and no websites? If AbuKhalil has this bizarre obsession with the American or Saudi media that he loves to hate, does that psychological fixation *ipso facto* deprive an entire nation of their defiance against tyranny, their agency in changing their own destiny?

What a terrible state of mind to be in! AbuKhalil has so utterly lost hope in us – Arabs, Iranians, Muslims, South Asians, Africans, Latin Americans – that it does not even occur to him that maybe, just maybe, if we take our votes seriously the US and Israel may not have anything to do with it. He fancies himself opposing the US and Israel. But he has such a deeply colonized mind that he thinks nothing of us, of our will to fight imperial intervention, colonial occupation of our homelands, *and* domestic tyranny at one and the same time. He believes that if we do it, then Americans and the Saudis must have put us up to it. He is so utterly lost in his own moral desolation and intellectual despair that in his estimation only Americans can instigate a mass revolt of the sort that has unfolded in front of his eyes. What an utterly frightful state for an intellectual to be in: no trust, no courage, no imagination, and no hope. That we, as a people, as a nation, as a collective will, have fought for over 200 years for our constitutional rights has never occurred to AbuKhalil. What gives a man the authority to speak so cavalierly about another nation, of whom he knows nothing?

I spent ten years watching every single Palestinian film I could lay my hands on before I opened my mouth and uttered a word about Palestinian cinema. I visited every conceivable archive in North America and Western Europe, travelled from Morocco to Syria, drove from one end of Palestine to the other, was blessed by the dignity of Palestinians resisting the horror of a criminal occupation of their homeland, walked and showed bootlegged videos on mismatched equipment and stolen electricity from one Palestinian refugee camp in Lebanon to another. Then I went to Syria and found a Palestinian archivist who knew infinitely more about Palestinian cinema than I did; I sat at his feet and learned humility. I still did not dare put pen to paper or open my mouth about anything Palestinian without asking a Palestinian scholar – from Edward Said to Rashid Khalidi to Joseph Massad – to read what I had written before I dared publish it. This I did not out of any vacuous belief in scholarship, but out of an abiding respect for the dignity of Palestinians fighting for their liberties and their stolen homeland, and fearful of the burden of responsibility that writing about a nation's struggles puts on those of us who have a voice and an audience.

For people like Slavoj Žižek, social upheavals in what they call the Third World are a matter of theoretical entertainment. It is an old tradition that goes back all the way to Sartre on Algeria and Cuba in the 1950s, down to Foucault on Iran in the 1970s. That does not bother me a bit. In fact, I find it quite entertaining – watching grown-up people make complete fools of themselves talking about something about which they have no clue. But when someone like Asad AbuKhalil indulges in cliché-ridden leftism of the most banal variety, it speaks of a culture of intellectual laziness and moral bankruptcy outrageously at odds with the struggles of people from which we emerge. Our people are not to conform to our tired, old, and cliché-ridden theories. We need to bypass intellectual couch potatoes and catch up with our people. Millions of people, young and old, lower and middle class, men and women, have poured in their millions onto the streets, launched their Intifada, demanding their constitutional rights and civil liberties. Who are these people? What language do they speak, what songs do they sing, what slogans do they chant, to what music do they sing and dance? What sacrifices have they made, what dungeons have they crowded, what epic poetry are they citing? What philosophers, theologians, jurists, poets, novelists, singers, songwriters, musicians, bloggers soar in their souls, and for what ideals have their hearts and minds ached for generations and centuries?

A colonized mind is a colonized mind, whether it is occupied by the European right or by the cliché-ridden left: it is an oc-cupied territory, devoid of detail, devoid of substance, devoid of love, devoid of a caring intellect. It smells of aging mothballs, and is nauseating.

Originally published in *Al-Ahram Weekly*, July 16–22, 2009

The Middle East is Changed Forever

Whatever the end result of the current electoral crisis in Iran, the dramatic rise of national politics has already cast a long and enduring shadow over the geopolitics of the region. No country can go back to business as usual. The climate has changed – for good.

Before the June 2009 presidential election, the realpolitik of the region had placed Iran, Syria, the Palestinian Hamas, the Lebanese Hezbollah and the Iraqi Mahdi Army on one side of the geopolitical divide, and the US and its regional allies on the other. With an extended foot in Venezuela, Iran even had a claim on the backyard of the United States.

In this precarious condition, the Islamic Republic emerged not out of its own capacities, but by virtue of serious follies that President George W. Bush had committed in its neighborhood as a regional "superpower." The presidential election of June 2009 suddenly has made that geopolitics something of an archeological relic.

With the commencement of the civil rights movement in Iran in June 2009, the moral map of the Middle East is being changed right in front of our eyes, with the democratic will of one nation having thrown a monkey wrench into the geopolitics of the region. The moving pictures of Iranians flooding colorfully onto the streets have forever altered the visual vocabulary of the global perception of "the Middle East."

Tehran, I believe, is ground zero of a civil rights movement that will leave no Muslim or Arab country, or even Israel, untouched.

"The unrest in Iran," the prominent Israeli columnist Gideon Levy of *Haaretz* said recently, "makes me green with envy."

However things may turn out, Mahmoud Ahmadinejad comes back to the global scene with a lame-duck presidency that may last anywhere from a few months, if the mounting opposition succeeds in demanding a new election, or else go to a full term, if it fails.

In either case, there is a domino effect from Ahmadinejad's weakened second-term presidency in the region.

Syria's position in its immediate regional context is seriously compromised. The rushed and injudicious siding of Hezbollah's Hassan Nasrallah with Ahmadinejad has wedded the fate of the Lebanese group with that of the discredited Iranian president.

Hamas would now be more inclined to strike a deal with Fatah and join President Obama's renewed peace process. And the Mahdi Army now has to fend for itself in more pronouncedly Iraqi (even nationalist) terms, making easier for the US military to leave.

The domino effect, however, is not limited to the allies of the Islamic Republic; it extends well into the domains of its nemesis, for now the options available to the United States and its regional allies regarding Iran's nuclear ambitions have also become categorically compromised.

The feasibility of an economic blockade or a military strike has become increasingly difficult to sell to the international community. The heroic fate of young Iranian men and women has become a global concern. How can you starve Neda Agha-Soltan's soulmates, or, even worse, bomb them?

We have to start thinking of a new term for "the Middle East." It is central, not to anyone's east or west. The Green Movement has recentered the world.

As Obama wisely keeps Ahmadinejad at arm's length, and as his task in securing a just and lasting peace between Palestinians and Israelis has just been made much easier, let it be known that this is the gift that thousands of young and old Iranian men and women have just handed him.

A severe crackdown has dampened the spirit of the civil rights movement in Iran. Scores of peaceful demonstrators have been killed or injured, and hundreds of civic leaders and public intellectuals arrested.

The leaders of the Green Movement are being accused of treason and threatened with execution. Human rights organizations are deeply troubled. Even worse news might still be in the offing.

But the morning has broken, and there is much that a simple march of the youth in the United States and around the globe, particularly across the Arab and Muslim worlds, all wearing a green bandana, can do for their momentarily silenced brothers and sisters in Iran.

They have sung their native song. They are awaiting the global chorus.

Originally published on CNN, July 21, 2009

An Epistemic Shift in Iran

About a decade ago, soon after the parliamentary election of 2000 in Iran, I wrote an essay, "The End of Islamic Ideology," in which I made a twofold argument: (1) there is an inner paradox at the heart of Shi'ism that makes it legitimate only when it is in an oppositional posture, and it thus loses that legitimacy when it is in power; and (2) the age of ideological convictions is over in Iran, and we have entered a post-ideological conundrum, the resolution of which is up for grabs. I had borrowed the idea from Daniel Bell's 1960 classic *The End of Ideology*, but radically altered its positivist and functional premiss with a dialectical relocation of the argument inside an anticolonial context.

This argument was based on my earlier book, *Theology of Discontent* (1993), in which I had demonstrated in extensive detail the formation of a militant Islamist ideology out of a dialectical force that was predicated on a false but enabling opposition between "Islam and the West." My argument in that book was that the false dichotomy was the single most creative catalyst in generating an Islamic ideology and then sustaining its political potency. I argued that "Islamic Ideology" was in fact the supreme sign of a fixation with "the West," a delusional mirage that loses its categorical authenticity the closer you get to it.

The radical Islamization of the Iranian Revolution of 1979 had paradoxically turned my own *Theology of Discontent* into an archeological verification of the exclusive Islamicity of that event, whereas I had in fact written it because that particular militant Islamism was so alien to my generation of activists in the 1960s and 1970s; a mixture of anticolonial nationalism (Nehru, Musaddiq, and Nasser read through Frantz Fanon and Aimé Césaire) and Third World socialism (Marx read through the Cuban Revolution) defined our perspective. In *Theology of Discontent* I wanted to excavate the hidden and distant layers of an Islamism that was in fact quite alien to my generation of leftist activists – not that we were hostile to it, but that we thought it (foolishly) outdated. In my subsequent work I proceeded to place the Islamic ideology inside a larger cosmopolitan political

culture that obviously included Islamism but was not limited
by or to a larger historical framework, in which I have always
thought Islam is integral but not definitive.

Having concluded that the age of ideology in general and
Islamic ideology in particular was over, throughout the 1990s
I took a partial leave of absence from Iranian politics, which I
found unbearably boring, and took an extended look at Iranian
literary, poetic, visual, and performing arts – film, fiction,
poetry, drama, video installations, underground music, photography, and so on. It was here that I noted that the creative
lexicon of a new generation was in full swing. They were
dreaming (what were to me) unfamiliar dreams. When I wrote
my *Masters and Masterpieces of Iranian Cinema* (2007), I opted to
write in an epistolary mode, addressing a younger generation
that I no longer knew intuitively. I had become, unbeknownst
to myself, a father figure to their dreaming otherwise. I was
walking on eggshells.

The work of Shirin Neshat was a path of liberation for me,
for in her visual reflections I found a sinuous subway into
the subterranean labyrinth of a creative imagination I sensed
was seminal in what was happening in the post-revolutionary
generation. I took the lead from Neshat and worked my way
toward contemporary Iranian, Arab, and Muslim artists around
the globe. I followed Iranian cinema very closely, read and
watched extensively, and wrote widely on its history, politics,
and aesthetics. Around and about Iranian cinema, I began following contemporary Iranian art – its visual, performing, and
aesthetic imaginary opening onto a whole tapestry of unfolding
panorama in front of me. I was now convinced that the children
of the Islamic Revolution had left the political hang-ups of their
parental generation behind and were sailing into uncharted

territories. They remained conscious and cognizant of poets and artists, filmmakers and novelists who had animated our souls a generation earlier, but they were making their own mark in newer and more exciting registers. For us, Forough Farrokhzad was a poet-prophet who kept us on our toes to reach out to her. For them she was a cute and cuddly grandma who was spoiling her grandchildren. *The sheer audacity of these kids...*, we thought quietly to ourselves, as they were giggling their ways around our revered icon and hanging lovely-looking pairs of cherries on her wrinkled earlobes.

At the writing of this essay, as we are both bruised and enthralled by the presidential election of June 2009 and its aftermath, two almost simultaneous contemporary Iranian art exhibitions, one in New York and the other in London, pretty much sum up the latest that is happening in this domain, where aspects of contemporary Iranian art are on display for the whole world to see – though the operatic panorama of what we are watching in Iranian streets has considerably overshadowed them – for those demonstrations are the variegated vineyard of the wine we are drinking in these exhibitions.

As the colorful drama of post-presidential-election 2009 was unfolding in ever more dramatic vistas in Iran, the global media took very little notice of this astounding presence of young Iranian artists in New York and London. Curated by Sam Bardaouil and Till Fellrath, the extraordinarily ambitious *Iran Inside Out* at the Chelsea Art Museum in New York was only one among a number of other sites in which some of the most poignant samples of contemporary Iranian art were on display. At the nearby Thomas Erben Gallery, another exhibition, *Looped and Layered*, had put together the works of twelve other Iranian artists; and uptown, the works of some forty other artists were also on display in *Selseleh/Zelzeleh: Movers & Shakers in Contemporary Iranian Art* at Leila Taghinia–Milani Heller Gallery. Yet another five Iranians were included among twenty-eight artists in *Tarjama/Translation* at the Queens Museum of Art. Entirely by serendipity, Americans now had all they needed to know about the civil rights movement in Iran right here in these exhibitions and yet the mass media were chasing after "experts" who had scarcely a clue that these pieces of artwork even existed, let alone what they meant.

Almost at the same time, in London, *Made in Iran*, a timely but mostly overshadowed exhibition, curated by Arianne Levene and Églantine de Ganay, brought the work of a number of Iranian artists to more global attention.

The trouble with the perfunctory media attention that these exhibitions did receive was that it maintained the habitual false bifurcation art critics make between politics and art – disregarding the far more important fact that the traffic between the two sublates the matter into the manner of a whole different way of seeing things. The operatic drama of the Green Movement in Iran was on full display, running the two complementary/contradictory urges of patricide and infanticide against each other, and yet journalistic art criticism was still caught in the congested traffic of art versus politics.

It was in the course of my getting closer to the contemporary Iranian visual and performing universe that the presidential election of 1997, and then the student-led uprising of the summer of 1997, came to complement what I was sensing in that universe and convinced me that we are witnessing a seismic change in Iranian youth culture – that a new generation of sensibility was fast upon us. The presidential election of 1997 and the student-led uprising of 1999 are the two most immediate antecedents of the current uprising in Iran. When Samira Makhmalbaf was invited to Cannes in May 2000 to participate in a conference on cinema in the twenty-first century, his father and I spent a couple of weeks together in Paris reflecting precisely on this sea change in Samira's generation. A few years later, in 2003, when I went to Cannes to see Samira Makhmalbaf's *Five o'Clock in the Afternoon* (2003), I also saw Parviz Shahbazi's *Nafas-e Amigh/Deep Breath* (2003). Shahbazi's film frightened me out of my wits and gave me countless sleepless nights. There was a quiet cruelty in the film that was entirely alien to me, a suicidal serendipity that convinced me we have entered a whole new matrix of existential anxieties in this generation – at once pregnant with possibilities and yet ruthlessly self-abortive. Shahbazi's film made Camus's *The Stranger* or even Dostoyevsky's *Notes from the Underground* read like *Tintin* comics.

Fast-forward to June, and the bloody murder of Neda Agha Soltan will now haunt the nightmares of the Iranian Islamic patriarchy for the rest of history. She has finally given a contemporary feminine face to the masculinist martyrological pantheon of Shi'ia Islam. A young and exceedingly eloquent Iranian-American, Melody Moezzi, was interviewed on CNN after Neda Agha Soltan was murdered. At one point she said: "When Neda was killed ... she became a martyr ... When we [perform any] physical exertion, Iranians say *Ya Ali* ... and now we're saying *Ya Neda*." There is a whole theology of discontent, a liberation theology of unsurpassed power, in that very twist of Melody Moezzi.

When in 2008, now deeply drawn to the post-9/11 syndrome, I once again turned back to the political parlance of this post-ideological generation and expanded my 2000 article on "The End of Islamic Ideology" into a book, *Islamic Liberation*

Theology: Resisting the Empire (2008). I was ready to make a case for a political culture in which any claim to a liberation *theology* had to move towards a *theodicy* – that is, be enabled to account for and assimilate its own shades and shadows, its political nemesis and emotive alterities. The work thus concluded with a chapter on Malcolm X as a figure whose revolutionary authenticity was predicated on cultural inauthenticity – for he kept shifting identity grounds, from a pre-Muslim to a Muslim, to a post-Muslim, in order to sustain his revolutionary disposition. Sustaining my argument throughout this book was Gianni Vattimo's revolutionary notion of *il pensiero debole*, weak thought, and, more so, Emmanuel Levinas's palimpsestic constitution of the face of the other as the ethical foundation of any future metaphysics.

I had come to this conclusion about "the end of Islamic ideology" and the epistemic exhaustion of ideological Islamism based on the argument that the binary opposition between "Islam and the West" had in fact exhausted its creative energies and thematically dissipated. The "West" had imploded by the end of the Thatcher/Reagan era and the collapse of the Soviet Union and Eastern bloc in the late 1980s, which had in turn prompted the publication of Francis Fukuyama's "The End of History?" (1989); the creative crisis of the East and West had depleted itself, and yet within a couple of years Samuel Huntington published his thesis on the "Clash of Civilizations" (1992) to resurrect an Islamic nemesis for the West. The events of 9/11 were a godsend for Huntington's apocalyptic vision of not just a clash but in fact the end of civilizations. As the world was distracted by that resurrection of an old cliché, I thought we needed to keep our eye on the ball inside the emotive universe of the younger generation, for whom the Internet and social networking had brought down all sorts of factual and fictive walls.

What we are witnessing today in Iran is predicated precisely on that end of ideological thinking, the surfacing of a whole new emotive universe, and the commencement, I believe, of a "civil rights movement" that marks a major epistemic shift in Iranian political culture. This, I propose, is not yet another iteration of a revolutionary uprising, as it is first and foremost evident in the collapse of the binary supposition between Islam and the West, the exhaustion of both Islam and the West as potent categorical entities that can generate ideas, sustain convictions, and launch movements in juxtaposition with each other. Bush and Bin Laden, in short, have been protesting too much, and creating a massive smokescreen with their "war on terror" and "jihad," blinding our insight. The ruling clerical establishment and the younger generation they are trying to chain speak two entirely different languages – one a cliché-ridden language of military coup, foreign intervention, and a manufactured "enemy"; the other the visual, performing, poetic, and dramatic lexicon of a far more fundamental liberation.

In an instant reaction to what is unfolding in Iran, Slavoj Žižek wrote a useful summary of the most useless and irrelevant readings of the current crisis and then offered his own. Žižek suggests that

> the green color adopted by the Mousavi supporters, the cries of "Allah akbar!" that resonate from the roofs of Tehran in the evening darkness, clearly indicate that they see their activity as the repetition of the 1979 Khomeini revolution, as the return to its roots, the undoing of the revolution's later corruption... We are dealing with a genuine popular uprising of the deceived partisans of the Khomeini revolution.

In other words, Iranians are not going back all the way to the time of the prophet 1,400 years ago, but to just thirty years ago, and they have started their march anew. William Beeman, a prominent anthropologist of Iran, has offered a similar reading. He thinks that

> People can only imagine what they can imagine. In Iran today both the people and the establishment have only one model for social and governmental change, and that is the original Islamic revolution of 1978–79. Because both sides are working with the same vocabulary of symbolism, they are groping to command those potent images that will galvanize public support in their favor.

Though his vision is foggy by his ethnographic lenses, Beeman at least offers an archetypal and not a reactionary reading: "The master vocabulary of revolution in Iran is the historical Martyrdom of Imam Hossein, grandson of the Prophet Moham-mad, who was killed on the plains of Karbala in present day Iraq in 680."

Both these gentlemen are out to lunch. Not everything that is round is a walnut, as we say in Persian. This is a post-ideological society: today's activists are not trying to reinvent an Islamic revolution that happened before they were born, or reiterating an archetypal martyrdom that has more than one way to skin a cat. Much has happened in Iran between 1979 and 2009, and neither a revolutionary nostalgia nor an anthropological dyslexia can account for it. Beeman is, of course, correct that "people can only imagine what they can imagine" (a truism), but he has no clue what this young generation has been imagining, and what their imagining has in turn imagined far beyond the distorted images of anthropological ethnography. A much more patient reading of the visual and performing arts of this generation is needed before we know what in the world they are doing as millions pour onto the streets of their cities, brandishing their poetry and sporting their green bandanas. The inherited universe of this generation has been atomized and then radically recast anew. They have reinvented themselves from an emotive ground zero on up. It was not just their parental generation and the aging clergy in the autumn and winter of their patriarchy who were fast and deep in slumber when they were out playing and acting out their future.

In the resurrected soul of this generation no metanarrative of salvation holds supreme, no sublime supposition of truth holds any water. They have been after the nuts and bolts of a more meaningful life, from which I have concluded that in specifically political terms what is happening today is far more a civil rights movement than a revolution; it is a demand for basic civil liberties, predicated on decades of struggle by young Iranian men and women to secure their most basic and inalienable rights. I could be wrong in my assumption, and there might well be yet another revolution in the offing, countered by a military coup, opposed by even more severe economic sanctions, even a blockade, perhaps even by a military strike by the US/Israel. No one can tell. But the singular cause of civil rights of 70 million-plus human beings, I dare say, will remain definitive to this generation. In the course of these thirty years, this generation has learned from its parental mistakes and might be given the allowance that it is marching forward through a major epistemic shift in Iranian political culture – seeking to achieve their most basic civil liberties within whatever constitutional law that cruel fate has handed them.

Originally published in *The Brooklyn Rail*, July/August 2009

The Crisis of an Islamic Republic

> These are the times that try men's souls … . Tyranny, like hell,
> is not easily conquered; yet we have this consolation with us,
> that the harder the conflict, the more glorious the triumph.
> What we obtain too cheap, we esteem too lightly: it is dearness
> only that gives every thing its value. Heaven knows how to put
> a proper price upon its goods; and it would be strange indeed if
> so celestial an article as freedom should not be highly rated.
>
> Thomas Paine, *The American Crisis* (1776)

The Islamic Revolution (1977–79) began with a concerted mobilization of political forces against the Pahlavi dynasty and
succeeded in establishing an Islamic Republic after a violent
distortion of the Iranian polity. The diverse aspects of Iranian
political culture not compatible with the militant Islamist perspective of Ayatollah Khomeini were brutally and systematically
eliminated. This worldly polity was and remains too cosmopolitan to be coded as simply "secular." Militant secularists are
distorting the multifaceted Iranian political culture in precisely
the same violent ways that the militant Islamists do. Thirty years
after the force-fed over-Islamization of Iranian cosmopolitan
culture, a new generation of public intellectuals, political and
social leaders, human and civil rights activists emerged from
the very bosom of the Islamic Republic, demanding their civil
liberties and wishing to correct the course of an Islamic Republic
that they saw had gone terribly wrong. These liberties, they
finally realized, are not only constitutional to any notion of a
republic to which the Islamic Republic seems to have a claim,
but also coterminous with the multifaceted Iranian political
culture that was systematically violated in order to make that
Islamic Republic possible. The crisis of legitimacy that has now
finally caught up with the Islamic Republic is not only evident

in its vile and violent behavior towards its own citizens but also coterminous with its very existence. Some thirty years after the violent crackdown on all alternatives, this crisis is now not merely political but infinitely more pointedly moral – going deeply to the very heart of the very idea of an "Islamic" republic.

The forced transmutation of Iranian political culture into a singularly Islamic site was an act of epistemic violence that could only be sustained by a militarized security apparatus that forced its intellectual and political oppositions into exile or else brutally eliminated them. But the Islamic Republic could not uproot and transform Iranian society at large, and from the older roots of the selfsame political culture new branches have sprouted – wiser, sharper, stronger, and more intelligent than their parental generation. Iranian civil society and political culture are not just ahead of the country's backward and retrograde leaders but also equally ahead of their stilted intellectuals – trapped inside a number of binary oppositions: in or out of Iran, left or right, religious or otherwise. The civil rights movement that has finally broken out in the aftermath of the 12 June presidential election is not reducible to either side of any such false binary – for it is, *ipso facto*, reaching out to retrieve Iranian cosmopolitan culture, to which Islam is integral but not definitive. Unless we come to terms with the worldly disposition of that cosmopolitan culture, the nature of the crisis that the Islamic Republic faces and the civil rights movement that has now ensued will not make sense or critically register.

After Mehdi Karroubi, a founding member of the Islamic Republic and an aging revolutionary, as well as others, disclosed that young Iranians are being raped and murdered in the dungeons of the Islamic Republic, and then hurriedly buried in mass graves, something far more crucial than the "republican"

claim of the Islamic republic was in jeopardy – it was its claim
on Islam, and thus Islam itself, that had to run for cover. After
violently denying, denigrating, destroying, forcing into exile,
or seeking to discredit the non-Islamist dimensions of Iranian
cosmopolitan culture – ranging from anticolonial nationalism
to Third World socialism in its political registers – the Islamic
Republic placed all its legitimacy eggs in one Islamic basket.
Once that basket was dropped onto the hard surface of mass
graves in Behesht-e Zahra cemetery, burying scores of young
Iranians murdered in cold blood on account of their political
positions, or simply having voted for one presidential candidate
rather than another, the Islamic Republic was pulling Islam
down to its grave too. It is now Islam, the faith of millions of
Iranians and other human beings, that must survive the banality
of this particular evil.

To retrieve the cosmopolitan culture of Iran, with the rightful
and democratic place of Islam in it, we have absolutely no choice
but to think of ways to reduce the magnitude of violence that
is unleashed upon us, upon the world in our name, first and
foremost by not falling into its trap and reciprocating it. Violence
is violence and must be condemned – genocidal, homicidal, or
suicidal. The Israeli genocidal violence against Palestinians does
not justify Palestinian suicidal violence against Israelis – it just
exacerbates it. American homicidal violence in Afghanistan and
Iraq does not justify Afghan or Iraqi suicidal violence either – it
just extends its madness. Muslims, Jews, Christians, and Hindus
are today at each other's throats. We have inherited a politics
of despair that has reduced us to taking desperate measures. In
revenge for what the world has done to Afghanistan, it is as if
the whole world is being reduced to Afghanistan – a disparate
people desperately in search of an illusive peace, robbed of

their dignity, commanding culture, sustained civility, moral whereabouts, and at the mercy of drug traffickers, highway bandits, and supersonic bombers alike. Iran is today ruled by a criminal band of militant Taliban lookalikes – savagely beating, raping, torturing, and murdering at point blank the people they are supposed to protect. They are, as Mehdi Karroubi once famously put it, worse than Zionists, for the Zionists do what they do to Palestinians, not to Israelis. The answer to that kind of indiscriminate violence cannot be violence, for it will plunge us all into even deeper layers of the hell that is now code-named "the Islamic Republic."

A Nakba of no less catastrophic consequence than that of the Palestinians, though perpetrated against now more than 72 million people, is casting its deadly and languorous shadow over an entire nation. A worldly cosmopolitan culture has been reduced to a narrowly exacting Shia juridicalism and the tongue-twisting legalese of a fraternity club that insists on speaking its clerically inflected Persian with Latinate obscurantism written into its very diction. Perfectly beautiful Arabic words, such as *Tanfidh* and *Tahlif*, are clumsily thrown at Persian syntax and morphology and made to look and sound strange and self-alienating in Persian when uttered by the clerically inflected obscurantism of a band of clerics who think Iran is their paternal inheritance and we ordinary folks are just a nuisance that ought to be regulated in the sanctified letters of their law. In this regard, it really makes no difference how progressive or retrograde a *Faqih* is – for they are identical in their excessive *fiqhification* of Iranian political culture. The only reason, as a result, that such prominent clerical figures as Ayatollah Montazeri, Ayatollah Sane'i, or Hojjat Al-Islam Kadivar are dearer to us than others is because they declare themselves and do their best (and sometimes they succeed) to speak a decidedly civil language, a language of our common citizenry. As one blogger put it so bluntly, referring to a famous story about the first Shia Imam Ali not being able to sleep because one of his soldiers had stolen an anklet off the feet of a Jewish girl, "they are now tearing the pants off our young brothers and sisters and violently raping them, and you want us to think highly of Imam Ali having lost sleep about an anklet?"

These are indeed terrifying times that are trying our souls, a time when principles sacrosanct to who and what we are have become the first victims of a vicious banality that has no regard for the most basic human decency. The moral and political crisis of the Islamic republic, however, is the emancipatory passage of both Islam and republicanism from a flawed and murderous mismatch. Like political Zionism, militant Islamism (and Christian and Hindu fundamentalism for that matter) has been a horrific historical faux pas. Once Muslims are released from implicating their multifaceted religion in a singularly militant ideology or a tyrannical theocracy they are freed once again to embrace their faith and piety in the cosmopolitan worldliness of its historical experiences; and once Iranians are freed from force-feeding their democratic aspirations down the narrow throat of an "Islamic Republic" they have *ipso facto* joined a public space in which their societal modernity gives birth to enduring democratic institutions. None of this is either to call for or to discourage the dismantling of the Islamic Republic altogether – a historical eventuality beyond any single person's wish or will. It is simply to begin to think through the current crisis of the Islamic Republic and the ungodly terror it has visited upon a nation for over thirty years, and to articulate the manner of civil liberties that will be needed to sustain enduring democratic institutions – during or after this Islamic Republic.

The difficult task ahead is that the barbarity of the violent custodians of the Islamic Republic is evidently determined to dictate the terms of not just obedience to it but, and far more dangerously, the manner of opposition. It is not that by violence the belligerent leadership of the theocracy demand and exact obedience; it is that by the selfsame violence they are determining the terms of opposition to their illegitimate rule. The Green Movement as a result needs to be exceedingly careful not to fall into that easy trap. In the writing of this passage, I cannot think of a more noble act of resistance to their barbarity than the peaceful, pious, and gracious gathering of the families of the unjustly incarcerated activists in Evin prison for their Iftar (breaking their fast) on the first day of Ramadan 1430 AH, 22 August 2009 – spreading their Sofreh and sporting their green plastic plates.

The organizational centre of the Green Movement is very conscious that it must not allow the violent behavior of the militarized security apparatus of the Islamic Republic determine the course of its actions, thoughts, and strategies. It insists on crossing the psychological barrier and coming to terms with a future bereft of violence. There is in fact no better way of fighting against this regime than celebrating life, embracing joy – *ba del-e khonin lab khandan biyavar hamcho jam*, as the contemporary Persian poet Houshang Ebtehaj teaches us:

> With a heart full of blood
> Bring forth a pair of smiling lips –
> Just like a cup of wine.

This assessment is not a wish. It is written on the body of the movement. "I am absolutely convinced," writes Fatemeh Shams, a prominent blogger whose own husband Mohammadreza Jala'ipour was arrested and charged with plotting to topple the regime, "that the incarceration of people like Somayyeh Towhidlu, Hamzeh Ghalebi, Mohammadreza Jala'ipour, Sa'id Shari'ati, and Shahab al-Din Tabataba'i is to target a young generation that both wishes to have faith and is committed to reform, is both preoccupied with [the betterment of] our homeland and committed to legal frameworks and societal principles. This time around, the fundamentalists have targeted a generation that was determined to follow a third path, the path upon which it was possible to be religious but not be retrograde, to be a reformist but oppose the toppling of the regime and violence."

Fatemeh Shams's appraisal of the movement, based on being born and raised in an Islamic Republic, is exceedingly important because there is always the danger that the moral dissolution of the regime and the systemic violence that it is perpetrating upon its own citizens might succeed in dictating the terms of opposition to its benighted rule. The transmutation of legitimate resistance to tyranny into tyrannous terms in the opposite direction is already very much evident among the quixotic expatriate "opposition" that speaks, writes, and acts in precisely the same vulgar manners that their counterparts in the Islamic Republic do. Outside the purview of the Islamic Republic and the violent expatriate "opposition" it has generated, the Green Movement needs to stay clear of both and turn to our extended literary humanism to sustain its moral rectitude. For all the terror that the Islamic Republic has perpetrated upon Islam and Muslims, the heart of Islam beats happily and resoundingly, strong and safe, where it has always been, in the best of our poetry, in our literature, in the solitude of our dis/belief: with one line of Sa'di we can rebuild our humanity, with one *ghazal* of Hafez we will learn how to love anew, and in the aromatic pages of Rumi we will look for God again – just before we turn to our sagacious Khayyam and play hide and seek with him.

Originally published in *Al-Ahram Weekly*,
November 12–18, 2009

Obama "Bearing Witness" is Crucial to Iran

If someone had asked me six months ago what would change on the national, regional, or global front after Iran's presidential election in June, I would have said that nothing would. And I'm supposed to know better.

Before events in Iran unfolded over the second half of 2009, national politics had become all but irrelevant in that troubled region.

From Pakistan and Afghanistan to Israel/Palestine, from Central Asia to Yemen, geopolitics was locked in a terrorizing balance of power, a stifling politics of despair.

More presidential, parliamentary, and city council elections have been held in Iran over the past thirty years than probably in the entire Arab and Muslim world. But these elections were not the signs of a healthy democracy. They were attempts by the Islamic Republic to legitimize its deeply troubled theocracy using the simulacrum of democratic institutions.

All that was exposed to the light by one simple edict this past fall. Grand Ayatollah Montazeri, the revered jurist who died in 2009 and was posthumously dubbed the moral voice of the anti-government Green Movement, declared that the Islamic Republic was neither Islamic nor a republic.

Outside Iran, national elections are either a ceremonial joke (from Morocco and Tunisia, through Libya and Algeria to Egypt and Sudan, to Jordan and Syria) or else barely consequential or positively damaging regionally (from Turkey to Israel). But not in Iran this year. Not since June, when the Islamic Republic emerged as the ground zero of a civil rights movement that will leave no stone unturned in the moral earth of the modern Middle East.

The Green Movement, helped by Twitter and Facebook, has taken the show onto a big stage. Iranian leader Mahmoud Ahmadinejad would like nothing better than to distract global attention away from his domestic troubles. Paradoxically, the man who could help Ahmadinejad in his determination to turn everyone's attention away is President Obama. One photograph of Obama with Ahmadinejad would be a dagger to the heart of the Green Movement. It would be remembered for longer than the CIA-engineered coup of 1953. It would traumatize US–Iran relations for another half century.

The creative civil rights movement unleashed by the June presidential election in Iran is writing a new page in the modern history of the country and its troubled region.

The children of the Islamic revolution, those one cultural revolution after another has sought to brainwash, are turning the rhetoric of the Islamic Republic on its own head. These Iranians have used every occasion since the last June election to challenge each instance of mendacity to which they have been subjected. This is a cosmopolitan uprising, forming in major Iranian cities. It is a gathering storm in the capital of Tehran, and is expanding to become a cyberspace rebellion.

In a New York cab on my way to CNN for an interview, I received an email from the streets of Tehran and read it on my iPhone. I used the message ten minutes later in the analysis I offered to a global audience. Then a former student in Tehran wrote to me to say he liked my analysis – and the cool color of my tie.

As the Green Movement gains ground, the regime is fighting back with all it has – kidnapping people off the street, murder, torture, rape, kangaroo courts. Official websites and news agencies are failing to report the truth, or else distorting it, ridiculing it, or attributing it to phantom foreigners. They have all failed.

The Islamic Republic is cornered; the public space is appropriated. Iranians within and outside their country, young and old, men and women, rich and poor, pious or otherwise, are all coming together.

Obama's reaction to the violent crackdown on protesters during the holy days of Tasu'a and Ashura has been measured. He has condemned "the iron fist of brutality," but continues to insist, and rightly so, that "what's taking place in Iran is not about the United States or any other country. It's about the Iranian people."

At the same time, Obama vows that "We will continue to bear witness to the extraordinary events that are taking place" in Iran. That "bearing witness" means and matters more than the president's critics can dream. The pressure on Obama "to do more about Iran," especially when it comes from a "Bomb, Bomb Iran" mentality, is hypocritical.

Iranian people have every right to peaceful nuclear technology within Nuclear Non-Proliferation Treaty regulations. Yet the international community has every right to doubt the trustworthiness of Ahmadinejad's government.

The worst thing that Obama could do now, not just regarding the best interests of Iranians but in furtherance of his own stated ideal of regional and global nuclear disarmament, would be to sit down and negotiate with Ahmadinejad. It would legitimize an illegitimate government and would never produce a binding or trustworthy agreement. The alternative to suspending direct diplomacy with Ahmadinejad is neither more severe economic sanctions nor a military strike, which would backfire and hurt the wrong people.

The only alternative for the American president is to believe in what he has said – to bear witness.

But that rhetoric can be carried further: Americans should send to Iran delegations of civil rights icons, film and sports personalities, Muslim leaders, human rights organizations, women's rights activists, labor union representatives and student assemblies. Let them connect with their counterparts there and expose the illegitimate government that has suffocated the democratic aspirations of a nation for too long.

"Bearing witness" is an investment in the future of democracy in a country that is destined to change the moral map of a troubled but vital part of a very fragile planet.

Originally published on CNN, December 30, 2009

FOUR

The War between the Civilized Man and the Savage

Imagining the Arab Spring: A Year Later

As we approach the first anniversary of the Arab Spring on December 17, 2011, when the young Tunisian street vendor Mohamed Bouazizi (1984–2011) set both himself and the Arab world alight, we may wonder what we are referring to when we speak of "the Arab Spring." Or perhaps the better question is, how do we characterize this unique phenomenon that spans multiple countries across North Africa and the Middle East that we insist on categorizing under a single phrase?

In less than a year, three tyrannical regimes in Tunisia, Egypt and Libya have collapsed: the first two with few casualties and a maximum degree of peaceful public participation, and the third with a violent crackdown by the ruling regime and a reactionary foreign intervention. The events in Yemen now suggest that the fourth tyrant is also on his way out, while in Syria heroic struggles for liberty continue to clash with a brutal dictator and his ruling junta. At the same time, from Morocco to Jordan, from Bahrain to Saudi Arabia, signs of unrest and popular discontent have manifested themselves in one form or another, and the year ahead might bring even more dramatic events in the Arab countries and extend to the entire Muslim world.

The transnational uprisings have been peaceful and gentle in Tunisia, violent and vicious in Libya, subdued in Morocco, tyrannous in Bahrain, off the radar in Kuwait, and in-your-face in Syria. How can we – those of us who believe in the veracity and tenacity of the phenomenon we call "the Arab Spring" – think and conceive of these events as a unified and cohesive whole? Don't the snapshots of these uprisings, in different countries and climes, only come together if we relate them with a beginning, a middle, and an expected end – in a meaningful narrative?

The mannered mimicry of revolts

There is a scene in the preeminent Palestinian filmmaker Elia Suleiman's *Divine Intervention* (2002) in which we see his alter ego ES driving on a highway in Israel/Palestine. We get a medium shot of ES driving while eating an apricot. He takes four bites of the apricot, chews and watches the road, and ultimately ends up with the pit in his hand. He casts a quick look at the pit, wonders what to do with it, and then throws it out onto the highway. It hits an Israeli army tank parking idly on the shoulder of the highway. Next, a long shot shows the tank exploding into shreds of metal that scatter to the widest reaches of the highway as it bursts into flames. The third shot of the sequence is back inside ES's car: the same medium shot with which we started as he continues driving, entirely oblivious to the spectacular explosion behind him. In the fourth and final shot of the sequence, we see a close-up of the destroyed tank with its metal remains strewn all over the highway, while ES's car continues to drive away in the distance.

In a panel discussion of the Arab Spring at the Institute of Contemporary Arts in London in late September 2011, the convener asked the panellists the simple leading question: "What just happened, and why?" He was referring to the Arab Spring, but he could have asked the same question about that scene in Elia Suleiman's film. What just happened? Where did it come from? What was the logical consequence? If you throw a pit into the middle of a highway and it unintentionally blows up a tank, how do we classify that event? Is it a disconnect – or not?

The mannered mimicry of Elia Suleiman's cinema in this scene and others defies reason or logic by challenging the original event. Instead, he constructs a moment of *rhetorical frivolity* that corresponds to his signature sense of humour. In this scene, perhaps the most immediate thought is to assume that ES's actions are the exemplification of a hidden wish that he lacked the capacity to carry out: he might be imagining the explosion. But why throw the pit? The pit is real – he just ate the apricot – and you can even hear the bang as it hits the tank (the soundtrack is pitch-perfect). In the scene, there is a reality check and a real gesture, as if he were actually throwing a grenade and not a pit at the tank. We see him eat the apricot and throw out the pit, and somewhere in between, the time in which he throws the pit accidentally – if we can think of it as an accident – and the time in which it hits the tank, something happens as the pit becomes a grenade, the accidental turns into the intentional, and the tank explodes.

A leap of faith

That transmutation, that *something* that sets off a chain of events
is a leap of faith, a nonviolent act of violence, a visual version
of what the distinguished contemporary Italian philosopher
Gianni Vattimo calls *Il pensiero debole* (the weak thought), or a
reconsideration of the events in question. But that *something* that
happens might not be in ES's mind; it only exists with certainty
for the audience. That is the only thing we can be sure of since
we have no way of knowing what goes on inside ES's mind. He
never speaks (and does not have a speech impediment). There
are many occasions when he is about to say something – but
he never does.

Neither before nor after the explosion of the Israeli tank
does ES show he is affected, surprised, or impressed by what
just happened. This adds another layer of ambiguity: it suggests
that the incident is actually a figment of the audience's imagination. In that case, ES is innocent and unaware of the illusion.
It is only *we*, the viewers, who are awe-struck; *he* is not. He is
completely nonchalant, indifferent, and perhaps ready to have
another apricot for all we know.

The rhetorical device at the heart of Elia Suleiman's mimicry is a *trace*, a reversal of the order in which things happen
whereby an original act of violence generates a *grammar* and
logic that then conceals the *rhetorical* violence, like the original
sin of a country wherein the *grammar* and *logic* of the myth of a
nation obscures the violence of stealing Palestine and building
a "democracy" on it.

The reversed tracing of Elia Suleiman's sequences exposes
the *deferred defiance* of Palestinians through an act of *mimetic
intransigence*. This mimicry, which is self-contained, does not
move from one shot to another in order to craft a narrative

teleology, for it is way beyond Edward Said's rhetorical demand
in "Permission to Narrate." The cinematic *trace* is the reversal
of the force of history, a visual *il pensiero debole* that exposes
the viral violence at the core of the mimetic crisis that deprives
the Palestinian any narrative. Instead of following in Edward
Said's footsteps, Elia Suleiman uses visual vocabulary to build
a narrative that leaves Zionism with a code no Mossad agent
can crack. It is no accident that Elia Suleiman's *The Time That
Remains* (2009) is the first *and* the last film that any Palestinian
could make about *Nakba* with such mimetic assuredness.

Years ago, I wrote: "When Palestine is free, Elia Suleiman
is there, waiting for it." That "then" is now – and that now is
called the Arab Spring.

As with Elia Suleiman's sublime frivolity regarding the real,
art refuses to follow the mimesis of power – assumed to be
reasonable and logical – that has concealed the rhetoric of its
original sin, its foundational crime, its primal murder, and the
violence written into the DNA of any state, whether a garrison
like Israel or a democracy like the US. Elia Suleiman reverses
that order by exposing it; he builds a logical progression that
does not lead up to the rhetorical conclusion, thereby leaving
the rhetorical conclusion to stand alone, unable to explain itself.
ES blows things up but he is removed from events. Instead,
the scenes collude purely in the mind of the audience, who are
guilty by historical association – just as they are in the primal
murder and the armed robbery of Palestine. The proof lies in
the *delayed defiance* of Arabs against tyranny, colonialism, and
imperialism, as they reclaim their historical agency.

Whether the events occur in ES's mind or in ours, this
sequence is a prime example of cinematic *rhetoric*. It is a visual
oratory. In medieval scholasticism, the *trivium* comprised the

three subjects that were taught first: grammar, logic, and rhetoric. The regiment follows both the *grammar* and the *logic* and
comes to a crescendo with rhetoric. Elia Suleiman's sequences
stage a visual rhetoric predicated on the *grammar* and *logic*
pertinent to his cinema. But the scene is also rhetorical because
it projects a *mimetic trauma* that stages a creative crisis predicated
on the absolute absurdity of the trauma, like stealing people's
homeland in a supreme act of terrorism and then calling *them*
terrorists. That *mimetic crisis* (the aesthetic impossibility of
representation) is at the heart of Palestinian art and cinema, in
particular. That *mimetic crisis* has now exploded into the full
bloom of the Arab Spring as people from multiple continents
cry out: "People Demand the Dismantling of the Regime."

It is not just a *political* predicament that Palestinians face.
It is also an essential crisis, an aesthetic challenge: how is
it possible to mimetically exaggerate that which has been
factually exaggerated? The scream is so loud inside one that
as an artist (or a revolutionary fighter) one can no longer hear
it, which explains the affinity between the mimetic crisis in
Palestinian cinema and the sacrificial self-staging in revolutionary outbursts.

Elia Suleiman turns that bitter, painful, and impossible
scream inside-out and stages it as cinematic sarcasm. Suleiman's cinema is the visualization of sarcasm that upends the
mimetic crisis that Palestinians have turned to in their art. This
is visible in Mahmoud Darwish's poetry, Ghassan Kanafani's
fiction, Naji al-Ali's Hanzala, Mona Hatoum and Emily Jacir's
art installations, Tarek Al Ghoussein's photography, May Masri's
documentaries, as well as Elia Suleiman's cinema, among others.

What we are thereby witnessing in Elia Suleiman's signature
frivolity is a cinematic will to resist power that stems from an

enduring mimetic crisis that has defined Palestinian cinema from its very inception. That mimetic crisis is then translated into art; its dreams of an Arab Spring, in Palestinian terms, have now spread all over the Arab world.

We may now see and visualize the Arab Spring as if we were watching a sequence in Elia Suleiman's cinema. What we see happening in *Divine Intervention* is nothing other than cinematic montage playing tricks on our mind. The individual shots are independent, but, like Sergei Eisenstein, Elia Suleiman slices them together and leaves the rest to the viewer. ES is entirely innocent; the pit had nothing to do with the explosion. It was just a pit – not a grenade. The explosion shot remains autonomous, and is punctuated by the third shot in which ES drives away, entirely oblivious to what had just happened. And the fourth shot just emphasizes the second, again showing the exploded tank. The four interpolated shots are two "parallel cuts," two by two, entirely irrelevant to each other on their own. While Suleiman plots them together, we are the ones who edit and interpret them for ourselves.

What we the audience think happened is the wishful thinking of our own hidden desires, multiplying the two by two and equating it with ES throwing a grenade at the Israeli tank. Poor ES: he did no such thing. And the poor Palestinian filmmaker: he cannot even eat an apricot in peace and throw out its pit. One can charge him with littering the highway, but not with throwing a grenade at an Israeli tank and blowing it to smithereens.

The Arab Spring as visionary montage

I have already suggested that the Arab Spring is the Third Palestinian Intifada writ large. Here I wish to suggest that the key sequence in Elia Suleiman's cinema as a visual simulacrum is the same as the manner in which we read the Arab Spring: a mode of narrative montage in which we sequence and edit specific historic events in the Arab world and give them a rhetorical consistency that banks on our dreams and thrives on our hopes. That act of creative and critical montage is what makes the Arab Spring both plausible and meaningful.

Individual uprisings, as well as both their immediate and their distant results, are scattered events with distinct local and national registers. But an emotive seepage creeps from one setting to another, which blends the colors, shapes, sounds and politics from places as different as Tunisia, Egypt, and Syria. This seepage then casts the shade of one event on that of its neighbor – just like a montage that creates the illusion of motion out of light.

In this transfusion, we do the montage – creatively, critically and hopefully – with Elia Suleiman and Sergei Eisenstein implanted inside our mind's eye. What we call the Arab Spring is the mental editing of a succession of shots that demand and exact a reading and a re-creation to render things meaningful. The individual shots produce a sequence with significance, and the sequence gives a teleological meaning to otherwise disparate shots. From all the recent and current incidents in the Arab world, distinct occurrences of histories proper to each nation-state have morphed into a regional narrative that we have come to call the Arab Spring.

There is a scene in John G. Avildsen's *The Karate Kid* (1984) in which Mr Miagi (Pat Morita) is teaching his young protégé Daniel LaRusso (Ralph Macchio) how to prune a bonsai. As soon as he is given the gardening shears, the rash young man starts cutting the delicate branches away. "Stop," says Mr Miagi.

"First close your eyes and imagine the bonsai you want to create. Now, open your eyes and start pruning."

That is exactly what we need to do with the Arab Spring.

Originally published on Al Jazeera on December 6, 2011

On Syria: Where the Left is Right and the Right is Wrong

When the Green Movement started in Iran in June 2009, there was a recalcitrant fraction of the left (taken in a very generic sense) that went on a rampage against it and denounced the civil rights uprising as a Saudi–US plot to dismantle the Islamic Republic, appease Israel, and pave the way for neoliberal imperialism. "I am only for revolutions that make Israel angry," one such sophomoric detractor of the Green Movement famously said at the time. "If Israel is happy with an uprising I am not happy."

More than two years after the Green Movement and a year into the Arab Spring, the selfsame segment of the left faces an even more crippling dilemma trying to formulate a sensible position vis-à-vis the bloody drama in Syria.

The dilemma that this component of the left faces in Syria is rooted in a more fundamental failure to read the Arab Spring in general; for if they denounced the Green Movement because the US had allocated millions of dollars for "regime change" in Iran, that sum was peanuts compared with the money that it had invested in the Egyptian army, and that the Saudis had committed to ensuring the Islamists had the upper hand in post-Mubarak Egyptian elections. So, what to do with the Egyptian revolution? Dismiss the whole thing just because the US and the Saudis were trying to control its outcome?

To be fair and to understand the predicament of the left vis-à-vis the Arab Spring in general and the Syrian uprising in particular, we must first have a clear conception of the right (understood equally in a generic sense) – to which the left is in part reacting.

No left turn

The position of the right is now self-evident: the Syrian regime is a murderous tyranny, it is butchering its own citizens, and "the international community" (by which they mean the US, its European and regional allies, through their machinations at the UN, the GCC, and the Arab League) must intervene to prevent the bloodbath, and anyone raising the slightest question about that narrative is an accomplice in the murderous acts of Bashar al-Assad. That the US, Israel and Saudi Arabia are actively involved in dismantling the Syrian regime for their own advantage either does not enter the calculations of the Right or, if it does, is considered a plus.

The right accuses anyone critical of the US–Saudi design for the region in general, or for Syria in particular, of being in cahoots with the ruling regime in Syria and/or Iran. People are risking their lives against tyranny, they charge on their moral high horses, and the left is not allowed to assume a "puritanical position" and pass judgment on what is right or wrong for these uprisings. The UN and the bombers of NATO and the US must be encouraged to do the job and get rid of these tyrants. For them, NATO and US interventions are forces of good, and the local tyrants are evil. The US must liberate the people and set them free.

The distinguished postcolonial feminist Gayatri Chakravorty Spivak had a phrase befitting these folks and their politics: "White Men saving Brown Women from Brown Men."

To be sure, the self-serving chicanery of this position of the right that is either morally blind or intellectually challenged is incapable of seeing the hypocrisy of the US/NATO position, cherry-picking their "humanitarian intervention" – a fact which makes people's blood boil – and thus encouraging the rush to the position that the left now assumes.

But such tit-for-tat is a useless tautology and will not help clarify the fault lines of the left beyond its current dilemma.

The center cannot hold
There can be little doubt that US, European, Israeli, Saudi and other Gulf states' special forces and financing are at work in covert operations in Syria, pulling and pushing the uprising in their own directions and for their own advantage. The gloves are now right off and the Saudis have come clean that they intend to arm (meaning they have been arming) the Syrian rebels.

"There ain't no such thing as a free lunch," as the colloquial American saying goes in the realm of economics – and in politics, likewise, there ain't no such thing as a free Uzi. The hand that giveth the Uzi today taketh back a share of post-Assad politics tomorrow.

Although the right is silent about such manipulations of revolutionary uprisings, it in fact approves of and endorses them: for them, the Libyan episode has been quite appetizing, entirely oblivious or even dismissive of the post-Gaddafi atrocities that have prompted the critical intervention of, among others, Trinity College professor Vijay Prashad, who has recently observed:

> There is a serious need to evaluate what has happened in Libya
> as a result not only of the Gaddafi atrocities, of the rise of a
> rebellion, but also significantly of the nature of the NATO inter-
> vention. And that evaluation has not happened ... I'm afraid
> that is really calling into question the use of human rights as
> a lubricant for intervention. If we can't go back and evaluate
> what has happened, I think a lot of people around the world are
> afraid of going forward into another intervention, where the
> lessons of Libya have not been learned.

The right dismisses all this as leftist hogwash. In response to
the outright hypocrisy or blatant imperialism of the right, the
position of the left becomes even more entrenched, and thus
morally ambivalent and intellectually challenged: yes, the Syrian
regime might be corrupt and murderous, they consent, but the
real danger to the Syrian revolution comes from the US and
Saudi Arabia, so they remain at best ambivalent towards and
at worst silent on the criminal Syrian regime. If anyone dares
to point to Assad's murderous spectacle, they accuse him/her
of complicity with the US and Saudi Arabia, or else of being a
mere simpleton manipulated by "the Western media."

The left contends that what started as genuine protest has
now been hijacked by "extremist Sunni groups" inside Syria
and by outside forces, from the US to Israel, Saudi Arabia and,
by extension, the Gulf states – all lining up against Iran and
Hezbollah, which, for them, evidently represent the forefront of
resistance against imperialism. Some on the left who approve
of the Arab Spring even suggest that the Arab revolutionaries
ought to develop a strategic alliance with the ruling regime in
the Islamic Republic. Yes, they say, the regime in Iran might
be murderous towards its own citizens, but it is standing up
to imperialism. Again, the moral depravity of this position is
informed by its political illiteracy.

Now even al-Qaeda (whatever that means) has entered the scene and wants to have a piece of the action. Ayman al-Zawahiri recently released a video denouncing Assad and urging Muslims to revolt against him – which has given the left more reason to denounce the Syrian uprising altogether. Now that even Hamas has dissociated itself from the murderous Assad regime and sided with the Syrian revolutionaries, the left is hung out to dry, wondering what to do or say about a world that is changing so fast that they can do little but chase their own tail.

Beyond the clichés

The problem with both positions, of the left and of the right, is that they speak from a position of power or counter-power – that is, from a *statist* position, a 100-meter spree to grab hold of the state apparatus and replace it as it falls. The right speaks from behind US–Israeli guns and from behind Saudi bank accounts, and the left speaks from the position of resisting that power and wishing to support an existing, evolving, or emerging state apparatus that can guarantee that resistance. The Assad regime is falling, and now we have a rush to get hold of the state apparatus, the military in particular. What the left and the right share, then, is an identical *statism*, because for both the Arab revolutions are about taking control of the *state* apparatus, of *state* power, about steering (or, more accurately, *trying* to steer) the falling regimes of power in their own direction.

Categorically absent from the calculations of both the left and the right are the people, the real people, ordinary people, those who occupy the *public space*, populate it, own it. For the left and the right, these people are mere puppets who are either used, or abused for facilitating US–Saudi machinations, or else duped into supporting a revolutionary uprising that has been hijacked from them. Neither the left nor the right has the slightest trust or confidence in, or even a politically potent conception of, the *public space* that ordinary people physically and normatively occupy.

Suppose Bashar al-Assad falls tomorrow, the Saudi and the Americans succeed in establishing a puppet regime and resume business as usual: is that the end of Syrians' uprising? Is that what the Arab Spring and Tahrir Square are all about? Now, suppose Russia, China and the Islamic Republic manage to keep Assad in power, is that the end of the Syrian uprising? No: the revolutions have only just started.

The fundamental flaw of both the left and the right is that – one from intellectual limitation, the other out of moral deprivation – they have no ground-up conception of what it is that is unfolding before their eyes, which we call the Arab Spring. They are both statists: power-hungry, reaching out to gain control of the state apparatus, or what Max Weber called the "external means" of any state, its violent means of domination, forgetting what in the same sentence he called the necessity of "inner justification" on the part of the people subject to those external means. Syrians, like all other Arabs from Morocco to Bahrain and down to Yemen, as indeed Iranians before them in the rest of the Muslim world, have lost that "inner justification." No "external means" – provided by the US/Saudis or by Russia/ Islamic Republic – can force them into obedience.

What we are witnessing in the Arab world is open-ended revolutions. What open-ended revolutions mean is that people matter, that the Egyptians are still out in Tahrir Square, and that these states, however they turn out and to whatever degree they are manufactured by external machinations, need a populace to rule – and that the populace will never be subject to one or other sort of tyranny or treachery. The Saudis and the Islamic Republic, along with the US and the Russians/Chinese, can perform all their machinations, but the Syrian people will remain resistant and defiant, and their revolution will remain open-ended, which is integral to the Arab Spring.

They say you can conquer a land on horseback, but you must descend in order to rule it. The same can be said about Syria: from the US and Israel to Saudi Arabia and the Gulf states, and from Russia and China to the Islamic Republic and Hezbollah, there certainly are many machinations at work to conquer Syria. But when all the dust is settled and these mighty maneuverings end, the new conquerors must descend in order to rule the country. And when they do, they will find themselves facing the indomitable spirit of the people, who have left their inner dungeons of fear, and who will never ever again be subject to either domestic tyranny or external treachery. Syrians have already won their revolution; for the next tyrants wishing to conquer Syria will have to come down from their horses, to face a nation that refuses to be frightened or fooled into obedience.

The Arab Spring has unleashed the power of ordinary people and staged the *public space* they occupy and the civic associations they will inevitably form in that space. The Arab Spring has already given birth to a robust revolutionary *Gemeinschaft* that will stay with these societies no matter who or what is in power. Unbeknownst to the political machinations that have divided the left and the right, the people of Syria – as indeed the people from across the Arab and Muslim world – are dispelling their agoraphobia and realizing the power of their communal gatherings.

Originally published on Al Jazeera in February 2012

The Spectacle of Democracy in the USA

"This is my last election. After my election I have more flex-
ibility." The unguarded remark of the US president Barack
Obama to the Russian president Dmitry Medvedev, captured
by television cameras, has once again drawn attention to the
increasing perils and undelivered promises of US presidential
elections. According to a transcript of the recorded remarks,
Obama told his Russian counterpart: "On all these issues, but
particularly missile defence, this, this can be solved but it's
important for him to give me space." Medvedev responded:
"Yeah, I understand. I understand your message about space.
Space for you."

What does this election mean? Does it make any difference?
Why does President Obama need "space" for his second-term
election – what did he do with the "space," indeed the mandate
he received, after his first election? Why should anyone believe
that the careerism that wasted that first term will not continue
to spoil the second term, the new "space" he will be given were
he to win the next election?

The implications of President Obama's asking for "space"
from the Russian president until he starts his second term is
obviously not limited to missile defence and can be extended
to just about any other domestic and foreign issue he faces –
giving false hope that in his second term he might indeed find
the courage of what seemed to have been his convictions.

So will he, for example, be more straightforward with the
Israeli prime minister Binyamin Netanyahu about the so-called
"Palestinian peace process" or the dismantling of the illegal
Jewish settlements in the most recently occupied territories, or
pushing the Israeli borders back to 1967?

Will the US president finally put his foot down regarding Israeli warmongering against Iran? Will he heed the rising course of the Arab Spring and yield to its free and democratic aspirations, rather than joining Saudi Arabia in trying to micromanage it for the specific and shortsighted benefit of the US–Israeli–Saudi alliance? Will he really push for a credible nuclear disarmament programme?

These questions can be extended to a whole host of other more domestic issues in the United States – all creating a delusional hope that Obama might be more courageous in his second term than he was in his first.

The grand spectacle

None of these questions can of course be answered at this point with any degree of certainty. But what is a fact is the pleading of President Obama with the Russian president to consider his predicament as he faces re-election. That question raises the more compelling issue of the general spectacle of American presidential elections – perhaps the grandest political bravura of our time, repeated ad nauseam every four years.

Americans, along with others around the world, were counting the seconds until the Bush presidency finally ended and Obama's started – but to what avail? What did Obama do differently to Bush? Just consider his speeches in front of AIPAC and take it from there. So what is the purpose, the function, the use of these American presidential elections? This is where it all starts – with the American presidential election. This is the political Oscars ceremony, the Macy's Thanksgiving Parade that starts the shopping season and the decorated windows down on 34th Street that attract the tourists more than the locals. Take this phantasmagoric show, this exercise in utter futility, away from the US and it has scarcely anything to parade and wave on its mass media when it invades countries, occupies them, and maims and murders people in the name of fighting terrorism and spreading democracy.

The globalized showmanship of American presidential elections is designed to sell one commodity and one commodity only: "democracy." The US is a democracy: by virtue of that fetishized commodity, it exercises the privilege of sending its aircraft carriers and fighter jets around the planet to drop bombs on people and their homeland and call it "humanitarian intervention."

As the paramount example of a product of the society of spectacle (Guy Debord), of the culture industry (Theodor Adorno and Max Horkheimer), and of the advertisement of "a bottle of wine" to sell health and happiness (Roland Barthes), the US presidential election is now the supreme bourgeois myth that sells "democracy," distinguishes military invasion from "humanitarian intervention," and justifies drone attacks to "combat terrorism" and "protect peace," the latest form of mass murder, its history stretching from My Lai in Vietnam in 1968 to Hadithah in Iraq in 2005, to Kandahar in Afghanistan in 2012.

This is the spectacle of democracy, lo and behold: the spectacle that every four years renews a pact with US imperialism and gives it the moral audacity to impose its will upon the world and wage "humanitarian intervention." The US Patriot Act, the Homeland Security Act, Guantánamo Bay and Bagram Air Base, or such draconian measures as the National Defence Authorization Act (NDAA), all the way down to illegal wiretapping and the move to Internet control and censorship, and the NYPD racially profiling and spying on Muslim communities and university campuses – these are facts of life in the US that are all camouflaged under the spectacle of a presidential election that (like Roland Barthes's bottle of wine selling health and happiness) sells "freedom and democracy."

Commodification of democracy

As the grandest spectacle of American politics, the presidential election looks like a massive television commercial, an advertisement, extended over more than a year, spread over the major and minor networks, cable television, cyberspace, selling one commodity, and one commodity only – always already "new and improved" like any other brand of detergent.

Having reached this point of self-negation, when the democratic will of a people is radically compromised by disfiguringly powerful warmongering foreign agents like AIPAC, this political culture has nothing to offer the democratic aspirations of the world except bombs and bullets, facilitated by the Orwellian newspeak of "human rights" and "humanitarian intervention."

All the neocon, con and even democratic NGOs have to offer the world is incorporating them into this vacuity so that fifty years from now Egypt may look like the US today and offer to the world Arab replicas of Newt Gingrich and Barack Obama. A platoon of native informers, comprador intellectuals, and fifth columnists are employed by this mendacity to make sure of that outcome.

The commodification of democracy in turn amounts to its fetishization into a global sign over which the US and its European and regional allies wish to have a solid monopoly – a monopoly that in turn justifies any means of violence at their disposal, in every way they deem necessary, to protect their values and their interests, as Obama put it when justifying US involvement in the NATO bombing of Libya to protect and promote democracy.

It is not accidental that Fanon in his *Wretched of the Earth* (1961) observed that "every time Western values are mentioned they produce in the native a sort of stiffening or muscular lockjaw... it so happens that when the native hears a speech about Western culture he pulls out his knife – or at least he makes sure it is within reach."

But the emperor's proverbial pants – left or right, Oriental or Occidental – are all on fire. That commodity is self-destructing as it seems with the combined forces and facts revealed and marching in the current course of the Occupy Wall Street Movement, the European Indignados, and the Arab Spring. It is the formal destruction of this political culture in the Occupy Wall Street Movement, inspired by the Arab Spring, that will have much to teach us in the near and distant future.

So, in the bizarre turn of events marking our historical moment, Americans face the same choice of opting not to vote in a sham presidential election in which their choice is between a Gingrich/Romney/Santorum and Obama – the Tweedledum and Tweedledee of American politics – in the very year when a vast spectrum of Iranians had decided to refuse to be part of the monumental joke that passed for parliamentary elections in March 2012.

It is not just the Arab potentates who have run out of time, exited the force of their historical destiny; so have European democracies, facing the systematic uprising of their people revolting against austerity measures they can no longer bear; and so, *a fortiori*, has the outdated and crooked political system of the US, deeply corrupted by corporate money and special interest lobbies (AIPAC is symptomatic of a much deeper sickness).

The charade of American democracy can no longer fool the world (if it ever did): a system that generates a Gingrich or a

Santorum at the top, and in comparison to whom Ron Paul suddenly sounds reasonable and sane, just to expose the hypocrisy and banality of Barack Obama, is no model of democracy to wage its war of "humanitarian intervention" anywhere in the world.

For the world at large, "democracy" is now a *tabula rasa*: there is no model, no template, and no blueprint. We have just entered a period of open-ended revolutions in search of a political ideal.

The center cannot hold

As was discussed on Al Jazeera's *The Stream* program, money has deeply corrupted US politics, perhaps beyond repair. "The landmark Supreme Court case *Citizens United* v. *Federal Election Commission*," the program reported, "has ruled that individuals working through corporations, unions or independent political action committees, known as SuperPACs, could make unlimited campaign contributions." This has resulted in a situation where "candidates can depend on a handful of the wealthy in America to fund their campaigns even when they lack strong grassroots support." What sort of δέμος (*demos*) "people" κράτος (*kratos*) "power" is that?

American political culture as it stands, from A to Z, has long ceased to be an arbiter of the truth, and is no measure of where humanity has been or is headed. Quite the contrary: it is the force singularly harmful to the cause of liberty anywhere in the world, including the US, as indeed was evidenced in the brutality of the police suppression of the Occupy Wall Street movement.

Instead of the delusion of American democracy aiding the cause of democracy anywhere in the world, the only source of hope for the future is the fact of the global democratic uprising aiding ordinary Americans in revolt against their own degenerate system.

Not just the American or European democracy, in fact no existing alternative has much to suggest itself. The ideals and aspirations of an alternative have now ended up in banalities like Chávez and Ahmadinejad on frequent flier programme to each other's capital, in search of business and legitimacy. Even Castro has no qualms giving honorary degree to "Dr Ahmadinejad."

Ideals and aspirations of political Islam have degenerated into the Islamic Republic and the horrors of Holocaust are abused by a colonial settlement cum apartheid garrison state called "Israel." We, the humanity at large, are at the cusp of a new dispensation, a moment of moral implosion when all has gone wrong and all has to change – and that is precisely why masses of millions of people around the globe are out in the street, sleeping in tents, withstanding militarized police brutality, claiming their public space, their hands in the cosmic dark looking for something that even they might not know what it is.

In the Occupy Wall Street Movement, Americans have joined the world and share in their struggles for the ground zero of a politics of emancipation. A young Iranian political activist and graduate student at Yale University, Ali Abdi, late last year began a solidarity campaign in which he is asking participants in the Occupy Wall Street Movement in the US and around the world to share with him their story and in return listen to the story of a political prisoner in Iran, and then prepare a hand-made poster with a message for that prisoner.

In recognition of the 99 per cent movement, Ali Abdi plans to prepare an exhibition of 99 of these posters. I know of no better sign of reimagining world politics beyond the banality of

US presidential election and the corrupt cruelty of the Islamic Republic than these budding signs of hope beyond political boundaries and ideological boxes. Ali Abdi was part of a movement boycotting the sham parliamentary election in Iran in March 2012. Come November 2012, Americans ought to join him boycotting yet another exercise in futility – for the "space" the President Obama is looking for and cannot see in Zuccotti Park.

Originally published on Al Jazeera in April 2012

The Syrian "Massacre of the Innocents"

In the early history of Christianity, "the Massacre of the Innocents" refers to an episode of infanticide by Herod the Great, the Roman client king of Judea. According to the Gospel of Matthew (2:13–23), Herod ordered the execution of all young male children in the village of Bethlehem, so as to avoid the loss of his throne to a newborn King.

That child was born and with it Christianity, a world religion.

The murdered infants, known as the Holy Innocents, are considered by later Christians to be the first "Christian martyrs." Though some biblical scholars question the historicity of the event, the matter has assumed iconic significance in early and subsequent Christian history. It has now become something of an allegory, a parable of murderous instincts, the infanticidal fear of the power and potency of the next generation – the birth of a truth: a future that might be already liberated from our inherited fears.

In works of art depicting the "Massacre of the Innocents" many European artists – ranging from Giotto di Bondone to Matteo di Giovanni to Cornelis van Haarlem to Peter Paul

Rubens and many others – have painted this episode for both the formal and the compositional challenge that it poses, and also iconically to connect it to the political events of their own contemporary time. Through these paintings, the parable has become a potent visual register of the artists' contemporary politics, and thus assumed even greater proverbial potency.

As an allegorical instance of infanticide, "the Massacre of the Innocents" is thus iconic as much for Christianity as for any other context in which innocent children are murdered for political expediency. The infamous case of the Children's Crusade (1212), dispatched to expel Muslims from the Holy Land or else to convert them to Christianity, although it ended up with most of them being sold into slavery, is yet another example. Modern instances might include the deployment of child soldiers in the course of the Iran–Iraq war (1980–88), the NATO bombing of Afghan schoolchildren, the Israeli targeting of Palestinian children, or even the more bizarre case of the US intelligence services torturing detainees at Guantánamo Bay and Abu Ghraib with music from Sesame Street. Examples can be multiplied across cultures and histories – in varied, though equally horrific, contexts. Joseph Massad has aptly diagnosed President Obama's categorical disregard for the plight of Palestinian children as a case of "Arabopaedophobia."

The Houla massacre

It is quite possible that the massacre in the Houla region of Syria on May 25, 2012 will go down in history, in the judicious words of the UN–Arab League envoy Kofi Annan, as "the tipping point" in the Syrian people's sustained struggle against the vicious tyranny that rules them. Richard Falk is right that this phrase may raise false hope for any imminent (but yet non-existent) solution. But that is only if we keep the politics of the matter uppermost in our minds, not the depth of moral depravity to which even Assad's regime can sink.

Those who managed to survive the carnage by hiding or playing dead have now come out and given grisly accounts of the horror that descended upon the defenseless children and their parents. They report that the massacre was perpetrated by the Syrian army and the notorious shabiha militia at the service of the ruling regime.

"Survivors who spoke to the BBC, and the local commander of the Free Syrian Army, said the people who carried out the killings were militiamen – shabiha – from nearby Alawite villages," reports the BBC, adding: "We can't confirm their accounts, but they are consistent with one another, and also with the reports given by activist groups on the ground in the immediate aftermath of the massacres." The report also confirmed that some of the 108 victims – many of whom were children – had been killed by close-range gunfire or knife attacks. Most witnesses who spoke to the BBC said they believed that the army and shabiha militiamen were responsible. "We were in the house, they went in, the shabiha and security, they went in with Kalashnikovs and automatic rifles," said survivor Rasha Abdul Razaq. "They took us to a room and hit my father on the head with the back of a rifle and shot him straight in the chin."

The Syrian authorities, meanwhile, "insist that what they admit was a massacre was the work of hundreds of armed rebels who massed in the area, and carried out the killings in order to derail the peace process and provoke intervention by Nato." The Syrian UN ambassador Bashar Ja'fari also claimed that his government is the target of a "tsunami of lies" regarding this massacre. President Bashar al-Assad has himself also denied his forces had any role in the Houla massacre: "And he again blamed 'terrorists', supported by foreign powers, for fomenting discord and creating 'a project of … dissent."

The blame game is thus set to go on apace for a while – the Syrian opposition blaming the regime and the regime blaming the opposition, while the Russian allies of the ruling regime in Syria divide the blame equally. According to the *Guardian*, "Sergei Lavrov says both Bashar al-Assad's regime and armed opposition were responsible for over 100 deaths in Houla."

So who killed these innocent children and their parents? The ruling regime in order to instill fear and end the revolutionary uprising; or the "opposition" in order to instigate a NATO military intervention on their behalf – or perhaps a combination of both? At least there is no historical record of Herod denying responsibility for the massacre of the children of Bethlehem.

Rashomon

In one of Akira Kurosawa's masterpieces, *Rashomon* (1950), we are witness to a murder and rape from multiple perspectives. A young samurai and his bride are passing through the woods when they are attacked by a bandit, who kills the samurai, rapes his bride, and runs away.

We get to know what actually happened through multiple narratives: the bandit's story, the young wife's account, the murdered samurai's version (summoned by a "medium"), and also via the account given by a woodcutter who chances upon the scene of the incident.

Many film critics and scholars have been tempted to read *Rashomon* as an indication of the relativism of truth, depending on the person's perspective and perhaps even interests. But evident in *Rashomon* is also the fact that whichever way we look at it, and whoever narrates the story, and no matter how responsibility for the murder and the rape keeps shifting, we end up with a man murdered and his bride raped. That singular fact stares us repeatedly in the eye no matter who tells the story. The power of the film is in fact precisely in revealing the overwhelming power of narratives, glossing over a fact that keeps showing itself through these narratives.

In other words, accounts, stories, renditions, successive shifting of blame, and narratives that are supposed to tell us what actually happened, based on the factual evidence we keep watching, do in fact paradoxically cover up precisely what we keep watching. The visual evidence is plain to see, while the multiple and conflicting narratives keep concealing them by distracting us – so much so that if instead of listening to these stories we were to cover our ears and just look at what Kurosawa's camera keeps showing us we would have no problem seeing what has happened: a man has been murdered and a women violated.

Our desire for truth, justice, and revenge constantly keeps us focused on multiple and varied narratives, while the tragedy itself – the supreme truth and the irreconcilable injustice – keeps staring us in the face. The desire for truth and the will to seek justice keep blinding us to the event itself, the daunting, frightful tragedy, the unalterable truth, and the irredeemable injustice.

But even that paradox is not the supreme twist of this cinematic masterpiece: before we know it, we the audience become narratively implicated in the desire for self-deception, for blindness, for not seeing what Kurosawa keeps showing us.

The holy innocents

The same applies to the Houla massacre: every party to this crime has a reason to put a different spin on the horror. But whichever way they spin it the fact of those perished young lives keeps staring us in the face and demanding our undivided attention. Bearing witness, we must not be duped into buying any one of those narratives, by the regime or by its opposition, by the now holier-than-thou European and American officials, or by the barefaced banality that rules, and yet does not represent, Syria – lest we too become distracted by these self-serving narratives and thereby implicated in our blindness to the massacre.

The resolution at the end of *Rashomon* comes when the woodcutter adopts an abandoned child. But the resolution of the Houla massacre has a far more historic scale.

Herod is reported to have killed all the children out of fear that one of them would be the author of his end. The ending of Assad's regime and the tyranny it has sustained for a very long time is contingent on no one child. It is the future of all Syrians. All those murdered children were, and are, and will forever remain the ending of that ghastly tyranny.

Any government, first and foremost, must both represent and protect its citizens; that is its very *raison d'être*. The ruling regime in Syria does neither. The Assad regime was buried along with those holy innocents.

Yes, there are many foreign elements who are abusing the Syrian uprising to their advantage: the Americans, the NATO countries, Israel, Saudi Arabia, Russia, Iran, even the morally and politically bankrupt al-Qaeda, it is said. But the final triumph of the Syrian people will be the defeat of all this treachery.

The terms of engagement with the future of democracy in our world are not any longer merely political but in fact entirely ethical. The discourse is radically shifting from the politics of power to an ethics of defiance – whether in opposition to NATO military intervention from Afghanistan to Libya, with its own civilian (including children) casualties, or a rejection of the corrupt and degenerate regimes that rule over our people's lives, liberty, and destiny.

We are given a false choice between a bloody ruling regime in Syria or the horrid Taliban in Afghanistan and the even bloodier NATO intervention in one or the other. The choice must begin with the facts on the ground, and those now buried in graves – facts staring humanity in the face; and we must never allow any story, any narrative, any spin, any version of the account, whether by the murderous ruling regime in Syria or by the even more treacherous militarism of NATO, or by the ghastly opportunism of Russia or the Islamic Republic of Iran, to gloss over those innocent bodies. It is not just the Syrian regime, its "opposition," NATO, ad nauseam, that is accountable to that murderous scene, but the whole of humanity.

Originally published on Al Jazeera in June 2012

Revolution: The Pursuit of Public Happiness

Mid-June 2012 marks the third anniversary of the Green Movement in Iran, and more than a year and a half into the dramatic unfolding of the Arab revolutions. Over the past three years, the Arab and Muslim world – from Morocco to Iran, from Syria to Yemen – seems to have witnessed more mass public demonstrations than in the entire history of all postcolonial nation-states combined.

Where do Iranians and Arabs – and, by extension, the rest of the Muslim world – stand today after shedding their fear of brutality, risking everything for a better, yet uncertain, future for themselves and their children?

Four dictators have fallen in Tunisia, Egypt, Yemen, and Libya, but their emancipated people face long and uncertain futures. The Iranian Green Movement was brutally suppressed – its leaders put under house arrest and its supporters and sympathizers reportedly murdered at point-blank range, arrested, jailed, tortured, even raped, or else forced to leave their homeland, suffering the indignities of exile. Syrians and Bahrainis are mounting stiff resistance to the entrenched tyrannies that rule over them, enduring massacres, mass arrests and torture – while, from Morocco to Saudi Arabia, many other Arab potentates await the turn of the historical screw – in one way or another.

But does too much myopic attention to one country or another, one event or another – the presidential election or the dismantling of the parliament in Egypt, the barbarity of the ruling regime in Syria, or the counterrevolutionary forces centered in Saudi Arabia trying to fish from the muddy waters and thus delay their own demise – perhaps dull our wits and prevent us seeing the larger picture, including where we are headed?

Revolution to reclaim the public space

In 1963, the distinguished political philosopher Hannah Arendt published a greatly influential book, *On Revolution*, in which she compared the two world historic American (1776) and French (1789) revolutions by way of putting forward her own contentious theory – in which she took both the liberal and the Marxist conceptions of revolution to task. Her primary concern was that the French Revolution had been much and widely theorized, so much so that it has in fact colored our very conception of "revolution," while the American Revolution has been entirely undertheorized. In this book she set herself the Herculean task of compensating for that fact and sought critically to theorize the American Revolution for her own time. Do Hannah Arendt's thoughts on revolutions have something to teach to us today about the Arab and Muslim revolutions?

In *On Revolution*, Arendt favors the American over the French Revolution because she considered that in the latter enduring and endemic economic issues (or what she called "the social question") diluted and confused the more primary concern of revolutions, which in her estimation was the constitution of the republic in a solid and enduring public domain and on the basis of legal institutions.

The French revolutionaries, Arendt thought, were distracted from their primary responsibility of establishing a free and democratic republic with the support of the masses, thus forcing them to address the ever expansive – and in her judgment insurmountable – economic issues, which turned the revolution towards chaos. Her preference for the American Revolution was precisely rooted in this revolutionary determination to constitute and stabilize the public domain of democracy; though she was equally critical of Americans for having limited their participation in their democratic institutions to periodic voting and abandoned the main objectives of participatory democracy.

Thus taking the French and the American revolutions as her model, she believes that initially these revolutions had a restorative force to them, but that in the course of events something of an epistemic shift occurred in the revolutionary uprising. It was in the aftermath of the French Revolution in particular, she thought, that the very idea of "revolution" assumed its radical (Marxist) disposition, aiming at eradicating economic and social injustices in society. It is at this point that in the eyes of "the leading strata in Europe … America ceased to be the land of the free and became almost exclusively the promised land of the poor." This was a flawed reading of the United States, she thought. The purpose of the revolution was not, and is not, to eradicate poverty, but to liberate from tyranny and enable the freedom of political participation.

Arendt's reading of revolutions is thus predicated on her conception of politics not as a codification of legitimate violence, as Max Weber, for example, would say, but as a haven and protection from violence, in a theoretical move more akin to Jean-Jacques Rousseau or even Thomas Hobbes, for whom the fate of humanity was otherwise "solitary, poor, nasty, brutish, and short." The aspect of the American Revolution that Arendt most admired was the fact that power was not directed toward the institutionalization of legitimate violence, as Weber understood it, but was a social contract, a covenant, that the public bestows on the state and can thus withdraw at will.

Arendt was critical of the view that economic factors could have political resolutions. Poverty was definitive of the human condition; only in modern times was it assumed that it could be addressed politically. That factor confused the political project of revolutions, which was no longer committed to liberating people from oppression but instead focused on addressing the problem of poverty. To Arendt, that political twist of the revolutionary project was dangerous and futile. The peculiar aspect of the American Revolution was precisely its having remained aloof from the social (economic) question, seeking rather to liberate from tyranny and safeguard freedom.

The very nature and function of revolutions for Arendt are to translate the momentary revolutionary zeal into a pluralistic, publicly based system of political participation and governance. In achieving that end, she makes a critical distinction between liberation and freedom. Liberation is an emancipatory act, and is liberation from tyranny, while freedom is the unfettered ability to participate in public life, in the public domain, through freedom of expression, freedom of peaceful assembly. Liberty she thus defined as liberation from unjustified restraint, freedom as the ability to participate in public affairs, a forceful expansion of the public space for political participation.

Central to Arendt's political thought is the active formation of this public domain, upon which citizens realize their political life. Hannah Arendt takes the proverbial expression of "the pursuit of happiness" in the United States Declaration of Independence – where pursuing "happiness" is considered an "inalienable right" – and offers a public reading of it, a reading that expands that happiness to include the freedom to participate in public life. The revolutionary spirit must translate into institutionalized forms of that public happiness. Public happiness is definitive of Arendt's very conception of politics.

Extending Thomas Jefferson's ideals, Hannah Arendt argues:

> If the ultimate end of revolution was freedom and the constitution of a public space where freedom could appear, then ... no one could be called happy without his share of public happiness, that no one could be called free without his experience in public freedom, and that no one could be called happy or free without participating, and having a share, in public power.

Tahrir Square

In a powerful piece for Al Jazeera, Murtaza Hussain briefly describes the significance of Tahrir Square in the course of the Egyptian Revolution:

> In Cairo's Tahrir Square, ground zero of the democratic uprising which overthrew the brutal 42-year dictatorship of Hosni Mubarak, the history of the 2011 revolution is literally drawn

on the walls. Down Mohamed Mahmoud Street, along the
sides of the American University of Cairo (AUC) compound
and all around the Square there are stunning and oft-emotional
testaments to the historic events which led to the fall of the
Mubarak regime and which galvanized the attention of the
world.

Then, with much concern, Murtaza Hussain rightly warns the
world:

> On an early Monday morning a work crew commissioned by
> the Egyptian government began covering the revolutionary
> murals in Tahrir with white paint, in what seemed to many to
> be a calculated and deliberate effort to erase the living history
> of the 2011 revolution.

But he concludes with an assurance – to himself and to us:

> No attempt at whitewashing by the government seems able
> to wipe away the collective memory of the Egyptian people, a
> memory which continues to manifest itself time and again in
> artistry on the streets where the battles of the revolution were
> fought and won.

Is "the collective memory of the Egyptian people," perfectly
reliable as it is, the only way to guarantee that the heroic
sacrifices on the historic square are not forgotten? If we are
not to fetishize the actual space of Tahrir Square in Cairo and
read it more metaphorically as the public space in which the
Egyptian Revolution (perhaps the most significant event of the
Arab Spring so far) happened, how are we to ensure that no
"calculated and deliberate effort to erase the living history of
the 2011 revolution" can actually take place?

There are Egyptians who think, and with perfectly good
reason, that the decision of their Supreme Court in mid-June
2012 to dismantle the newly elected parliament and allow the

former Mubarak-era prime minister Ahmed Shafiq to run for office amounted to "a judicial coup" against their revolution. But will the Supreme Court also take away the memory of Tahrir Square and be able to ban Egyptians from gathering in their meeting place forever?

How exactly will the memory of Tahrir Square not be erased; in what manner can we think that the public sphere that was magically crafted with heroism and sacrifice – and upon which, as Hannah Arendt might say, we need to cultivate our "public happiness" – will not be whitewashed away?

Suppose the Egyptian Supreme Constitutional Court succeeds in dissolving parliament, or suppose either Mohamed Morsi or Ahmed Shafiq does become the next Egyptian president: has the Egyptian Revolution failed?

What will happen, not just to the memory or the art produced and perhaps whitewashed in Tahrir Square, but to the square itself? Not just its physical or metaphorical meanings for Egyptians, but the manner in which it has crafted a new meaning of public space for the Arab and Muslim world.

For Hannah Arendt, wards, districts and boroughs were "the elementary republics" that defined the public domain and safeguarded freedom. But in Egypt, what would be the functional equivalent of those wards today? Community organizations and voluntary associations or Facebook pages and Twitter accounts, or somewhere in between, or a combination of both?

These are the critical questions that not just Egyptians but all Arabs, all Iranians, and all Muslims face every day and on every anniversary of their uprisings.

Originally published on Al Jazeera in June 2012

To Protect the Revolution,
Overcome the False Secular–Islamist Divide

It is impossible to exaggerate the significance of the momentous events that have drawn global attention to Egypt as its people continue to struggle with the unfolding drama of their revolution.

Two evidently opportunistic events have come together to signal a dreadful attempt by the Muslim Brotherhood to claim the entirety of the Egyptian Revolution for themselves, on pretty much the same model that the Shia clerics hijacked the Iranian Revolution of 1977–79 – with the crucial difference that Egyptians in their tens of thousands have poured onto their streets and are far more alert and vigilant to protect the totality of their revolution than Iranians were more than thirty years ago.

The first event revolves around President Morsi grabbing (and then rescinding) more power than he was granted by the free and fair election that – with a narrow margin – sent him to the presidential palace. The other is the draft constitution that a Muslim Brotherhood-dominated Constitutional Assembly – the president's political allies – has hastily drafted and put out for referendum.

But the devil is in the detail. What is it exactly that we are witnessing? A president that was freely elected suddenly made a power grab and placed himself above the rule of law. Egyptians who cared deeply for the future of democracy in their homeland poured onto their streets and opposed this move. Soon other Egyptians joined them, expressing their solidarity with their president and for his decision – which they insisted was only temporary and intended to overcome the obstacles that elements of the old regime were placing in his way – to implement the will of the people, the whole point of the revolution. Clashes have ensued; some Egyptians have died in the protests, and many more have been injured. The blood of these Egyptians is entirely on the hands of Mohamed Morsi, who began this cycle of abuse and mistrust. But the historic fate of the Egyptian revolution is now far too urgent to engage in a blame game.

That President Morsi has now rescinded what he had illegally granted himself is a good sign and a victory for the revolution. However, that he is proceeding with the referendum on the basis of this flawed constitutional draft – in so far as the process and thus the outcome are concerned – is a cause for continued concern for the leading oppositional bloc, which is rightly suspicious of this half-measure. Egyptians thus face Egyptians in a fateful moment in their history. What is the underlying cause of this unfortunate confrontation, which, if it remains unresolved, could potentially unravel the entire course of the Egyptian Revolution?

Egyptians versus Egyptians

Both factions are Egyptians who had come together to topple the old regime. It is constitutionally wrong to demonize one or other of these two groups. Much of the US and European news coverage of the events in Egypt is drawing a demonic picture of Egyptians who support Morsi and a heroic image of those opposing him. Underlying this binary is a very old-fashioned Islamophobia. Legitimate criticism of President Morsi and the Muslim Brotherhood and their factional power grab must not degenerate into Islamophobia. This is a nasty and debilitating divide, which Egyptians must not fall for. They must think beyond this momentary and false binary between Islamists and secularists. But how, exactly?

The position of the judiciary is key here. But so is the nature of the Constitutional Assembly drafting the constitution, which a significant portion of Egyptian representatives had already quit. The judges may indeed have had ulterior motives, for some doubtless still harbour a nostalgia for the old regime. Be that as it may, the assembly that drafted the constitution was not representative of all the revolutionary forces and thus was not democratic, but in fact illegitimate, and therefore so is the constitution they have now put out for a referendum.

The Muslim Brotherhood, perfectly entitled to play an important role in shaping a common vision for the future of Egypt, cannot manhandle an entire nation into voting for a constitution that a politically significant portion of the population have played no part in drafting.

The power grab and the draft constitution are being heatedly contested and debated not just in the streets and squares of Egypt but also by Egyptian journalists, essayists, legal scholars, constitutional experts, university professors, public intellectuals, within and outide their homeland. Some Egyptians think the draft constitution fair and balanced and perfectly compatible with a democratic nation-state, whilst acknowledging the flawed political process through which it was drafted; others have all manner of substantive issues with it. One prominent Egyptian, the Nobel Peace Prize winner Mohamed ElBaradei, has already relegated the draft constitution to the "garbage can of history." The fact that ElBaradei is a liberal, and that the US and the EU seem to prefer him to others, does not disqualify him and his supporters from their fair share of this revolution.

Morsi and his supporters say that his grabbing more power than he was granted by the people was a temporary measure – and only for a few months. But you cannot abrogate democracy to protect democracy for even a few seconds – no matter that the judiciary might be corrupt or peopled by elements from the old regime. It is the body of democracy, its formal structure and its skeletal vertebrae, that must by all means, on this ground zero of Egyptian democratic history, be protected. But why is this simple fact not seen, and what is the underlying cause of the mistrust of Morsi and his Muslim Brotherhood supporters that underlies this bloody twist in the Egyptian Revolution?

Who is a Muslim?

The battle between some Egyptians and others is predicated on a phantom fear, one group of the other, "Islamists" of "secularists," and "secularists" of "Islamists." This false and falsifying binary must be dismantled immediately.

The Muslim Brotherhood is a political faction, predicated on a political ideology, formed in the course of the Arab and Muslim encounter with European colonialism and its domestic extensions, which just happens to have a name that claims Islam for itself. By calling themselves "secular," the opposition is in fact granting the Brotherhood an exclusive claim on Islam, which they categorically lack. Islam, the Quran, sharia, al-Azhar, and so on are all false flags raised by the Brotherhood to protect their class and ideological interests, thereby manipulating the inner sanctum of millions of Muslim Egyptians for their political purposes, the same (almost identical) way that Muslim clergy, led by Ayatollah Khomeini, appropriated the Iranian Revolution of 1977–79 entirely for itself, far beyond their rightful claim.

Here at this historic juncture we must rethink Islamic doctrinal history and reconceive the notion of what it means to be a Muslim, to which Islamic law and Muslim jurists have falsely laid a total claim. Neither Muslim jurists nor Islamic law (with its own varied schools and normative tropes), and certainly no nativist Islamist ideology formed in the course of the Muslim encounter with European colonialism, has any prerogative to decide or define what it means to be a Muslim. A Muslim philosopher is also a Muslim; a Muslim mystic is also a Muslim; nevertheless Muslim jurists have historically expressed animosity toward these equally legitimate ways of being a Muslim, and have refused to come to terms with that fact, particularly over the last 200 years and under colonial duress when they fallaciously assumed a disproportionate power and authority to define who is a Muslim and what Islam is. The Muslim Brotherhood in Egypt today is the final product of that colonial development, as Shia clericalism was the beneficiary of the selfsame development in Iran. Egyptians have now been given the historic opportunity to overcome it once and for all. By calling themselves "secular" – and even, almost imperceptibly, partaking in Islamophobia – the opponents of the Muslim Brotherhood are paradoxically partners in preempting that overcoming.

Muslims – all 1.3 billion of them scattered around the globe, defined by their class, gender, and racialized identity, and informed by the juridical, mystical, and philosophical aspects of their collective faith – decide what is "Islamic" and who is a Muslim, not Islamic law (let alone any clerical order in Iran or Muslim Brotherhood in Egypt, or their kindred souls among the professors of Islamic Studies on North American or West European university campuses). In the crisis that we are witnessing in Egypt these fateful days, we observe the dismantling of the misplaced notion that has informed the Brotherhood's false assumption that they are the only Muslims in town. They are not.

In the current bloody battles raging on the streets of Egypt, the false and falsifying divide between the "secularists" and the "Islamists" glosses over the far more critical issue of citizenship. It is the citizenship rights of Egyptians that must be debated, not whether or not these citizens are Muslim or secular. Egypt, just like Tunisia, is on the cusp of overcoming this debilitating and flawed divide between "the secular" and "the religious" – a colonially manufactured gulf that has for the entirety of colonial and postcolonial history divided Muslims to rule them better.

To begin to think of the rights of that prototypical citizen, we should not start with the misleading distinction between "seculars" and "Muslims" but with non-Muslim Egyptians, with Copts, with Jews, and with any other so-called "religious minority." The whole notion of "religious minority" must be categorically dismantled, and in the drafting of the constitution the rights of citizenship irrespective of religious affiliation must be written in such sound terms that there is no distinction between a Copt, a Jew, or a Muslim, let alone a so-called "secular," who is also a Muslim in colonial disguise.

The false battle between "the seculars" and "the religious" disguises the far more critical task of building a free and democratic republic based on the inalienable rights of non-Muslim Egyptians, followers of other religions, which must be the defining moment, the building block, the single most important unit of citizenship rights in the new constitution. That is to say that the rights of the so-called "religious minorities" are not to be "recognized" by the magnanimity of the majority, but rather the whole notion of majority/minority in religious terms must be categorically dismantled and overcome.

If the most vulnerable are emphatically protected by the constitution, then all citizens' rights are protected. This is the real issue that the false battle between "the seculars" and "the Islamists" is disguising. The drafting of the constitution must start from the weakest of the weak and not from the most powerful – the exact reverse of what took place in the process after the Muslim Brotherhood suddenly found itself in a position of power. While its presidential representative suspends judicial oversight and leaps into dictatorship, its rank-and-file parliamentary representative seeks to smuggle in a constitution that is to their liking and not to the benefit of the most vulnerable Egyptians.

Muslims are all Muslims

When we turn to consider Muslims as citizens, we might say that Muslims are all Muslims, but not all Muslims are of the Muslim Brotherhood, which nevertheless falsely equates the two, while at the same time forgetting that it does not even include its own "Sisterhood."

Egyptians who consider themselves "secular" must in the name of the Egyptian Revolution go and claim the mosques for the site of the public sphere and not allow the latter to be claimed, as the Brotherhood have done, as an extended definition of the mosque. These mosques belong to all Egyptian Muslims – liberals, seculars, socialist, feminists, and so on. They must go and redefine that site, reasssert their right to what belongs to them, and thereby overcome the nasty and debilitating divide between the "Islamist and secular" figments of the imagination that we have inherited from our lingering colonial history.

The two sides of this fictitious and fetishized divide are equally to blame. No one died and made the Muslim Brotherhood the custodians of Islam and the right to define what it means to be a Muslim. There are as many ways to be a Muslim as there are Muslims. The self-described "secularists" should also overcome this ghastly colonial construct and realize once and for all that they too are Muslims – who can be socialists, feminists, nationalists, even atheists or agnostics, if they choose to identify themselves as such. The history of Islam, after all, includes many Muslim atheists and agnostics, for example. The term "Muslim" needs to be rescued from the ideologically manufactured and politically violent juridicalism that defines Shia clerics and Sunni Islamists alike. Egyptian "secularists," like all other "Muslim seculars," need to recognize and overcome their streak of Islamophobia.

Muslims, in the sanctity of their consciences, in the privacy of their hearts, and in the publicity of their normative and moral behaviors, will collectively decide what it means to be a Muslim. Egypt, along with the rest of the Arab and Muslim world, is going through magnificent historic changes: the collectivity of Muslims will eventually decide who is and what constitutes a Muslim. This historic eventuality is guaranteed; it is happening as we live through these historic days. But collective public recognition of this fact can spare much of the hardship and violence that is now marring the glory of the Egyptian Revolution. Egyptians owe it to themselves, and they owe it to the rest of the Arab and Muslim world, to lead the way at this critical moment.

Principled reasoning, not rocks

The only way out of the crisis and the bloodshed is dialogue – immediate and unconditional – and that dialogue must begin now. President Morsi's decision to rescind the power he granted himself was a necessary but insufficient move. He must also immediately postpone the date of the referendum in order for the Constitutional Assembly to reconvene. This must include all Egyptian factions and work to resolve all pending issues before it is sent to the Egyptian people to vote on. In that reconvened Assembly, Egyptians who think of themselves as "secular" must abandon the false anxiety of that colonial designation and enter into dialogue with their own Muslim brothers and sisters.

Meanwhile, if Netanyahu and his Zionist supporters in Washington DC think that by bombing Gaza and encouraging Morsi towards this power grab they have thrown a monkey wrench at the Egyptian Revolution and the Arab Spring, they are mistaken. Egyptians will overcome this obstacle and emerge stronger through it. And bankrupt ideologies – from the militant Islamism of Ayman al-Zawahiri to the violent Zionism of Binyamin Netanyahu – will not benefit at all from that triumph.

Originally published on Al Jazeera in 2012

Wresting Islam from Islamists

In a magnificent new essay, "Egypt's Revolution: As It Might Have Been; As It Could Be," published on the occasion of the second anniversary of the January 25, 2011, revolution, veteran journalist Hani Shukrallah muses over its course. In the rhetorical guise of a series of "what ifs" he charts the course of the unfinished revolution in Egypt. In a key passage of this long but very important essay, Shukrallah writes:

> Under somewhat different circumstances, and a relatively greater level of political and organization experience, the Revolutionary Youth Coalition could have been transformed from the largely behind the scenes field leadership that it had been into the core formation of a national revolutionary leadership

able to speak openly, clearly and forcefully on its behalf, indeed, to make of itself – to use the common phrase – the sole legitimate representative of the revolution. Theoretically, it had all that it takes to do so. Made up of popular organizations rather than the ideologically-based and largely bankrupt political parties inherited from the Mubarak era, the RYC was also reflective of a broad revolutionary front, encompassing a whole range of political and ideological persuasions, transcending in particular the "secularist–Islamist" divide that had plagued the nation's growingly diminutive political space for decades.

Radically expanding that "diminutive political space," the Egyptian Revolution will go down in history as the paramount occasion when the public sphere became the transformative location where Muslims began wresting Islam from Islamists and thereby reclaimed their religion beyond any false and falsifying divide.

On a previous occasion, when President Morsi had made a power grab beyond the Egyptian electorate's degree of investment in him, I wrote on the necessity of overcoming the false binary of the "secularist–Islamist" divide which Hani Shukrallah reports having occurred in the throes of revolutionary momentum. What I theorized, Hani Shukrallah verifies: Egypt is today the epicenter of activity wherein Muslims are reclaiming their collective faith, retrieving it from its false custodians.

From Shukrallah's reports from the heart of the Egyptian Revolution, correlating with the principal theoretical thrust of my book *The Arab Spring: The End of Postcolonialism* (2012), a larger frame of reference comes into view, which the distinguished sociologist Asef Bayat has aptly called "post-Islamism," and which I have expanded to call "post-ideological" – in the sense of the historical matrix of postcolonial knowledge production of the last 200 years. It is in the context of that postcolonial epistemic exhaustion of militant Islamism, as we have known it (in combative conversation with Third World Socialism and anti-colonial nationalism), that the current dramatic events in Egypt and the rest of the Arab and Muslim world should be understood.

Militant Islamism

After decades of ideological build-up and political opposition, the Muslim Brotherhood is now the ruling regime in Egypt. Although Mohamed Morsi was democratically elected as the Egyptian president, and although the current constitution was democratically ratified by a majority of Egyptians, nevertheless Egyptians at large are not entirely happy with the prospect of the ideologically outdated and politically heavy-handed Muslim Brotherhood ruling over their homeland. It is precisely this paradox that reveals a moment of epistemic breakthrough.

Those who oppose the rule of the Muslim Brotherhood are not Christians, Jews, or aliens from another planet: they are also by and large Muslims. But these Egyptians, born and raised to Muslim parentage, are today burning the offices of the Muslim Brotherhood to the ground and raising banners that read "People Demand the Overthrow of the Muslim Brotherhood."

Until just before the revolution, a mere two years ago, the Muslim Brotherhood thought they were God's gift to humanity. But today, other Muslims – whatever their political persuasions – are comparing Morsi to Mubarak and consider the Muslim Brotherhood an impediment to their revolution.

This moment of ideological, moral, and political crisis for political Islamism of one brand or another is not exclusive or peculiar to Egypt. It is widespread and symptomatic of something deeper. In Iran over thirty years ago, a tyrannical

Shia clerical order confiscated a multifaceted revolution and with it the cosmopolitan political culture that had initiated it, and is now violently ruling a vast and complicated country that has long since outgrown the outdated ideology of an "Islamic Republic." It is not Martians or creatures from another planet who are contesting their rule.

The most serious challenge to the rule of the tyrannical clergy in Iran comes not from expatriate monarchists or from the equally militant Islamism of the MEK type, or from any other kind of discredited expatriate opposition. It comes, in fact, from other Muslim revolutionaries – people like Mir Hossein Mousavi, Mehdi Karroubi, Abolfazl Ghadyani, and Mostafa Tajzadeh, all of whom were among the founding figures of the Islamic Republic, people who now see their ideals and aspirations betrayed by the current ruling regime. Above them all towers the figure of the late Ayatollah Montazeri (1922–2009), the theorist of *Velayat-e faqih*/Authority of the Jurisconsult, who went to meet his creator having publicly declared that the Islamic republic he helped establish was "neither Islamic nor a republic."

In Egypt and in Iran, Muslims are contesting the rule of the Muslim Brotherhood and the tyranny of the clerical custodians of Islamic law. The ludicrous neocon Americanism of pitting "moderate" versus "radical" Muslims is simply a silly camouflage that conceals a far more serious epistemic breakthrough.

Egypt and Iran are only the tip of the iceberg. In the larger Muslim world something radically transformative is taking place. In Syria, the US and its regional allies are busy trying to remote-control the various opposition factions, allowing Assad's regime to slaughter the militant Islamist groups so that the outcome is more palatable to Washington and Tel Aviv.

Be that as it may, the militant Islamism that wishes to kidnap the democratic aspirations of the Syrian people is categorically alien to them, as is now best evident in the streets and squares of Egypt. Any militant Islamist group that thinks it will rule Syria when Assad is gone will meet the same sort of resistance in Damascus and Aleppo that the Muslim Brotherhood is facing in Cairo and Alexandria. Sooner or later Assad will lose, as will the various militant Islamists, and a fortiori the imperial will of the US that wishes to micro-manage the Arab revolutions.

Militant Islamism was the co-product of European colonialism, yielding to American imperialism. The battle between the militant Islamists and their imperial nemesis has nothing to do with the tsunami of revolutions running through the Arab and Muslim world. They are breeds apart. French neocolonialists are fighting an Islamist militia in Mali to secure access to gold, uranium, phosphates and other minerals. What has that to do with the livelihood of 14 million-plus human beings, of which some 90 percent are Muslims? Nothing.

In Mali, a new brand of outdated militant adventurists are running amuck and allowing the French to practice the perfect subterfuge to reassert their colonial claims on a critical corner of Africa. As is evidenced by their matching abuse of human rights, Ansar Dine, the ruling regime in Mali, and their French backers are using each other as the excuse to legitimize their own brand of violence. The silent 14-million-plus Malians are quietly wresting their collective faith from Ansar Dine and the French alike.

A new generation of resistance
In Europe and the United States, rampant Islamophobia has given rise to a new generation of resistance by Muslims – immigrants

or born and raised in their new homelands – who are not going to be intimidated by the vile racism of people like Michele Bachmann, Pamela Geller, or Geert Wilders, and are striking back with reason, sanity, and magnificent creativity – for example, categorically reclaiming the concept of jihad to assert their identity within an incessantly hostile and vicious environment.

From the heart of the Arab and Muslim world to Europe and the US, Muslims have entered a world historic moment when neither domestic tyranny, nor vulgar militant Islamism, nor vicious Islamophobia, nor indeed racist imperial hubris prevents them from rethinking their collective faith and reasserting their collective identity in a vastly different world to that which their parental generation had bequeathed to them.

It would not be an exaggeration to suggest that Muslims around the world are collectively engaged in a massive global endeavor to reclaim their religion, to take it back from the ruling regimes, from the Islamophobes and Islamists alike, from militant mercenaries stealing their liberties and distorting their sacrosanct faith, all the way from Mali to Afghanistan.

An average Muslim living in North Africa, in Western Asia, in Europe or in the US has absolutely nothing in common with the gangs of militant adventurists engaged in a turf battle with European or American imperialism; nor will they stand idly by, allowing racist European and American Islamophobes to define their faith for them. The Islamophobes are identical in their fanatical bigotry to those militants they hate and at the same time resemble.

The Islam that the ruling regimes in Iran and Egypt project is the Islam that came to be in the context of anti-colonial struggles of Muslims, and so is the Islam of the Salafis, the Wahhabis and the Muslim Brotherhood, and likewise the Islam of the thugs ranging from Mali to Afghanistan, as crafted and narrated by the US and its allies. This Islam is ideologically outdated, politically outmaneuvered, and emotionally entirely out of touch with the factual evidence of millions of Muslims living around the world.

Both the ruling regime in Iran and the Muslim Brotherhood in Egypt and elsewhere are out of touch with reality, left behind by a postcolonial history that no longer has any use or space for them. They may continue to delude themselves that they are ruling their people, but, as evidenced in the streets of Tehran three years ago and Cairo today, they are not.

In his recent visit to Egypt, Ahmadinejad was pressured by a Sunni cleric at al-Azhar regarding the presumed growth of the Shia sect. There is scarcely anything more alien to both Egyptians and Iranians and their democratic aspirations than such silly mothballed sectarianism.

A combination of divisive imperial intervention and the militant Islamism they engender has given rise to a horrid cycle of sectarian violence and hostility in the Muslim world. In Pakistan, Shias are being slaughtered. In Bahrain and Saudi Arabia, people are denied their civil liberties just because they are Shias.

There are high-ranking clerics in Egypt who categorically dismiss the democratic aspirations of the Bahrainis just because they are Shias. Meanwhile, the divisive policies of the US and the conniving interference of the Islamic Republic in Iraq have generated massive resentment against Shias on the part of Sunnis, while in Syria the atrocities of the ruling regime are ascribed to the Alawites.

These sectarian hostilities are categorically a byproduct of hostile encounters between imperial militarism, on the one hand, and militant Islamism, on the other. Like two parasitical organisms feeding off an otherwise healthy body, they sustain and encourage each other.

"Behind these media statements and calls for dialogue," as Yassin Gaber puts it about the current unrest in Egypt, "the ideological chasm is apparent in every line of each side's rhetoric. The two sides speak of two different Egypts, and consequently believe they are actively responding to popular sentiment."

He is of course right, except that there are not two Egypts but just one, striving fiercely in the middle of a historic dialectic, giving birth to itself anew, beyond the "religious–secular," "Islamist–secularist" divide, Muslims wresting Islam from the Islamists and letting it breathe the fresh air of the world at large.

Rescued from the Islamists – their triumphalist politics and totalitarian jurisprudence alike – Islam will resume its multifarious course of creative and critical conversation with the world, and will thus become what it has always been to Muslims: integral to their expansive cosmopolitan cultures but not defining of them.

Originally published on Al Jazeera in February 2013

The Arabs and Their Flying Shoes

It all began with an Iraqi throwing his shoes at George W. Bush. "This is a farewell kiss from the Iraqi people, you dog," Muntadhar al-Zaidi reportedly said when he threw his shoes at the US president on December 14, 2008, during a press conference in Baghdad. Bush managed to dodge both shoes.

There are interesting mixed metaphors here: why would one want to dodge a farewell kiss from the Iraqi people one has just liberated, and what's wrong with being a dog? inquiring minds want to know.

Then the act was repeated in Cairo in February 2013 – this time with a Syrian throwing his shoe at Mahmoud Ahmadinejad. "Mahmoud Ahmadinejad's visit to Cairo, which started with an affectionate welcome on Tuesday from Egypt's new Islamist president," reports the *New York Times*, "turned less pleasant as the day wore on. First, Mr Ahmadinejad, the Iranian president, was lectured by a senior Sunni Muslim cleric and then was nearly struck with a shoe by a man furious at Iran's support for the Syrian government."

On both of these occasions the work of generations of anthropological scholarship on the Arab and Muslim world – their *mentalités* and manners – was invoked in order to inform the American and European publics. What were they to make of such a bizarre gesture as throwing shoes at people?

"In the Middle East it is traditionally considered highly insulting to hit someone with the bottom of a shoe, which is considered dirty." This according to a piece of news in *ABC News*, in which we read about an Egyptian protesting against President Ahmadinejad in Egypt. Anthropologists are enlightening on other people's "traditions," identifying what they are and explaining them to their own very modern people.

"Showing the sole of your shoe to someone in the Arab world is a sign of extreme disrespect, and throwing your shoe is even worse." This amplification is according to another news report dedicated to making sure that non-Arabs are properly informed as to the nature and the hermeneutic nuances of such shoe-throwing incidents.

The more recent origin of such vital anthropological clarifications goes back to the Bush incident, when the BBC informed its website readers in the UK and around the world: "In Arab culture it's considered rude even to display the sole of one's shoe to a fellow human being." By way of further ethnographic elaboration, the BBC adds: "The sensitivity is related to the fact shoes are considered ritually unclean in the Muslim faith." Now that makes a lot of sense, and should BBC website readers wish to keep the matter firmly in mind for future visits to the Muslim world they are advised that "Shoes should either be left at the door of the mosque, or carried (preferably in the left hand with the soles pressed together)."

The source of such delicate insights into Arab and Muslim culture for the benefit of non-Arabs and non-Middle Easterners who need these sorts of glosses to understand the world-historic events "in that part of the world" is entirely thanks to generations of dedicated, courageous and insightful North American and Western European anthropologists – all the way from Bronislaw Malinowski (1884–1942) down to the youngest generation of graduate students being trained in top-notch Ivy League universities and other liberal arts institutions. Were it not for their sustained body of anthropological insights, how else would contemporary Europeans and Americans know what to make of the bizarre shoe-throwing business?

It is not accidental that the US military has been so keen to hire anthropologists to help them rule Afghanistan and Iraq better. "It is sending 'mine-resistant, ambush-protected' vehicles into the battlefield," the BBC reports of the US military; "It is also using cutting-edge biometric technologies to identify insurgents. But that is not all. The US military has developed a new programme known as the Human Terrain System (HTS) to study social groups in Iraq and Afghanistan. The HTS depends heavily on the co-operation of anthropologists, with their expertise in the study of human beings and their societies" – and their shoe-throwing habits, one might add.

The HTS has, of course, a grand cultural anthropologist to look up to – a man named Raphael Patai, who in fact taught at my own university in New York, among many other Israeli and American centres of higher education, and who wrote a popular book titled *The Arab Mind* (originally published in 1973; revised and updated in 1983 and again in 2007), which soon after the US-led invasion of Iraq became the American military's most trusted handbook to help it understand Iraq and Iraqis so they could be made to behave better. As Brian Whitaker of the *Guardian* discovered,

> According to one professor at a US military college, *The Arab Mind* is "probably the single most popular and widely read book on the Arabs in the US military." It is even used as a textbook for officers at the JFK special warfare school in Fort Bragg.

Had it not been for this masterpiece of American cultural anthropology, the US military would never have known that we in the Arab and Muslim world are categorically and genetically lazy, sex-obsessed, owners of at least four wives and plenty of sex slave concubines, which anthropological insights were subsequently used in Abu Ghraib by the US military by way of enhancing the already enhanced interrogation techniques. No "Franz Boas Award for Exemplary Service to Anthropology" can come close to appreciating the significance of such anthropological services. It took a great work of art like Kathryn Bigelow's *Zero Dark Thirty* to show to the public at large the invaluable services that these techniques can provide in order to save American lives.

Heeling the sole of the world with humanitarian interventions

These sorts of anthropological insights are, of course, absolutely necessary not just for the smooth operation of US military humanitarian interventions around the globe and often foreign lands, but also for pragmatic journalistic exegesis back on the home front: for an average American in New York, Chicago, Washington DC, or San Francisco this whole business of throwing shoes to insult people is completely bizarre, because in New York, for example, throwing your shoe at someone is a sublime sign of respect and admiration. Stopping people – friends or strangers – in the middle of street and showing them the sole of your shoe, or better still just tossing it their way, sole first, makes them just want to kiss and cuddle you to show how moved they are with your delicate yet assertive expression of affinity, camaraderie and solidarity.

Now one can understand why the late Edward Said was so adamant that people in the Middle East should start having departments of American studies: so that Arabs and Muslims know how drastically different is their perception of shoes from those of Americans, Canadians, Israelis, or even the British. In Israel, in particular, we know from top shoe designers like Tamar Shalem and Noa Luria that precisely because "life in Israel is intense, so clothes and shoes must be comfortable, easy and practical."

Here in New York, where life is no less "intense," the symbolic significance of shoe-throwing is not limited to respect and admiration. How many love affairs and happily-ever-after romances have in fact started with a simple, elegant and yet timely throwing of a smelly sneaker at your object of affection and desire. It is precisely for that reason that some enterprising entrepreneurs have made it their business to make shoes out of delicious chocolate – so that once the magnificent object is tossed your way you cannot resist but must taste and savor the romantic gesture.

One of the most difficult tasks we people of Oriental descent face when we live here in North America is precisely this urgent need to explain to our friends and colleagues why is it that our folks "back home" so loathe their shoes that they throw them at their enemies, while here in North America the anthropological fact we immediately notice is exactly the opposite: people so utterly adore their shoes that throwing them at a person is nothing short of a stirring sign of adoration and even flirtation, depending on the season of the year, region of the US where the ritual takes place, and/or the age and sex of the shoe-thrower.

In some extreme cases, this American love affair with shoes develops into full-blown shoe fetishism, as we can see in one particularly poignant episode of *Sex and the City* – "La Douleur Exquise!" – where Charlotte meets Buster, a shoe salesman who keeps giving her discounts just for the joy of seeing her wear the shoes.

Yet these anecdotal observations need the support of far more serious "fieldwork," of the kind that only cultural anthropologists know how to conduct. Perhaps universities in Jordan, Egypt, Tunisia, or even Turkey could provide some of their students with "travel grants" for a short summer visit to New York to conduct this fieldwork. Many American-trained anthropologists have done extraordinary work studying Iranian or Iraqi women and their dress, and (taking their cue from the doyen of their discipline Raphael Patai) even their sexual habits. They have subsequently published their books with major university presses and received generous endorsements from their former professors; in some cases anthropological journals have reviewed them very positively indeed.

Here I am thinking particularly of an absolute masterpiece of this genre of anthropology, a book titled *Passionate Uprisings: Iran's Sexual Revolution* about the sexual orgies that Iranian women were conducting just before the rise of the Green Movement by way of collective political protest. Though not an anthropologist by training, but writing rather from the vantage point of an eminent historian, Bernard Lewis had also made comments about Arabs' sexual frustrations and the rise of the Arab Spring.

"Another thing," Bernard Lewis suggests, regarding the rise of Arab revolutions we call the Arab Spring, "is the sexual aspect of it."

> One has to remember that in the Muslim world, casual sex, Western-style, doesn't exist. If a young man wants sex, there are only two possibilities – marriage and the brothel. You have these vast numbers of young men growing up without the money, either for the brothel or the bride-price, with raging sexual desire. On the one hand, it can lead to the suicide bomber, who is attracted by the virgins of paradise – the only ones available to him. On the other hand, sheer frustration.

One reads these astounding insights and wonders why it is that we do not have similar groundbreaking scholarship and insights about young men, women and sex in the Occupy Wall Street movement or the Eurozone crisis? People in the Middle East and the Arab World do not even know as little as what a simple swing of a pair of smelly sneakers means here in New York, let alone the nuances embedded in every episode of *Sex and the City*. Much detailed research by cultural anthropologists needs to be done in that respect. One of those splendid anthropological studies of Egyptian soap operas, for example, needs to be simply copied and conducted here in New York too.

I am convinced that in the same way that some of our anthropologist graduate students here in the US who were born and raised in the region but are now working on their Ph.D.s pay a summer visit to their cousins and aunts and come back with a splendid doctoral dissertation, we also need to have grad students from the Arab and Muslim world come here to North America and study American ways, write doctoral dissertations on the American culture of shoes and other related objects (boots, socks, underwear, jeans, T-shirts, chewing gum, Frappuccino, the works) and return to write and defend their theses, publish them with the university press in Cairo or Tehran and move on to become tenured professors of American Studies. I bet these published dissertations would considerably reduce the enormous degree of cultural misunderstanding that causes so much confusion and even war among people.

This field of research is now particularly important for young anthropologists from all the other non-Western countries, for we have just learned, according to a BBC report, that "European Trade Commissioner Peter Mandelson says China and Vietnam are dumping shoes in the European Union." Yes, "dumping" – can you imagine? What sort of behavior is that? The possibilities for comparative anthropology that considers this Chinese, Vietnamese, and evidently even Brazilian custom can hardly be exaggerated. It could literally revolutionize the field of cultural anthropology. There are obviously plenty of government grants and potential for lucrative marketability in this emerging field.

Sometimes a shoe is just a shoe – no sir!

Such ethnographic works on the American or European culture of shoe-throwing and related romances, as I suggest, are absolutely necessary because they are so susceptible to misinterpretation, particularly by people who have a radically different conception of shoe-throwing. Freud famously said that sometime a cigar is just a cigar – but not so in the US, and certainly not here in New York, where a shoe has a loaded symbolic significance carrying the deepest signs of affection, respect and solidarity. Here in North America, hitting someone with your dirty, smelly shoe, or rushing to show them the dirty soles of your loafers is the supreme sign of respect and admiration. This is specially the case here in New York where people walk their dogs on pavements covered with animal feces, which inevitably end up on people's shoes, and provide friends, families and those of potential romantic interest with the perfect opportunity to impress upon them how much one dearly loves and adores them.

It is not just Arabs but Persians too who have been such a source of confusion in the West regarding their shoes. The European aristocracy first ran for high heels because of their enchantment with things Persian. Evidently, the Safavid cavalry in the sixteeth century was wearing high heels for a better horseback riding posture. Once they had visited Europe, European aristocratic men imitated them and began wearing high heels. But before you knew it, in the next wave women rushed to imitate European aristocracy and sported high heels. "You start seeing a change in the heel at this point," says Helen Person, a curator at the Victoria and Albert Museum in London, according to a BBC piece; "Men started to have a squarer, more robust, lower, sticky heel, while women's heels became more slender, more curvaceous."

This is one excellent example of how Arabs and Persians (not to speak of Brazilians, Chinese, and Vietnamese) confuse, confound, and cause a nuisance by way of their sleeper-cell shoe designers who threaten the homeland.

Every time I must take my shoes off in an airport here in North America or Western Europe, I have noticed how Americans and Europeans look lovingly at each other's shoes and exchange longing glances basd on the prospect of sharing their innermost soles with a friend or colleague. I am no trained anthropologist, alas, but I can imagine what a group of Arab, Iranian, Indian, Chinese, Brazilian, or Vietnamese anthropologists can do in a scene like that – become participant observers and start throwing, sharing, and dodging shoes at JFK Airport. An enterprising visual anthropologist may well make a documentary about the incident and premiere it at the Tribeca, Sundance, or Berlin Film Festival.

That they have not yet done so I consider chiefly responsible for the "Shoe-Bomber" character, Richard Reid, who had completely confused his metaphors when he loaded his shoes – evidently not with chocolate or rose petals as he should have in the proper American and British ways, but with explosives al-Qaeda style, wanting to blow himself and everyone else in the vicinity to smithereens. Fortunately he did no such thing, but he did manage to create a bizarre setting for shoe-sharing orgies in airports around the world. "The son of an English mother and Jamaican father," as the BBC describes Richard Reid, the "so-called 'shoe bomber' … was born in 1973 in the London suburb of Bromley." Had he been properly educated in Bromley by the British anthropologists about the cultural differences between Muslims and those in the Judeo-Christian tradition, no such confusion would have happened to the nice British boy.

Another enterprising bomber evidently used the vicinity of his underwear to try to smuggle in some explosives, but to the best of my knowledge no anthropologist has yet offered any insight into the Muslim significance of boxer shorts. Perhaps the matter is just too touchy.

Awaiting a promising revolution in the field of cultural anthropology, all I can do in a spirit of collegiality is to admit here publicly that I have been repeatedly tempted to throw my shoes at the president of my own university, Lee Bollinger, but have never managed to whip up enough courage to do so. For I have no clue how he would interpret the gesture – in the common culture of New Yorkers as a sublime sign of love, respect, and admiration, or, given my Oriental origin, more in the spirit of Muntadhar al-Zaidi throwing his shoes at President Bush. My own dilemma in this regard is another perfect example of the need for extensive anthropological study in order to clarify the confusion and to create better conditions for dialogue among civilizations, the way former Iranian President Mohammad Khatami had envisioned it.

So, as you see, we Orientals may move to North America and live here for decades, but still not manage to master fully the ins and outs of the culture of shoe-sharing in our adopted homeland. This inability I attribute categorically to the failure of Arab, Iranian, African, Asian, and Latin American anthropologists to study North America in the same way that American and European anthropologists have studied us and regularly informed their publics about our culture of lazy and obnoxious shoe-throwing and suchlike, while parading our four wives and our harem full of concubines.

Originally published on Al Jazeera in 2013

Can the Arab Revolutions
Survive Syria and Egypt?

The hopeful wave of uprisings that started in Tunisia seems to have given way to despair and violence.

The continued carnage in Syria has given rise to staggering numbers of people dead and displaced.

As we mark the commencement of year four of the Arab revolutions, a quick glance around the Arab world may leave much to be desired from the initial promise of the crescendo of events that warranted the term "Arab Spring."

Mohamed Bouazizi's self-immolation on December 17, 2010, his death on January 4, 2011, and the subsequent uprising in Tunisia that resulted in the fall of Zine El Abidine Ben Ali on January 14, 2011, triggered a series of uprisings all the way from Oman and Yemen to Egypt, Syria, and Morocco. Now, more than three tumultuous and groundbreaking years later, things seem to be different: the Arab Spring seems to have become a premature Arab Winter.

In Egypt, the democratically elected president was toppled by a military coup, and what is even more unsettling is the fact that leading Egyptian intellectuals seem to be cheering along the sidelines. In Tunisia, mass demonstrations demanding the resignation of the Islamist-led government continue. In Libya, private and public sectors have staged a general strike demanding the government confront the armed militias. In Yemen, the shady shape of al-Qaeda seems to have staged a comeback. In Bahrain, all signs of resistance to the ruling regime seem to have been uprooted, to the point that even an art exhibition depicting the uprising is not tolerated. Any sign of protest in Saudi Arabia is brutally suppressed, Moroccan constitutional reform now seems bogus, Iraq still reels under sectarian violence, and Kuwait and Jordan are dormant.

The case of Syria

All these events, however, pale in comparison with the continued carnage in Syria. The numbers are staggering. According to the United Nations Office for the Coordination of Humanitarian Affairs, from an estimated population of 22.4 million, more than 100,000 people have been killed; 9.3 million people are in dire need of help inside Syria, while some 6.3 million people have been internally displaced. Syria as a country, to all intents and purposes, has disintegrated, while Bashar al-Assad stands morbidly still and entirely unfazed.

A quick look at the composition of the external forces now turning Syria into a proxy war clearly shows that all of them have a single, common purpose: to put an end to the momentum of the Arab revolutions. They have successfully shifted the discourse away from the democratic will of the Syrian people and degraded it into one of civil war. That narrative transmutation of "revolution" into "civil war" is by far the most dangerous threat facing the Arab revolutions today.

Revolutions are destabilizing. The United States, as an imperial project with vast material and strategic interests in the Arab world, is not happy with these revolutions that destabilize the region, endanger its allies, and potentially embolden its adversaries. Israel has even more at stake to thwart the revolutionary tide. For the entire duration of its colonial project, Israel has relied on corrupt Arab potentates like the ones the Arab revolutionaries are overthrowing. The apartheid state prefers a tyrant like Assad over messy unfolding democratic movements like those in Egypt and Tunisia.

Saudi Arabia is a staunch ally of the US and Israel in this opposition to the uprisings. As a retrograde monarchy with no democratic institutions ever having been allowed to disrupt its tribal rule, it is naturally opposed to any mass revolution that *ipso facto* exposes its political obscurantism. Iran is a strange bedfellow with Saudi Arabia in this endeavor. Having swallowed a vastly cosmopolitan political culture, and eliminated all its ideological rivals in the aftermath of the Iranian Revolution of 1977–79, the custodians of the Islamic Republic are not happy with a tsunami of revolutions that returns to the global stage what they are doing their best to repress. Initially they branded these revolutions an "Islamic Awakening," but when Egyptians revolted against the Muslim Brotherhood, they learned their lesson and let a moderate like Hassan Rouhani become president and began negotiating a better deal for their future with "the Great Satan."

Is Turkey next?

The "deep state" successfully hiding behind the democratic facade in Turkey has a singular mission in its political DNA: to be a major player in the region, in its own interests. And these interests have no principles: they collaborate with Israel, deny the Armenian genocide, suppress Kurdish demands for autonomy, squarely partake in NATO's military projects in the Mediterranean, and in every turmoil seek their own immediate and distant advantage. The potential success of the Arab revolutions can be a model of revolt for Turks as well, as we saw in the course of the Gezi Park uprising.

Russia and China, in different but complementary ways, are strategic allies in opportunism, one primarily in political and the other in patently economic terms. They are no allies of any revolutionary cause. Russia and China merely haggle and negotiate with the US for a bigger share of the pie they perceive in every conflict and chaos.

Tunisia marks the third anniversary of the uprising

Though these players may appear to be at odds with each other, in fact they are united in doing all they can to divert the revolutions. The combined interests of these forces have successfully turned a popular democratic uprising in Syria into a civil war in which there are obviously two sides that are to be separated and their interests adjudicated.

As Iran, Russia, and Hezbollah help Assad, the US, Israel, Saudi Arabia and other Gulf states aid and abet an entire army of mercenary fighters who sport one Islamist brand or another. They are all categorically mercenaries; no amount of branding them "Islamist" should detract from that fact. The representation of a Sunni–Shia fight constitutes an entirely bogus claim. This is a fight between Saudi Arabia and Iran, one supported by Russia and the other by the US/Israel; a fake fight to divert attention from the real issue – the Arab revolutions.

From the very beginning there were two kinds of reaction to the Arab revolutions: on the one hand, the distrustful nay-sayers who thought the whole thing was a passing fever, or else manipulated and "kidnapped" by the US; and, on the other, those who were deeply invested in these revolutions, never blinded to the tumultuous road ahead, and yet unflinchingly hopeful.

We did not inherit the postcolonial world of 2011 overnight. It took the combined calamity of domestic tyrannies and European imperialism of some 200 years or more to bring us to where we were when Bouazizi set himself alight. It will not take another 200 years to set things right; nor will the counterrevolutionary forces from Washington DC, Tel Aviv, Riyadh, or Tehran just pack up their interests and disappear into thin air overnight.

Buy into civil structures

Resistance to these regional and global counterrevolutionary forces must be local – domestic to the Syrian people themselves and their peaceful desire for a transition to democracy. This, therefore, is the time for the formation of voluntary associations, labor unions, women's rights organizations and student assemblies.

In Syria, as elsewhere, the brutes that are gathered around Assad, and the mercenary thugs among those who are fighting him, are categorically incapable of governing a civilized society. Syrians, along with other Arabs and Muslims, must be busy translating the civilized will of their democratic uprising into institutions of resistance to tyranny – right now, as those who know nothing but the language of violence are busy discrediting and destroying each other.

The question of the Kurds is also critical here. The Syrian Kurds now have a historic opportunity to provide a template for democratic change, if they can put an end to the abuse by every major and minor player who takes advantage of their aspirations for a unified Kurdistan. If they abandon that dream and channel its legitimate aspirations into the democratic will of the Kurdish people now scattered in Iran, Turkey, Iraq, and Syria, they can become a game-changer.

The Syrian debacle has put a damper on the Arab revolutions and beyond. Every country from Afghanistan to Iran to Morocco now points to Syria as justification for the view that all these revolutions were in vain, that the ruling regimes and all their atrocities are better than this carnage. This is a bogus binary. The choice has never been between the carnage we witness in Syria and the corrupt elite and the deep states that rule from Morocco to Turkey, from Afghanistan through Iran to Saudi Arabia. The choice is between the will of the people and their revolutionary uprisings and the conspiracy of counterrevolutionary forces to put an end to these aspirations.

In between these two forces, what has irreversibly changed is the calculus of the democratic will of the people at large, 422 million Arabs and 1.3 billion Muslims. That calculus of liberation represents the major momentum of our contemporary history – and it will not be reversed.

FIVE

Postcolonial Defiance or Still the Other

Revolt Spreads against Politics of Despair

A revolt against the politics of despair is sweeping across the Arab and Muslim world – signs of which are on full display from Afghanistan and Iran to Palestine, and most spectacularly in Tunisia. The protests against Zine El Abidine Ben Ali, the Tunisian dictator and a chief ally of the United States in the Arab world, had received relatively little notice in the US until they ended dramatically with his ignominious departure.

One can only imagine if it had been Mahmoud Ahmadinejad or Ali Khamenei leaving the Islamic Republic with an overnight flight to a neighboring country how jubilantly it would be greeted with banners in major US media. But in "the post-American world," as Fareed Zakaria has described the current condition of our globe, it no longer makes any difference if Americans pay much attention to seismic changes around them.

Those living in the immediate vicinity of Tunisia in the Arab and Muslim world have far more reason to follow closely every sign of revolt against tyranny. Within seconds of the departure of Ben Ali from Tunis, Iranian bloggers and Facebook aficionados were making a pun on the name of the country: "Tunis" in colloquial Persian means "they could." They wonder why the Tunisians could so swiftly topple the tyranny that rules over them while the Iranians could not.

Different countries have different levels of social momentum, even with similar circumstances.

While a series of mass demonstrations against Iran's fraudulent presidential election and for civil liberties has been brutally suppressed, the Green Movement is more widespread and rooted more deeply than ever in the Islamic Republic. Three grassroots movements – labor, women, and students – continue their struggles despite violent suppression.

If the Iranian uprising of the summer of 2009 was an inspiration for the Tunisian insurgency of the winter of 2011, the success of the Tunisian democratic revolt is ten times more inspirational to Iranians.

The ruling theocracy in the Islamic Republic might be able to outmaneuver a morally compromised and militarily over-stretched United States, but it cannot stop the inspiration that Tunisian students, labor organizations, and women's rights movement convey to their Iranian counterparts.

And if the Islamic Republic thought all it had to deal with was more severe economic sanctions and computer worms to delay its nuclear projects, the Tunisian uprising should be a wake-up call that its real problem is with the democratic will of its own people, who are now looking with awe and admiration at Tunisians. This same hunger for change is arising in many countries out of the prevalent politics of despair that engulfs the region.

In a recent statement, an anonymous group of Palestinian students publicly expressed their frustration with Hamas's intolerant politics, Israel's destructive occupation of their homeland, and the political games played by Fatah and the United Nations. "Here in Gaza," the statement reads,

> we are scared of being incarcerated, interrogated, hit, tortured, bombed, killed. We are afraid of living, because every single step we take has to be considered and well-thought, there are limitations everywhere, we cannot move as we want, say what we want, do what we want. Sometimes we even can't think what we want because the occupation has occupied our brains and hearts so terribly that it hurts and makes us want to shed endless tears of frustration and rage!

Even in war-ravaged Afghanistan, people cannot be prevented from expressing their will to be free.

After a recent demonstration in front of the Iranian embassy in Afghanistan, the Islamic Republic demanded that the Afghan government arrest and punish those responsible for the rally. The demonstration was organized to condemn the Islamic Republic for not allowing oil tankers to cross the Iranian border en route to Afghanistan and also for the general ill treatment of Afghan refugees in Iran.

"Kabul is not Tehran" was the response from Afghan officials to their Iranian counterparts. "People can rally in protest against anything they wish." Within minutes of that Afghan declaration, Iranian opposition websites and Facebook pages were echoing it with admiration.

Of these four countries, one is the principal nemesis of the United States and its regional allies (Iran), one used to be its ally (Tunisia); of the other two, one is torn by war, the other under military occupation (Afghanistan and Palestine).

Compare this widespread rise in multiple nations for liberty with the recent fraudulent and corrupt election in Egypt, identical to many others from Morocco to Saudi Arabia. But the tide of liberty rising in these countries seems irreversible.

Arab leaders from Syria to Egypt to Yemen are already nervous about the possibility of similar uprisings in their own countries, as many observers are wondering whether "the spring of Arab democracy" is finally upon us. But this axis of liberty does not split along national, ethnic or even religious identities. The will of a young and fed-up population will bring down these regimes, whether the US considers them friends or foes.

Economic malfunctions, massive social unrest, fundamental political failures, and pervasive cultural alienation from the status quo are going to shake the very foundations of these societies and reshape the geopolitics of the region.

The self-immolation of young Tunisian street vendor Mohamed Bouazizi, whose act of desperation in protest at the confiscation of his vendor cart set in motion the cycle of demonstrations that toppled Ben Ali, is now being emulated across North Africa. It's a clear sign of pervasive despair in the region.

A brutal theocracy may crack down on Iranians today, and US foreign policies might disregard the human rights abuses of its corrupt allies on another day. But the tide of change has a logic of its own and will triumph.

President Barack Obama was quick in applauding the democratic change in Tunisia, but if I were him I would not wait for the next Arab or Muslim dictator to run away from his own people before realizing that siding with brutal potentates is not in the spirit of American ideals and aspirations.

Originally published on CNN in January 2011

Green and Jasmine Bleeding Together

The democratic sirocco that is blowing beautifully eastward from North Africa has refreshing ripples and fragrance of jasmine across the River Nile, towards the Persian Gulf, beyond the Arabian Sea, over the Indian Ocean and right into the farthest reaches of Iran and Afghanistan and then into Central Asia.

The triumph of the democratic will of the Tunisians – and now Egyptians – is a simultaneous victory for the identical aspirations of Iranians, who did precisely what we are witnessing in Tunisia and Egypt a year and a half earlier and yet failed to reach for the dream-like finale.

Iranians in and out of their homeland are taking vicarious delight in the swift success of the Tunisian uprising and in the heroic determination of Egyptians. Although they have yet to dislodge a far more vicious and entrenched dictatorship that has destroyed their land and distorted their culture for three decades, they are following with punctilious attention details of the dramatic unfolding of events in Tunisia and Egypt.

In Facebook and tweets, on websites and webcasts, Internet forums and transnational news portals, email listservs and text messaging – in Persian, French, English, and Arabic – Iranians from around the globe post and repost, watch and rewatch the YouTube clips and Al Jazeera streams, following the unfolding events, offering advice, soliciting details, congratulating their Tunisian and Egyptian friends and colleagues. They have already come up with moving posters and graphics uniting their fates – "The future is ours" reads one in Persian, Arabic, and English.

Revolutionary fervor

This delight need not be only vicarious. There is every reason for Iranians to partake in the joy and delight of their Tunisian and Egyptian brothers and sisters, for the spread of the Jasmine Revolution is a solid victory for the Green Movement in precise and measured ways. This wind of freedom knows no colonially manufactured or racialized demarcation. The root cause of these uprisings is the same – from Afghanistan and Iran to Iraq and Palestine, Tunisia, and now the biggest apple of all, whose fall will create a new Newtonian law of plenary motion about us: Egypt! – namely, defiance of a politics of despair, an economics of corruption and cruelty.

It is imperative that the events in Tunisia and Egypt not be assimilated backward into a blind retrieval and habitual regurgitation of Arab nationalism, tempting as the cliché of "Arab Spring" seems to be these days. It is not merely as "Arabs" that Tunisians rose against tyranny. It is not just as "Arabs" that Egyptians have revolted against corrupt government.

It is as citizens of betrayed republics that have been denied them since the end of European colonialism that Tunisians and Egyptians, Yemenis and perhaps others in the region, are rising against the tyrants who rule them – and the US and European interests that keep those tyrants in power against the will of their people. The commencement of that postcolonial buildup of nations is a deferred promise to all those in the extended shadows of European colonialism, and not just the Arab world. Abusing the memory of the colonial history, and the trauma of the US-sponsored coup of 1953, are the *raison d'être* of the Islamic Republic, and the brutish theocracy long ago lost its legitimacy.

The Tunisian and Egyptian achievements are victories for the Green Movement in Iran. For it is not just the US with its heavy-handed presence that is deeply troubled by the prospect of losing its chief allies in the region; the opportunistic Islamic Republic, too, is losing its main enemies – and in this region losing enemies is worse than losing friends. Over the entirety of its lifespan, the Islamic Republic has been the singular bene-ficiary of the politics of despair that has ruled the region, with the pains of Palestine the epicenter of that opportunism.

The ruling banality in the Islamic Republic has been and remains the direct beneficiary of every catastrophe that befalls the Arab and Muslim world, from Palestine and Lebanon to Iraq and Afghanistan. There is a balance of terror in the region between the US and its regional allies, on one side, and the Islamic Republic and its sub-national allies (Hamas, Hezbollah, and the Mahdi Army), on the other. Any change in that balance is potentially damaging not just to the US but, even more so, to the Islamic Republic – and that is good for the cause of liberty in Iran and the region. The will of the people in Tunisia and Egypt, and perhaps the rest of the Arab world, is denying the Islamic Republic its insatiable appetite for enemies.

There is one more, equally powerful, way in which the triumph of the Jasmine Revolution is a source of joy for the Green Movement in Iran. Over the last year and a half, the US/Iranian neocon contingency that has (in vain) tried to kidnap the Green Movement has been repeating ad nauseam the false clichéd mantra that there is no democracy without neoliberal-ism – that democracy and the free market are two sides of the same coin.

So far those forces within the Green Movement that have fought against this nonsense have simply provided sustained theoretical arguments. But the spectacular flight of Ben Ali from Tunisia to Saudi Arabia dispelled the aura of that delusion. Ben Ali's Tunisia was the World Bank and IMF wet dream of yielding to neoliberal recipes. The European Union (Sarkozy's France in particular) was so pleased with Ben Ali's neoliberal policies – even more than President Bush was with his role in the "fight against terrorism" – that, in effect, it considered Tunisia an extension of the EU.

And yet, lo and behold, inside this very neoliberal haven, where the desperate suicide of a jobless young man set the revolution alight, a ruthless and corrupt dictator had run the state for the luxurious benefit of himself and his corrupt family, entirely unbeknownst to the defenders of the contention that "the source of the free market is democracy."

In denying the Islamic Republic its insatiable need for enemies, and in exposing the banality of the assumption that without US aid and neoliberal economics there is no democracy, the spreading Jasmine Revolution is also a solid victory for the Green Movement.

Originally published on Al Jazeera in February 2011

Delayed Defiance

Muammar Gaddafi's defiant speech, refusing to let go of power even after his army had massacred Libyans in their hundreds to suppress the February 2011 uprising, will go down in history as the rambling soliloquy of a mad colonel who had fallen so deeply into the depths of his own delusions that it called out for a Gabriel García Márquez to conjure up the scene in a revised version of *The Autumn of the Patriarch*.

The wandering soliloquy, at once sonorous and lethargic, would have been exceedingly sad were it not so murderous; the wretched tyrant stood there Lear incarnate, mumbling in fear and fury upon the heath of his own tormented mind, entirely oblivious to what had befallen his land, threatening Libya:

I will have such revenges on you ...
That all the world shall – I will do such things –
What they are yet I know not, but they shall be
The terrors of the earth!
You think I'll weep;
No, I'll not weep:
I have full cause of weeping; but this heart
Shall break into a hundred thousand flaws,
Or ere I'll weep. O fool, I shall go mad!

"We're witnessing," as the Libyan novelist Hisham Matar has recently said of Gaddafi's brutal crackdown on his own people, "the violent lashings of a dying beast." Cries and whispers have now become thunderous obscenities.

Postcolonial defiance

The eloquent discourses of defiance against the corrupting condition of European coloniality reached their poetic crescendo last century with Léopold Sédar Senghor, Aimé Césaire, and Albert Memmi, and came to a conclusion with the theoretical passion and precision of Frantz Fanon, Edward Said, and Gayatri Spivak. After the feverish gibberish of Muammar Gaddafi – the decadent and defiant relic of domestic tyranny picking up from European colonial domination – the colonial discourse has finally degenerated into mere Tourette's syndrome.

Rambling ceaselessly about how he was "a fighter, a revolutionary from tents," and that he "will die as a martyr at the end," and then threatening "I have not yet ordered the use of force ... when I do, everything will burn," Gaddafi stood there in the midst of the rubble of a US-bombed building, like Márquez's "Patriarch," "the All Pure," "the Magnificent," "Zacarias," like his literary prototype somewhere between 107 and 232 years old: paranoid, ruthless, superstitious, broken, fallen, pathetic. Ben

Ali's and Mubarak's exits were princely in comparison. From Ayatollah Khamenei to Ali Abdullah Saleh, other tyrants in the neighborhood should look at that video and wonder.

Gaddafi's speech on February 22 brought the discourse of postcoloniality as we have known it over the last 200 years to an end – not with a bang but with a whimper. Following that speech we need a new language – the language of postcoloniality, having had a false dawn when the European colonial powers packed and left, has just started. After forty-two years of unsurpassed banality and cruelty, Gaddafi is among the last vestiges of a European colonial destruction not just of world material resources but, far more crucial, of a liberated moral imagination. There are a number of these relics still around. Two have been deposed. But still the criminal cruelty and the identical gibberish of many more – from Morocco to Iran, from Syria to Yemen – are to be taught the dignity of a graceful exit, an ennobling silence.

Like Tunisia and Egypt, Libya has arisen in a collective act of deferred postcolonial defiance, to demand and exact what is Libyans': their national sovereignty, predicated on democratic institutions, rule of law, and the human decency of a just economic distribution of their national resources and the wealth they generate – the prerequisites of the dignified life that was due to them in the gruesome aftermath of the obscene and ludicrous era of Italian colonialism (1911–51). Like all other Europeans, the Italians packed and left Libya having not only plundered its natural resources; they also left it bereft of any enduring institutions of democracy. Gaddafi was the nativist aftertaste of European colonialism – the bastard son of its militarism, charlatanism, and barefaced barbarity.

The last vestiges of European colonialism that robbed nations of their natural resources, enslaved them as abused labor in order to fortify the material foundations of a now globalized capitalism, fomented tribal and sectarian hostilities – Arabs and Persian, Sunnis and Shi'is, Muslims and Hindus, Muslims and Christians – left no possibility of any enduring institution of political modernity. A functioning democracy is what was supposed to have happened in the aftermath of European colonial barbarism. But charismatic lunacies – ranging from Gaddafi, Mugabe, and Ahmadinejad back to Saddam Hussein, Ayatollah Khomeini, and Idi Amin – is what was left behind.

The nightmare is over

Today we are awakening from a nightmare. We have been dreaming of this day for a lifetime, as did our parents, with the same determination that our children will never know the indignity of being ruled by the most pernicious of our fears. What we are witnessing around the Arab and Muslim world is the birth of the first postcolonial nations, beyond the post-independent pathologies of European colonialism, when native tyrants replaced their European counterparts and for decades abused our noble anger, banked on our fears, plundered our resources, wasted our hopes, robbed us of our democratic dignity, and delayed any meaningful formation of sovereign and liberated nation-states. So, the dawn has broken, long and arduous days lie ahead, and we are full of anxious hope – this time for real.

For forty-two years Gaddafi ruled Libya with charismatic banality and carnivalesque cruelty. To save his throne his corrupt army (minus the courageous who have deserted and joined their people) has carpet-bombed Libyans with the military machinery that American and British arms manufacturers have sold him. For just a little shy of half a century, as Marwan Bishara has noted, "he's used political blackmail and financial bribes and unveiled threats of force to stay at the helm of the regime. In the process, much of the country's wealth was wasted. And so was any chance of development as his dictatorship suppressed pluralism, creativity and freedom of expression."

Some historians believe that by the time the Italians had left Libya in 1951, almost 50 percent of its population had been killed in the course of their anti-colonial struggles. Today scarcely any Libyan remembers life without Gaddafi – thus rendering ever more powerful their dreams of liberation.

Their differences notwithstanding, the specific sites of the uprisings in the Arab and Muslim world and beyond are connected by the common denominator of a shared and sustained struggle. What is happening in Libya, Tunisia, Egypt, Bahrain, and Yemen cannot be separated from what has happened in the Arab and Muslim world over the last half-century. From the armed robbery of Palestine to the betrayed dreams and aspirations of the Iranian Revolution of 1979, to the military invasion and colonial occupation of Afghanistan and Iraq – all are integral to the democratic aspirations that have now swept across our homelands. We as a people are defying the politics of despair that more than half a century of colonial and imperial domination has imposed on us.

A new geography

What we are witnessing as a result is not just the demise of the delusions of "the end of history" and "the clash of civilizations" that the prognosticators and strategists of US imperialism were harboring, but in fact the moral contours of a new imaginative geography of liberation, mapped far from the false and falsifying binary of "Islam and the West" or "the West and the Rest."

The US and Israel may think that by having Omar Suleiman or the compromised upper echelons of the Egyptian army in charge of the democratic transition in Egypt they will have everything under their control. They will not. They may think of "the Turkish model" as an ideal blueprint for them to hope for and expect. But these uprisings we are witnessing will not subside.

The insurgencies are positing an open-ended hermeneutics of political possibilities that will remap the world – far beyond the obscenity of Hugo Chávez ignoring the brutalities of the Islamic Republic and being a frequent flier to Tehran, or even the more absurd banality of the Nicaraguan president Daniel Ortega's recent call to Gaddafi to express his solidarity. That kind of corrupt "anti-imperialism" has now been lost to the rising democratic will of nations that will demand and exact their right to freedom from domestic tyranny and imperial hubris alike.

What we are witnessing is a new planetary awakening far beyond Arab or any other ethnic nationalism. The world is giving birth to a new geography. We must allow and prepare for a different mode of postcolonial thinking (not yet dreamt of by Bengali intellectuals) that will allow the synergy among these revolutionary uprisings to work themselves out, rather than assimilating them back into an arrested jingoism of one sort or another.

The imaginative geography of this uprising maps out a whole new topography of the world for us to navigate and discover. Though every Arab from Morocco to Yemen has reason to be proud of what the world is witnessing in awe and admiration, neither pan-Arabism nor any other colonially racialized category is a sufficient hermeneutic parallax within which to understand, interpret, and take forward what is happening today in our liberated world. The geography of this uprising goes far beyond the Arab or even the Muslim world. From Senegal to Djibouti similar uprisings are brewing. The birth of the Green Movement in Iran almost two years before the uprising in the Arab world has had far-reaching implications deep into Afghanistan and Central Asia. Today, as far away as China there are official fears of a "Jasmine Revolution."

Giving birth to ourselves beyond our colonial condition we are the fortunate witness of the dawn of a whole new discovery of who and what we are – from Morocco to Afghanistan, from Turkey to Yemen, from Central Asia to the extended domains of the Indian Ocean. We must simply wake up, catch our breath, and wash our eyes. We are the discoverers of a brand new world – a world whose geography it is ours to map, as opposed to the colonial map we inherited and are now finally leaving behind. Our deferred defiance against domestic tyranny and globalized imperialism is, at one and the same time, the creation of a whole new horizon for world history.

Originally published on Al Jazeera in February 2011

De-racializing Revolutions

Soon after the brutal crackdown on Iran's post-electoral uprising in June 2009, rumors began circulating in cyberspace and among ardent supporters of the Green Movement that some of the Islamic Republic's security forces, recruited to viciously attack demonstrators, were in fact not Iranians at all but "Arabs."

Snapshots began circulating with red circles marking darker-skinned, rougher-looking members of the security forces, who it

was said were members of the Lebanese Hezbollah or Palestinian Hamas. Iranians like me, who, coming from the southern
climes of our homeland, look like those circled in red, and
who remember a long period of being derogatorily dismissed
as "Arabs" by our whiter-looking northern brothers and sisters,
were not convinced by the allegations.

We also recalled that in the aftermath of the Soviet invasion
of Afghanistan and the massive influx of Afghan refugees into
Iran, all sorts of crimes and misdemeanors were attributed to
"Afghanis," with that extra "i" carrying a nasty racist intona-
tion in Persian.

Cut to almost two years later, when "the mercenaries" who
were deployed by the Gaddafi regime to crush the revolutionary
uprising engulfing Libya were reported to have been "African."
"As nations evacuate their citizens from the violence gripping
Libya," Al Jazeera reported, "many African migrant workers
are targeted because they are suspected of being mercenaries
hired by Muammar Gaddafi, the Libyan leader." The Al Jazeera
report further specified: "Dozens of workers from sub-Saharan
Africa are feared killed, and hundreds are in hiding, as angry
mobs of anti-government protesters hunt down 'black African
mercenaries,' according to witnesses."

Revealing the "other"

These travelling metaphors of racially profiled acts of violence
– violence that is always perpetrated by "others," and not by
"oneself" – now metamorphosing as they racialize the transnational revolutionary uprisings in our part of the world, are
a disgrace, a nasty remnant of ancient and medieval racism
domestic to our cultures. They were exacerbated, used and
abused to demean and subjugate us by European colonialism

to further its own interests, and are now coming back to haunt and mar the most noble moments of our collective uprising against domestic tyranny and foreign domination alike.

The manifestations of this racism are multifaceted and are not limited to the revolutionary momentum of street demonstrations or the anonymity of web-based activism. It extends, alas, well into the cool corners of reasoned analysis and deliberations.

The racist identification of certain "Arabs" among the security apparatus of the Islamic Republic by some pro-democracy activist Iranians was in turn reciprocated by some leading Arab public intellectuals (by no means all), who are still on record as having dismissed the massive civil rights uprising in Iran as a plot by the US and Israel and funded by Saudi Arabia, condescendingly equating it with the "Cedar Revolution" in Lebanon.

That astonishing sign of barefaced inanity was in turn reciprocated by equally (if not more) inane reactions on the part of some Iranian activists who have ridiculed and dismissed the Egyptian and Tunisian revolutions as a "glorified military coup" or else boasted that "Arabs" were doing now what "we" did thirty years ago, concluding that "they" are backward at least by the factor of a thirty-year cycle.

This closed-circuit cycle of racism feeds on itself; its cancerous cells must be surgically removed from our body politic.

The Arab "other"
The roots of Arab and of Iranian racism, both toward each other and toward "black Africans," are too horrid and troubling to justify full exposure at this magnificent moment in our histories. Aspects and dimensions of these pathologies need to be addressed only to the degree that they point to a collective

emancipation from the snares of racism transmuting into cycles of racializing violence.

On the Arab side, as Joseph Massad has demonstrated in his *Desiring Arabs* (2007), in the course of Arab nationalism the trope "Persian" was systematically racialized and invested with all sorts of undesirable and morally corrupt and corrupting "sexual perversions," and thereby a "manly" and "straight" heteronormativity was manufactured for "Arabs."

In much of the dismissal of and the derision heaped on Iran's Green Movement, Massad's insight has been fully borne out. Iranians in this estimation have in effect been considered to be too feminine, too pretty, too weak, too middle class and bourgeois, too chic (look at all those pretty women and their hairdos and sunglasses) to stage their own uprising, and, like all other women, they have needed help from the superpower.

The "real revolution" was what "real men" did in the "Arab world," not just without American help but in fact against American imperialism.

Whereas the Iranian Green Movement was thus feminized (by way of its dismissal as feeble, flawed, and manipulated by "the West"), the Egyptian and Tunisian revolutions are assimilated aggressively into a pronouncedly masculinist Arab nationalism.

The Iranian "other"

The pathology of Iranian racism has a different genealogy. Engulfed in the banality of a racist Aryanism, a certain segment of Iranians, mostly monarchist in terms of political disposition, has been led to believe that they are in fact an island of pure-bred Aryans unfortunately caught in a sea of Semitic ruffians, and that they have been marred by Arab and Muslim invasion and need to reconnect with their European roots in "the West" to regain their Aryan glory.

Predicated on the historic defeat of the Sassanid Empire (224–651) by the invading Arab army in the Battle of al-Qadisiyyah (636), in particular, this national trauma has always been prone to xenophobia of the worst kind.

Not just "Arabs" but "Turks" and "Mongols" – corresponding to successive invasions of Iran from the seventh to the thirteenth century – have been the repository of Iranian racism. This racism also has an internal manifestation in the derogatory and condescending attitude of self-proclaimed "Persians" toward the racialized minorities such as Kurds, Azaris, Baluch, and so on.

External and internal racisms then come together to manufacture a fictitious "Persian" marker that is the mirror image of its "Arab" invention. The binary Persian/Arab, rooted in medieval history and colonially exacerbated, in turn becomes a self-propelling metaphoric proposition and feeds on itself.

Racializing revolutions

Predicated on these dual acts of racialized bigotry, pan-nationalist political projects have been the catastrophic hallmark of our postcolonial history over the last century.

As pan-Iranism has competed with pan-Turkism in Central Asia and exacerbated pan-Arabism in West Asia and North Africa, their combined calamity, mimicking "the West" they have collectively helped manufacture, and which they loathe and copy at one and the same time, comes together and coalesces in an identical act of bigotry against "black Africans."

The current proclivity toward the racialization of transnational revolutionary uprisings in our world partakes in that ghastly history; if we fail to surgically remove it, it will send us on a wild goose chase precisely at the time when we think we are being liberated.

As the Zimbabwean journalist and filmmaker Farai Sevenzo has noted,

> In the violence of the last fortnight [mid-February 2011 in Libya], the colonel [Gaddafi]'s African connections have only served to rekindle a deep-rooted racism between Arabs and black Africans. As mercenaries, reputedly from Chad and Mali fight for him, a million African refugees and thousands of African migrant workers stand the risk of being murdered for their tenuous link to him.

He further reports:

> One Turkish construction worker told the BBC: "We had 70–80 people from Chad working for our company. They were cut dead with pruning shears and axes, attackers saying: 'You are providing troops for Gaddafi.' The Sudanese were also massacred. We saw it for ourselves."

This ghastly manifestation of racialized violence is not exactly why millions of people from Senegal to Djibouti, from Morocco to Afghanistan, and from Iran to Yemen, are dreaming for better days for their children.

Racializing violence

Racializing violence is the last remnant of colonial racism that knew only too well the Roman – and, later, Old French – Republic logic of "divide and conquer," or "divide and rule" (*divide et impera* or *divide et regnes*), a dictum that was ultimately brought to perfection by Machiavelli in his *The Art of War* (1520).

The criminal record of European colonialism in Asia and Africa is replete with this treacherous strategy. Germany and Belgium both put the dictum to good use in Rwanda by appointing members of the Tutsi minority to positions of power. The Tutsi and Hutu groups were re-manufactured racially, an atrocity at the heart of the subsequent Rwandan genocide. The British had a similar use for the colonial maxim when they ruled Sudan and sustained a divide between the North and the South, which in turn resulted in successive Sudanese civil wars.

The colonial history of the rest of Africa reveals many similar divides, as does the history of Asia – particularly in India where the British were instrumental not only in reinscribing the caste system to their colonial benefit, but also in fomenting hostility between Muslims and Hindus, which ultimately resulted in the catastrophic partition of India and Pakistan along religious lines.

The old colonial adage has renewed imperial usages. Soon after the US-led invasion of Iraq, a US military strategist, Seyyed Vali Reza Nasr, wrote an off-the-cuff analysis on the Sunni–Shia divide, *The Shia Revival: How Conflicts within Islam Will Shape the Future* (2006). He effectively blamed the carnage in Iraq on ancient Sunni–Shia hostilities and linked it to the strategic hostility between the Islamic Republic and Saudi Arabia – a well-thought-out strategic intervention that turned the US, in the US-led invasion and occupation of Iraq, into a good Samaritan and entirely innocent bystander.

The strategy was so successful that the book became a bestseller in the US. Its author was subsequently recruited into US diplomatic meandering to manufacture a similar lullaby from the continued fiasco in Afghanistan.

Solidarity of a younger generation
These tired old clichés are the dying metaphors falling behind the trails of a liberated world, free to map itself afresh, with different, more embracing, horizons.

Today, beyond the reach of these colonial and imperial treacheries, we as a people have a renewed rendezvous with history. But if the revolutions are allowed to be assimilated back into outdated and frightful racializing elements, evident ad nauseam in pan-Arab, pan-Iranian, pan-Turkic frames of reference, we will all be back where we were two centuries ago and the heroic sacrifices will have been for naught.

Fundamental demographic and economic forces are driving these revolutionary uprisings from Asia to Africa to Latin America and even to Europe and North America. Events we have seen in Iran, Egypt, Tunisia, and Libya, with vast and variegated resonances from Morocco to Bahrain and from Afghanistan to Yemen, are changing the very planetary configuration of who and what we are.

We cannot allow nasty colonial vestiges to cloud the horizon toward which we are headed. And we will not do so. Not everything in our midst attests to our worst fears. Quite the contrary: the younger generation of Arabs, Iranians, and Africans speaks an entirely different language and acts on the basis of new sentiments. Transnational solidarity is what ignited the uprisings in the first place and will sustain them for years to come. Evidence of this is abundant in the streets and squares of our Tahrir and Meydan-e Azadi alike.

In reaction to the anti-Arab sentiments in the Green Movement, other activists wrote articles on the Palestinian artist Naji al-Ali's character Hanzala: soon the Palestinian figurative hero appeared with a green scarf keeping demonstrators company in Tehran. And the day Hosni Mubarak left office, the first young Egyptian that the BBC interviewed said in solidarity with his Iranian counterparts that Iran would be next. Likewise, Wael Ghoneim, the young Egyptian Internet activist, sporting a green wristband when addressing the rallies in Tahrir Square, indicated his delight that Iranians were interpreting it as an expression of solidarity with their cause.

From their economic foundations to their political aspirations, these revolutionary uprisings are the initial sketches of a whole new atlas of human possibilities – beyond the pales of racialized violence, gender apartheid and, above all, obscene class division.

Originally published on Al Jazeera in March 2011

Muslims as Metaphors

The frightful mass murder in Norway on July 22, 2011 and the instant, knee-jerk reaction of a number of leading European and American news organizations – including the BBC, the *Financial Times*, the *New York Times*, the *Wall Street Journal*, the *Washington Post* and a wide range of television and radio stations, websites, and blogs – in assuming, and indeed globally publicizing their assumption, that the heinous crime was perpetrated by Muslim terrorists. This was before a single fact was officially known about the suspect or suspects. The event evoked largely repressed memories of the Oklahoma Bombing of 1995, in which another white, blond, terrorist had gone on the rampage, murdering hundreds of people, injuring even more and terrorizing an entire nation. Here the same racist disposition set about blaming Muslims – until the terrorist turned out to be the white Christian fundamentalist American named Timothy James McVeigh. I still remember a Columbia University "colleague" (a white, Anglo-Saxon male) accosting me on our campus on that dreadful Wednesday, April 19, 1995, to tell me that a massive terrorist attack had been perpetrated in Oklahoma and that in connection with it "three Iranian suspects" had been arrested at the airport. He then just stared at me, waiting for my baffled look to jell into embarrassment and shame. It did not.

The two identical reactions in the span of some sixteen years that bracket the events of 9/11, one before and the other after, have once again widely exposed the politically motivated racism operative not just in the mass media, but at the heart of the societies they represent. Now that the dust of the initial frenzy around the Norway massacre has settled, the suspect arrested and identified as a blonde, blue-eyed, Norwegian named Anders Behring Breivik, who has confessed to his crime, and now that we know he is a man with a sustained record of hating the left and Muslims (the left for allowing Muslims to come to Europe and the United States and thus pollute his race, and Muslims just for being Muslim), we need to attend to the enduring disease at the root of that knee-jerk reaction. Why is it that every time there is a ghastly crime of such magnitude perpetrated in Western Europe or North America, the gut reaction of these societies, as evidenced in and perpetuated by their mass media, is to suspect a Muslim.

The question is not straightforward, but the answer is. This time around we are fortunately no longer at the mercy of the ghastly news organizations, ceaselessly practicing their bigotry and frightening our communities out of their wits. Even when they are caught red-handed expressing their horrid racism, all they do is publish a cursory "correction" and consider the matter over. Yet the miracle of the new media – from Al Jazeera and Jadaliyya to countless blogs, Facebook pages, YouTube clips, tweeters, and so on – has made it possible to force these white supremacist racists to confront their conceited mendacity and contemplate their ugly behavior. The age of European colonial hubris and American imperial arrogance is over. This is the season of the Arab Spring. We talk back. This gang of badly educated, monolingual, provincial goons, who masquerade as responsible journalists and are quick to assume the posture of a respectable institution, and who even congratulate themselves as the paper of record and award themselves the Pulitzer Prize, despite the fact that they have for generations intimidated our parents and children, cannot be let off the hook this time around. They frightened the last generation into silence. We will not allow our children to be sent to school in fear of their names and their parents' faith and by whom and what they are. They have terrorized us for long enough. It is time to get even and theorize them.

Muslims and the left

Consider the following titles: *Unholy Alliance: Radical Islam and the American Left* (David Horowitz, 2004), *The Enemy at Home: The Cultural Left and Its Responsibility for 9/11* (Dinesh D'Souza, 2007), *The Grand Jihad: How Islam and the Left Sabotage America* (Andrew C. McCarthy, 2010). The list is almost interminable – hold your nose and look it up on the Internet, whether it be Amazon or the websites that pop up like mushrooms, or else just visit your local bookstore anywhere in North America or Western Europe. These books are usually on the "Bestsellers" desk. The phrases fulminate: "the modern left and Islamic fascism," "unholy alliance of Islam and leftists," "exposing liberal lies: the odd marriage between Islam and the left." It is quite an industry: books, articles, websites, blogs, tweeters, think tanks, white supremacists, native informers, comprador intellectuals, terrorist experts, entrenched Zionists, neoconservatives for hire.

The message is simple: the left and Islamists have come together to destroy Western civilization, beginning with its first and final line of defense, the good state of Israel. One of the grandest charlatans among them published a book entitled *The Professors: The 101 Most Dangerous Academics in America* (2006) – I am one of them – in which he lists the leading American academics who are either characterized as on the left or else profiled as Muslim.

This "left" is a generic term, a sponge-word. It includes feminists, gay activists and scholars, as well as activists and academics in the fields of African-American Studies, Race and Ethnic Studies, and whatever it is that the white masculinist imagination means by "multiculturalism" – in short, all the undesirable elements populating the nightmare of those authors who write these books, their publishers, the people who buy and read them. In Zach Snyder's movie *300* (2007) all the creatures who populate Xerxes' army are the visual summation of "Muslims and the Left."

Let us consider just one of these bestselling authors – Dinesh D'Souza. Reflect on the titles of some of his books: *What's So Great about Christianity; What's So Great about America; Ronald Reagan: How an Ordinary Man Became an Extraordinary Leader; Life After Death: The Evidence.* The man has one simple idea: America and Christianity are the greatest things that ever happened to humanity; everything else – the left and Islam in particular – represents the darkest evil that has existed, categorically condemned to hell unless, like him, they see the light, join his church, and are saved. D'Souza used to be in the company of like-minded people at the Hoover Institute in California, which evidently specializes in such antics. He is now the president of an entire college, responsible for the education of an entire generation of students.

Reflect on those titles and ask yourself, is Dinesh D'Souza for real? Is he a used-car salesman or does he actually believe in what he writes? Should we call him delusional, wanting in his mental make-up, or should we consider the possibility of career opportunism – that the man realizes that the nonsense he peddles actually sells. He is a Christian fundamentalist warmonger who hates gays, hates Muslims, hates feminists, hates the left. In fact he hates anything and everything that is non-Christian – according to his understanding of Christian-ity– but he loves the abstraction he calls "America," which to him means white America. However, and here is the rub, he himself is not white. What sort of paradox is that? The man is a dark-skinned Indian; yet he sees himself as a white warrior of Greek mythology in Zach Snyder's movie. Muslims and the left, gays and blacks, feminists and multiculturalists – these are the creatures he sees in front of him, his nightmares. But he is not alone. He is a *New York Times* "bestseller," as they say. People buy what he sells in America – and thus prominent editors seek him out, offer him lucrative contracts, publish him with pomp and ceremony; in consequence, countless numbers of his books are sold, read, discussed, reviewed in print and electronic media, on the basis of which he then receives invitations to give public lectures, interviews, and so on. The cycle is self-perpetuating, endless, implicating an entire industry, not just a person and his own ideas, whether these are considered outlandish or plausible by those exposed to them. Let's consider some vintage D'Souza:

> The cultural left in this country [USA] is responsible for causing 9/11 … the cultural left and its allies in Congress, the media, Hollywood, the non-profit sector and the universities are the primary cause of the volcano of anger toward America that is erupting from the Islamic world.

The cultural left and Islam together, with their allies in government and media, were responsible for an act of terrorism... Does that ring a Norwegian bell? Before an insanity plea is entered and accepted on behalf of Anders Behring Breivik, which seems to be his lawyer Mr Geir Lippestad's intention, the office of the Norwegian attorney general may want to take a look at these sorts of books, their authors, publishers, audiences, readerships. An entire industry caters to precisely the sort of "insanity" with which the Norwegian mass murderer is afflicted – an industry that banks on people fusing the left and Muslims and sees the result as the supreme metaphor of menace to civilized life.

The larger picture

The history of American slang is filled with racial slurs that reflect a condescending contempt toward people at the receiving end of North American military invasions and/or conquests: "Commie," "Brownie," "Buffie," "Camel Jockey," "Chinaman," "Chinky," "Coolie," "Darkie," "Gooky," and so on – and, soon after the US-led invasion of Iraq, "Haji," referring to any Iraqi or Arab in or out of sight of American GIs. These are derogatory terms of condescension and disdain used to distance and denigrate the person they were fighting, subjugating, conquering. These are dehumanizing terms, which turn "the enemy" into a "thing" before he is dispensed with – with a clear conscience.

Since the 1950s and the McCarthyite witch-hunt, "the left" has been presented by "the right" as the nightmare of America. "The left" is held to be a fifth column, the enemy within. If the Soviet Union was the enemy without, the left was the enemy within, the entity that wanted to sabotage the system to further the cause of the enemy without: the same way that the early Catholics were accused of being more loyal to the Pope in Rome than to the American Constitution, and the same way that now Muslims are considered to be the enemy within, the enemy that has come into the heart of the empire, threatening it on behalf of Muslims around the world. There is a siege mentality at work here. "The West," commentators ranging from Bernard Lewis to Niall Ferguson have been declaring to their lucrative market, is threatened by these Muslims invading the heart of their empire. Looking for this enemy within squarely fits the trope of witch-hunt. Arthur Miller in *The Crucible* (1953) went all the way back to the 1692 witch-hunt in Salem, Massachusetts, to diagnose the pathological fear that had engulfed Americans during the so-called "Red Scares" of 1919–20 and 1947–57. Today the identification of the left with the Muslim – the way we see it articulated from bestselling American authors to the Norwegian mass murderer Anders Breivik – is straight out of the witch-hunt genre, from Salem in 1692 to the Oklahoma Bombing of 1995, to the list of neoconservative and Zionist bestsellers.

What Dinesh D'Souza and the whole platoon of less talented but more pestiferous old and new conservatives he represents have been doing over the last few decades in the United States is to help transfer fear and loathing of the left to fear and loathing of Muslims – and they have succeeded. This transmutation of the left and Muslims into each other is a very recent development, which dates back to a time before the ghastly events of 9/11, and which began in earnest soon after the hostage crisis of 1979–80. A key contributory factor here is, of course, the Israeli propaganda machine, which has succeeded in persuading Americans that (facts be damned) all Palestinians are Muslims, Muslims are terrorists, and thus Israel is really fighting for Americans in the frontline of defense against barbarity. The "clash of civilizations" thesis of Samuel Huntington, a leading theorist of American imperialism, which perceives Islam in civilizational terms as the number-one enemy of "the West," is the acme of this process of transmutation. The practice is straight out of the thinking of German Nazi political philosopher Carl Schmitt (1888–1985): without an enemy there is no concept of the political. That is, The very concept of *the political* is predicated on the existence (fabrication) of an enemy.

A combined hatred of the left and Muslims (being a gay, black, radical Muslim is the full Sunday-best regalia here) informs a wide range of public commentary in the United States, which goes far beyond Dinesh D'Souza and Samuel Huntington and which has employed a whole regiment of less intellectually gifted but nevertheless rather verbose characters. These two neoconservative icons are symptomatic of a much more widespread syndrome.

The demonization of Muslims

What we are witnessing in this transmutation of the left and the Muslim is but one critical element in the constitution of the Muslim as a menacing metaphor. The systemic machinations behind the demonization of Muslims as a menace to humanity is not limited to the neoconservative and Zionist operation. When it comes to characterizing Muslims as the epitome of evil, the list in fact swings all the way from the right to the left. The anxiety of identifying the Muslim with the left is the anxiety of the enemy within. But when we catch the left itself using the Muslim as a metaphor of banality and terror, then we are onto something far deeper within the inner anxiety of the entity that calls itself "the West."

Consider this statement: "He is a caliph, I suppose, almost of the Middle Eastern variety." These are the words of Robert Fisk, the distinguished British journalist, who is probably the furthest in political disposition from Dinesh D'Souza and Samuel Huntington and their ilk, and are the opening sentence of an article he wrote on July 11, 2011 for the *Independent*, in which he shared his thoughts on Mr Rupert Murdoch at the height of the phone hacking scandal in the UK. Why that curious opening – why a "caliph," of all things, of "the Middle Eastern variety"? What other variety of caliphs do we have, anyway? Scandinavian caliphs? Australian, British? There is only one kind of caliph. The word comes from the Arabic *khalifa*, meaning representative, vicegerent. It was first used in its historical sense in the aftermath of Prophet Muhammad's death in 632 CE, when Abu Bakr, his comrade, succeeded him.

Abu Bakr and his supporters opted for the humble title "representative of the Prophet of God," not wishing to pretend they were equal to him. Other successors of the prophet followed suit and kept calling themselves "caliph," until finally the first and second Arab dynasties of the Umayyads (661–750) and the Abbasids (750–1258) were formed and they called their institution a "caliphate." Other dynasties such the Ottomans (1299–1923) also at times used this title.

Now, were some of these caliphs (as any other monarch or queen or caesar or pope) corrupt, authoritarian, and wealthy? Of course they were. But why, when it came to choosing a metaphor for corruption, banality, and tyranny, could Mr Fisk not think of one from his own backyard: pope, caesar, a British monarch (perhaps "Bloody Mary"), *Duce*, or *Führer*? Why invoke a Middle Eastern caliph when referring to Rupert Murdoch, AC, KCSG, an Australian-American global media baron (the

AC after his name standing for Companion of the Order of Australia, an order of chivalry established by Elizabeth II, Queen of Australia; KCSG standing for Knight Commander of the Pontifical Equestrian Order of St Gregory the Great (Ordo Sancti Gregorii Magni), established by Pope Gregory XVI in 1831)? There are plenty of metaphors to work with there. So why "a caliph ... almost of the Middle Eastern variety?" Why could Robert Fisk not "suppose" differently and reach for "almost" something else other than a "Middle Eastern" metaphor?

It is not just Robert Fisk: the syndrome is an epidemic. The Muslim is a metaphor for menace, banality, and terror everywhere. Let's consider another prominent example. Lewis H. Lapham, the distinguished former editor of *Harper's Magazine*, a singularly progressive left-leaning American critic of US imperialism, also would not hesitate for a minute to invoke Islamic metaphors when he wants to denigrate and dismiss his conservative opponents. In a critical review of David Frum and Richard Perle's *An End to Evil: How to Win the War on Terror* (2003), Lapham unabashedly ridicules the book for having taken their inspiration from "the verses of the Koran," for issuing "fatwas" like Osama bin Laden, and for summoning "all loyal and true Americans to the glory of jihad" – all the while calling them "Mullah Frum," "Mufti Perle," and "the two Washington ayatollahs," concluding: "Provide them [Frum and Perle] with a beard, a turban, and a copy of the Koran, and I expect that they wouldn't have much trouble stoning to death a woman discovered in adultery with a cameraman from CBS News."

When Lapham needs an analogy to illustrate what he considers to be unquotable propagandist prose, he cannot think of a better source than the Quran. Nor does he pause for a moment to think through the implications of what he says.

As with all forms of propaganda, the prose style [of Frum and Perle's book] doesn't warrant extensive quotation, but I don't do the authors a disservice by reducing their message to a series of divine commandments. Like Muhammad bringing the word of Allah to the widow Khadija and the well Zem-Zem, they aspire to a tone of voice appropriate to a book of Revelation.

Likewise, Islam and Quranic language are handy for providing an appropriate allegory for the indoctrination of hatred and terror:

> The result of their [Frum and Perle's] collaboration is an ugly harangue that if translated into Arabic and reconfigured with a few changes of word and emphasis (the objects of fear and loathing identified as America and Israel in place of Saudi Arabia and the United Nations) might serve as a lesson taught to a class of eager jihadis at a madrasa in Kandahar.

Examples abound and are not limited to *Harper's Magazine*. Pages of *The Nation* magazine, another left–liberal US periodical, are replete with derogatory references to conservative adversaries again employing Islamic metaphors: mullahs, madrasa, turbans, verses from the Quran, and so on. The Florida pastor Terry Jones, who burned the Quran, is an easy target: he is just a simple and honest racist man wearing his bigoted heart on his sleeve. Whereas those with a far superior claim – to progressive, liberal, left, and tolerant ideals – have been at work sustaining "the Muslim" as a metaphor of evil for a very long time.

Muslim scholars help perpetuate the Islam–West dichotomy

The issue here is not the catching of these people red-handed. It is understanding how Muslims became a singularly dominant metaphor for menace, terror, and mendacity. In thinking through the transmutation, a larger frame of reference is required. For it is not just Europeans and Americans, not just the left and the right, who use and abuse Islamic terms freely as metaphors of dismissal and denigration, vilification and disparagement.

The practice is predicated on a more fundamental binary opposition established between "Islam and the West" – a binary that Muslims themselves have been historically instrumental in using and thus corroborating.

This binary has been manufactured, corroborated, and driven home by no other Orientalist, dead or alive, more adamantly, more doggedly, more persistently than by Bernard Lewis. But Muslims themselves have bought into it. Every time, to this day, that a Muslim or Arab scholar, journalist, activist, or public intellectual uses the term "the West" uncritically – "the West did that" or "the West will do the other thing" – she or he is corroborating the binary "Islam and the West" – two vastly vacuous appellations that rob reality of its paradoxes, ironies, contradictions, self-effacements. It makes no difference if one says, as Dinesh D'Souza or Niall Ferguson would, that "the West" is God's grandest gift to humanity, or reverses that and holds that "the West" is the source of all horror in the world – in either case one is corroborating the amoral authenticity of a reference that *ipso facto* posits and negates "Islam" and thus transmutes Muslims into a solid metaphor of threat and deceit.

In the battle of metaphors between "Islam and the West," "the West" is good, "Islam" is bad. "The West" is cowboys, "Islam" the Indians. As an Arab or a Muslim one may reverse the order, but one will only exacerbate the binary opposition, the delusion that clouds reality. Arabs and Muslims are equally at fault for cross-authenticating "the West" and positing it as the primary frame of moral reference, within which Islam and Muslims are staged as metaphors of evil and banality.

Where the left and the right come together is thus the constitution of Muslim as *the civilizational other*, the ontological alterity, of the sandcastle that must call itself "the West" or else doubt and dissolve itself back into the shadow of its own nullity.

In seeing through this epistemic free play of signs, it is not sufficient, necessary, or even advisable to go back to the European history of Orientalism, to Dante's *Divine Comedy* (1308–21), to Mozart's *The Abduction from the Seraglio* (1782), or even to Aeschylus' *The Persians* (472 BC) on a wild goose chase seeking the origin of "the Oriental" and later its rendition of "the Muslim" as the supreme other of "the West." There was no "West" at the time of Aeschylus or even Dante – and the Orientalism of each era differs from the other.

That kind of historicism dilutes the issue and confuses the focal point of *iteration* through which the delusion of "the West" is sustained in order to continue to believe in itself. We need surgical precision in defining how, when and for what purpose the figure of the Muslim is posited as the supreme metaphor of menace – to produce an instant, knee-jerk reaction. Who benefits from this spontaneity, who invokes it, and to what effect?

The constitution of "Muslim" as a metaphor of mendacity and menace to civility and society is indeed predicated on older tropes. But today it is the handiwork of North American, Western European, and Israeli journalism (three specific sites for three specific reasons), and as such is exposed for the hideous lesion that it is on the body politic of a constitutionally flawed narrative that has perpetrated unfathomable terror on generations of Muslim children and their parents around the globe, convincing them that there is something constitutionally wrong with who and what they are.

The world is no longer at the mercy of this corrupt cacophony of power and wealth. They have analyzed and terrorized us enough. It is time to get even, to understand and expose them for what they are.

Originally published on Al Jazeera
in two parts in July and August 2011

Žižek and Gaddafi: Living in the Old World

Just a couple of days before the fall of Tripoli to Libyan rebels, Saidj Mustapha, a prominent Algerian political scientist, was asked his opinion about the Arab Spring. He responded by outlining a number of key factors that he thought had contributed to the making of the dramatic transnational revolutions, particularly the aging leadership and the young population, mixed with the corruption of the ruling regimes, concluding that "The young people who launched this revolution do not come from the traditional political institutions, such as political parties or military coup elites. This makes us look forward to a phase of democratic transition from an authoritarian regime to a pluralistic, democratic system."

When Mustapha was asked to predict what would happen in Libya (in an interview conducted in Algiers on August 19, 2011, just before the Libyan rebels entered Tripoli), he gave a detailed answer, scenario by scenario, analyzing the possibilities of (1) civil war that would split Libya like Sudan, (2) the triumph of the Transitional National Council, and (3) the nightmare of Iraq or Somalia and civil strife in which he feared that al-Qaeda in Maghreb might be the beneficiary. In the very short interview, in very precise terms, Saidj Mustapha was meticulous, caring, optimistic, and above all celebratory of the Arab Spring and the new horizons of open-ended politics it had occasioned.

As fate, or the metahistorical force of events, would have it, on the same day as the interview the *London Review of Books* published an essay by the famous European philosopher Slavoj Žižek, frivolously titled (as is his wont) "Shoplifters of the World Unite," in which he gave his take on the recent UK riots.

Žižek's worldless world

In his article, Žižek concurred with Alain Badiou, his French counterpart, that "we live in a social space which is increasingly experienced as 'worldless': in such a space, the only form protest can take is meaningless violence." Žižek continued to suggest that "the riots should be situated in relation to another type of violence that the liberal majority today perceives as a threat to our way of life: terrorist attacks and suicide bombings." But, he stipulated, "the difference is that, in contrast to the riots in the UK or in Paris, terrorist attacks are carried out in service of the absolute Meaning provided by religion."

So, as Žižek saw it, what we have here, defined by shoplifters and terrorists, is a "worldless" world (informed by Badiou and shoplifters) and occupied by "absolute Meaning" (suggested by Hegel and Osama bin Laden).

Žižek then turned his attention to the Arab Spring: "But weren't the Arab uprisings a collective act of resistance that avoided the false alternative of self-destructive violence and religious fundamentalism?" This should have given the European philosopher a sign of hope in what appeared to be a worldless world filled with absolutist religious meanings thrown like grenades by terrorist Hegelians. But it did not. The European philosopher has lost all hope: "Unfortunately, the Egyptian

summer of 2011 will be remembered as marking the end of revolution, a time when its emancipatory potential was suffocated."

The end of revolution? So early? It would seem that, early in
the game, the European philosopher has utterly lost all hope.
How did he come to that conclusion?

> Its gravediggers are the army and the Islamists. The contours
> of the pact between the army (which is Mubarak's army) and
> the Islamists (who were marginalized in the early months of the
> upheaval but are now gaining ground) are increasingly clear:
> the Islamists will tolerate the army's material privileges and in
> exchange will secure ideological hegemony.

This has, to be sure, by now become a clichéd concern
among a certain segment of Arab intellectuals too, but more
as a defiant rallying cry than a metaphysical fait accompli, the
air in which Žižek was delivering his ruling. There were other
Arab activists and intellectuals who were even more concerned
about their revolution being derailed and hijacked by the perfectly business-suit-clad and clean-shaven neoliberals, by the
IMF, by the World Bank, by NATO bombings, by American
neoconservatives "helping Arabs transit to democracy," while
they put "boots on the ground" and signed up to lucrative
business deals.

Žižek: out of touch

It is strange that the (evidently Marxist) European philosopher
had no concerns about those acts of "suffocating" the revolution.
On a previous occasion I suggested that distinguished European
philosophers like Žižek who wish to say something about other
parts of the world need to consult a more diverse selection of
native informers. But, alas, Žižek seems not to have listened
to my advice. "The losers," he warns Europeans, "will be the

pro-Western liberals, too weak – in spite of the CIA funding they are getting – to 'promote democracy', as well as the true agents of the spring events, the emerging secular left that has been trying to set up a network of civil society organizations, from trade unions to feminists."

These key confusions of Žižek – his "secular left" in particular is a giveaway – should warn him to start shopping around (with a proper credit card of course, for shoplifting is nihilistic) for more reliable information. The counsel he is currently receiving is no good. In a "worldless" world, filled with the Absolute meanings of militant Islamists stealing revolutions like shoplifters, Žižek's diagnosis is that "today's left faces the problem of 'determinate negation': what new order should replace the old one after the uprising, when the sublime enthusiasm of the first moment is over?"

In this "worldless" world we have, it seems, a lack of organization; yes indeed, party politics. Žižek mourns precisely where and what Saidj Mustapha celebrates. Žižek dismisses not just the UK shoplifters, the Muslim terrorists, and the Arab revolutions, but even the Spanish Indignados:

> In this context, the manifesto of the Spanish *indignados*, issued after their demonstrations in May, is revealing. The first thing that meets the eye is the pointedly apolitical tone: "Some of us consider ourselves progressive, others conservative. Some of us are believers, some not. Some of us have clearly defined ideologies, others are apolitical, but we are all concerned and angry about the political, economic and social outlook that we see around us: corruption among politicians, businessmen, bankers, leaving us helpless, without a voice."

They make their protest on behalf of the "inalienable truths that we should abide by in our society: the right to housing, employment, culture, health, education, political participation, free personal development and consumer rights for a healthy and happy life." Rejecting violence, they call for an "ethical revolution":

> The *indignados* dismiss the entire political class, right and left, as corrupt and controlled by a lust for power ... And this is the fatal weakness of recent protests: they express an authentic rage which is not able to transform itself into a positive programme of sociopolitical change. They express a spirit of revolt without revolution.

So, there's no hope in Spain either, where people are revolting without having a revolution. Is it not entirely predictable that the European philosopher goes back to Greece, his fictive birthplace, for solace and hope: "The situation in Greece looks more promising, probably owing to the recent tradition of progressive self-organization (which disappeared in Spain after the fall of the Franco regime)."

But even good old Greece is not a happy scene for "the Absolute Professor" (Søren Kierkegaard 's choice term for Žižek's idol Hegel), for "even in Greece, the protest movement displays the limits of self-organization: protesters sustain a space of egalitarian freedom with no central authority to regulate it, a public space where all are allotted the same amount of time to speak and so on."

This to Žižek is anarchy, lacking in revolutionary discipline, the necessary cadre of political party apparatchiks of the old Soviet sort.

> When the protesters started to debate what to do next, how to move beyond mere protest, the majority consensus was that what was needed was not a new party or a direct attempt to take state power, but a movement whose aim is to exert

pressure on political parties. This is clearly not enough to impose a reorganization of social life. To do that, one needs a strong body able to reach quick decisions and to implement them with all necessary harshness."

The abyss has opened and the postmodern professor has become positively punctilious – indeed, dare we say it, conservative. All it takes is a riot in London (retail therapy on steroids), a terrorist attack in New York, and a misinformed native informer of the Arab Spring in the philosopher's company to turn the world dark and worldless, filled with Absolute fanaticism, and expose the postmodern existential angst unable to read the signs of the time.

Is the Arab Spring half-full or half-empty?

Whence derives the difference between these two perspectives, the Arab intellectual morally invested and politically engaged, his European counterpart morally aloof and politically pessimistic? One has everything to gain, a world to live; the other has nothing to lose, having lost his world to worldlessness. The Algerian political scientist thrives on a visionary reading of a world that Žižek dismisses as already worldless. Why is Saidj Mustapha not afraid of a conspiracy between the Islamists and the generals? Why is Joseph Massad far more afraid of American neoliberals and neoconservatives than of Islamists? A world is unfolding right in front of Žižek's eyes and yet he sees the world as worldless, the Egyptian revolution suffocated, the Arab Spring lost. How and why is it that the Algerian intellectual celebrates precisely what the European philosopher mourns: the absence of party politics, the rise of a politics beyond cliché?

Žižek mourns worldlessness, and designates absolute Meaning as the cause of terrorism. He does not see the world that is unfolding right before him as hopeful, purposeful, worldly, life-affirming. This is because, just like Gaddafi, Žižek is stuck in his old ways. He cannot believe his eyes, he cannot accept what is happening to him: that *his* world has ended, not *the* world; that *he* (embodying a European philosophy at the losing end of its dead certainties) lives in a worldless world, not *the* world.

Žižek and Gaddafi are identical souls, sticking to the worlds they know, militantly, the world they are losing – defiant rebels banging at the Bab Aziziyeh compound of their habitat, a world that is either theirs or it will not exist: *Après moi, le déluge*. Although it has barely begun, Žižek dismisses the Arab Spring and then mourns the loss of idealism among the shoplifters.

It is in fact the European philosopher himself who is the gravedigger of history, having nothing to see, nothing to say, nothing to celebrate, because this history is not *his* history, is not History, for History has always been His and not anyone else's. It is quite a moment in History when the Hegelian cannot tell the difference between signs of a disease (shoplifting and terrorism) as the *thesis* and the sight of a cure (the Arab Spring) as *antithesis* – giving it up to generals and Islamists. The London riots and terrorism of one brand or another are the symptoms of a disease, of capitalism and its imperialist fighter jets running amok from top to bottom.

The Arab Spring is the renewed ground zero of history, the sight of a world that is beginning to reveal itself, precisely at the moment when the European philosopher – just like Colonel Gaddafi – sees the world as "worldless" because it is not *his* world; as a world in which he cannot imagine himself, for he has been imagining the world for everyone else. The Arab Spring is the opening horizon of a hope for emancipation, for a renewed reading of the world, of worlds. But Žižek does not see this because it is not the world of his making, the visage and force of a world Hegel had relegated to pre-History, non-History. Žižek has already proclaimed the obituary of the Arab Spring, because what appears as a worldless world to the European philosopher is one he cannot fathom, as it is inhabited by others he cannot read.

Originally published on Al Jazeera in September 2011

Repairing the Soul of the Empire City

Almost a decade has passed since the mournful, heartbreaking collapse of those two gentle giants of the WTC in New York City – a decade that has just ended with a leading credit rating agency, Standard & Poor's (S&P), downgrading the United States' AAA standing to an AA rating, for the first time in history.

Empires: they don't make 'em like they used to. Which is worse, the two giant AA phallic symbols of an empire cut deep and down in the full daylight of history, or its AAA rating circumcised by one notch to AA for the whole world to see? Is this what Fareed Zakaria meant, perhaps, by "the post-American world"?

Did anyone remember – or did we all miss – the tenth anniversary of March 2, 2001, when the Taliban began dynamiting the twin Buddhas of Bamiyan on the orders of their leader, Mullah Omar? Between the two mirror images of the Buddhas of Bamiyan and the towers of Manhattan, falling to the terror of fear and fanaticism, how many more monuments, buildings, innocent lives, have perished in Herat, Kabul, Kandahar, Baghdad, Basra, Kazmain, Gaza, Beirut, Tripoli, how many widowed and orphaned, how many victims of intentional and accidental drone attacks, how many refugees, how many nightmares? "We don't do body counts," US General Tommy Franks once said. What do generals count? Will empires ever be held accountable?

Whether or not generals count, things don't look good on the home front for the monopolar empire. Just short of two years after the severe financial crisis of 2008 that ushered Barack Obama into the White House, on the tenth anniversary of 9/11 the American empire has something far trickier than al-Qaeda to fear and fight. The deficit reduction plan passed by the US Congress has evidently not gone far enough for the agency to keep the superpower at its AAA standing. The finicky investors are losing confidence. With huge debts, unemployment running at 9.1 per cent, and amid fears of a double-dip recession, the man at the helm, who preached "the audacity of hope" to get there, is now facing a home front weaker than on that frightful Tuesday morning on September 11, 2001.

Empire in decline

This enemy comes from within, and it ain't no "Muslim sleeper cell." It is homegrown. It is greed. It is the Republican Party giving birth to a nightmare it calls the Tea Party. If during the Bush era (2000–2008) the world was menaced by the neocons, the Obama era is plagued by a Tea Party that makes the neocons look like pussycats. If the neocons were psychopaths taking their class notes from Leo Strauss's lectures for global domination, these Tea Party sociopaths are targeting the very foundation of civil society.

The decade marks a downward spiral: the Republicans begat the conservatives, the conservatives begat the neoconservatives, and the neoconservatives begat the Tea Party. We thought Newt Gingrich was an antiquity. Now we need to decipher Rick Perry.

The criminal attacks of 9/11 unleashed the state-sponsored terrorism of the neocons upon the world, and the terror of the Tea Party now threatens to cripple the functioning of the state apparatus and with it the very fabric of civil society.

Their darling, Minnesota Representative Michele Bachmann, just won the Iowa straw poll, adding momentum to her populist Christian evangelical fundamentalist campaign for president. Sarah Palin was a decoy. The UK should dispatch a "supercop" (James Bond?) this way to sort out the political riots. Imagine the world's predicament: you run away from an Islamic republic, fearful of a Jewish state and its matching Hindu fundamentalism, just to end up in a Christian empire – where Florida pastor Terry Jones is burning the Quran and the Christian Zionist John Hagee is preparing for Armageddon, before Reverend Harold Camping revealed that the "Rapture" would take place on May 21, 2011, at which point the world would end.

The empire – what empire? Forget about Muslim terrorists; China, to which the US owes more than it can afford to pay back, is now asking the US to address its "structural debt problems," even demanding international supervision over the US dollar. Senator Joseph McCarthy (1908–1957) is turning in his grave.

All of this is Greek to New York. New York is not a city. It is an apparition, a phantom, a vision – a frontier outpost of a territory yet to be conquered, possessed, named. Americans will have conquered and colonized another planet sooner than claim New York as the capital of their empire. It is not. New York is unruly; it is a trojan horse, its belly full not of terrorists, but of insomniac workaholic immigrants all on a heavy dose of stimulus.

The capital of this would-be empire is somewhere else – a Romanesque architectural lookalike meeting clumsily with the forsaken Southern gentry, held together inside "the Beltway" for fear of contaminating the rest of the world. New York City is farther from Washington DC than from the moon. Washington DC is J. Edgar Hoover; New York City is Joe Pesci.

NYC: in a class of its own

New York City is the physical embodiment of its own memorial gathering – for otherwise it has absolutely no memory. It is gloriously afflicted with a short attention span. It cannot remember anything. It is drastically different from London, Paris, Tehran, Cairo, Casablanca, Istanbul, or any other cosmopolis. The best way to compare New York City to other major cities is on New Year's Eve. Paris has its Eiffel Tower, London its Eye, Sydney its Harbour Bridge, and so on. Each becomes the center of festivities.

What about New York? Times Square is a vacant space. Nothing is there: no monument, no structure, no edifice. All that defines Times Square on New Year's Eve is the people who have gathered there to celebrate. Their celebrations done, champagne popped and kisses exchanged, they go home and sleep, and tomorrow morning nothing is there – except huge billboards crawling over the walls, and yellow cabs and tourist buses sneaking up and down Manhattan. There is nothing at the center of Times Square – any more than there is in Tahrir Square. People define each of them, creating a makeshift human monument at their centers; and when they leave, so does the monument – that's why people stayed in Tahrir until Mubarak left. If there ever were to be a revolution in America it would have to start in Times Square: *Silmiyya, Silmiyya!*

New York does not flaunt its character. It tailors itself around every character. Paris has a "take it or leave it" attitude, as do London, Istanbul, Mumbai, and Tokyo. Not New York. New York is too big to be arrogant like that. If you come to visit New York, it will charm and tease you, but it will not bother you – for New York is exceedingly shy; it has built the facade of all those glitzy billboards to hide its modesty. To conceal its shyness from strangers, it pretends it is busy doing something else – always something else – but in fact it is watching you closely, from somewhere up in one of those high-rises.

But if you go there to live, New York treats you differently, with respect; it opens itself to you, shows you all its nooks and crannies, all the while trying to figure you out – who *you* are, what *you* want, where *you* want to be, how much insomnia fate has invested in *you*. Then, before you know it New York has wrapped itself around you, made itself your city – and you will never be able to live anywhere else. New York belongs to no empire. It is a frontier town, comprising millions of insomniac immigrants, with memories of their parents, the birthplace of their children, having made a picture-perfect image of their unfolding dreams they call "New York." New York is the tweet of Planet Earth to the possibility of life in our galaxy.

The self-surfacing soul of New York City is self-regenerative. It dies every evening and is born again from its five boroughs every morning – remembering nothing. New York is immemorial – it could not care less for histories, for it is busy making and remaking them. When militant Zionists occupy Fifth Avenue to flaunt their power on "Salute to Israel Day," just a few blocks away from the parade New Yorkers are watching the leading Palestinian filmmaker Elia Suleiman's *The Time that Remains*. Frustrated Zionists, watching Edward Said commanding global attention for the Palestinian cause from Columbia University in the City of New York, called my university "Birzeit-upon-Hudson."

The Iranian filmmaker Amir Naderi – a New Yorker now for more than three decades – was shooting his exquisite homage to New York, *Marathon* (2002), during the fateful year of 2001, one of four films he has made in his beloved city, while serving as an inspiration to the widely celebrated Iranian-American filmmaker Ramin Bahrani, whose *Man Push Cart* (2005) and *Chop Shop* (2007) are among the first post-9/11 visions of the city from the vantage point of its labor immigrants, from within and outside the Empire. Between Naderi and Bahrani, New York has revealed its self-regenerative soul to its native immigrants, while Zach Snyder and imperial Hollywood were busy making the testosterone-fueled CGI image of their juvenile delusions in *300*.

New York is for real – and, as Dominique Strauss-Kahn learned the hard way, it will cost you a lot if you try to fake it.

We New Yorkers neither remember nor forgive that gang of criminals who violated the physics and poetry of the Twin Towers – you cannot forgive what you cannot remember, and for that gang the fate of anonymity is worse than ignominy. We New Yorkers categorically denounce the neocon abuse of our sorrows to wage war against humanity. To many of us in New York, Osama bin Laden and Donald Rumsfeld are the same charade on different banners – one perturbed soul in two crooked bodies. One of them has now met his creator; the other should be put on trial for crimes against humanity.

What Rumsfeld did to Baghdad was a hundred times worse than what Muhammad Atta did to New York, and a hundred thousand times worse than what the Mongol warlord Hulagu did to Baghdad in the thirteenth century. Rumsfeld may have gotten away with it – but the US didn't. In just a decade, and precisely due to the "campaign of shock and awe" that Rumsfeld launched, the United States has gone from the presumption of a superpower to the daunting recognition of its economic bankruptcy, political impotence, and global irrelevance, with the democratic rise of the Arab Spring exposing the sheer banality of its military might and of its garrison state of Israel alike.

Against the avalanche of memories and identities, a New Yorker is just a New Yorker, citizen of an Empire City made of many races, creeds, and nationalities – Jews, Christians, Muslims, and blessed atheists, or else Arabs, Iranians, Afghans, Pakistanis, Turks, Koreans, Chinese, Africans – and from any and every exit off the New Jersey Turnpike you can count or imagine.

On the tenth anniversary of 9/11, the National September 11 Memorial and Museum, located at the World Trade Center site, on the former location of the Twin Towers destroyed during the September 11 attacks in 2001, is planning the inauguration of a major landmark. A forest of trees with two square pools in the center, designed by Michael Arad, an Israeli architect, on the footprints of where the Twin Towers once stood, is to commemorate the fallen giants and the victims who perished on that day. The design is both somber and majestic.

The politics of mourning

But what is it exactly that the memorial is supposed to memorialize, in a city that thrives on too many memories to recall every night and thus gets up in the morning having completely forgotten itself? If one looks at the southern tip of Manhattan these days, one may notice the imperceptible rise of a new, soon-to-be 1,776-foot-high, centerpiece of the resurrected Ground Zero, just like the newborn child of Afghan or Iraqi parents who perished in the campaign of "ending states" by "shock and awe."

Soon after the dreadful events of 9/11, Jacques Derrida delivered a public lecture at Columbia University in which he talked about "the mourning of the political." The Algerian sage was teaching his audience that day, in an auditorium with standing room only, that what we were witnessing in the US was not just the mourning of those who perished on 9/11, but of the very notion of "the political" as we have known it. At the conclusion of his speech a curious member of the audience asked Derrida, point blank, if he thought that "the politics of mourning" that we were witnessing in the city would perhaps preempt "the mourning of the political." He pondered the question exquisitely, publicly – though not to his own satisfaction. He said he had no crystal ball. New York is a crystal ball.

The events of 9/11 could have brought the US to the bosom of the world if, as Derrida had taught, we were to have allowed a proper mourning of "the political" as we had known it, and as it has marked us. Within days, George W. Bush was on the site of 9/11, his war machine was throttling full blast, the neoconservative chicanery of the Project for the New American Century was dusting off its plans to dominate the world, and *the politics of mourning* (to this day, and marked by an Israeli architect winking at a Muslim atrocity) had preempted that *mourning of the political.*

The wounded soul of New York was restored by the evening of 9/11, as Kandahar, Baghdad, Gaza, and Beirut were waiting to be burned. On Wednesday morning, 12 September, New York was back to normal, buzzing, humming, working, feeling, building – oblivious, as always, to "history." New York dies with the death of every New Yorker, and New York is born again with the birth of every child in its five boroughs. We mourn the death of New Yorkers we have lost in and by the blessing of those born to us every day.

New York is not an imperial city. It is the Empire City – an empire of its own. No other city in the United States is quite like it, and thus they all aspire to be it. It is not America. It is what America wants to be – but cannot be. It is the worst aspect of America that there is always hope for it.

Originally published on Al Jazeera on September 11, 2011

The Third Intifada Has Already Begun

No amount of global revulsion at US President Barack Obama's mendacious speech at the UN General Assembly in September 2011, unabashedly seeking to preempt the possibility of the Palestinian statehood bid, can ever match the unsurpassed hypocrisy with which Mr Audacity of Hope has opted to put his signature to his presidency.

After this speech it will no longer matter if Obama wins the next US presidential election or loses it to Attila the Hun on the Republican side. He will be remembered in history for the fireworks of his having stirred a nation to seek their better angels in 2008 and then for the crude cowardice with which he betrayed that dream, throwing a bucket of iced water on those who trusted his words.

Reverend Jeremiah Wright was right about him: "He is a politician" – a polite way of saying "He lies."

It no longer matters if one is a Democrat, a Republican, or any other colorless shade of bought-and-paid-for politician in-between: Israel has finally dragged the United States – not just its elected officials, but the nation that actually elects this corrupt calamity to power – down to its level, while the rest of the world is mapping a different future for itself.

The only hope for the United States now is a band of visionary heroes camping out for days and nights, occupying the site of that Ponzi scheme that calls itself "Wall Street," all the while being brutalized by militarized New York police with evident impunity.

Not just one but three retrograde speeches (Obama's, Ahmadinejad's, and Netanyahu's) marked this season of discontent – matched by one rousing pronouncement (by Mahmoud Abbas), the aura of its noble cause having overcome its not-so-eloquent speaker. The noble cause of Palestine shone on that graceless building in lower Manhattan, as Obama, Netanyahu, and Ahmadinejad took turns depositing themselves ignobly in the dustbin of history.

Condemnation of all three of these hypocritical speeches, in one way or another, has been global. But one particular point raised by Robert Fisk deserves closer attention. Responding to Obama's speech, he has observed that,

> as the days go by, and we discover whether the Palestinians respond to Obama's groveling performance with a third intifada or with a shrug of weary recognition that this is how things always were, the facts will continue to prove that the US administration remains a tool of Israel when it comes to Israel's refusal to give the Palestinians a state.

The Arab Spring

Palestinians are, of course, not waiting for Israel to deign "to give them" their state – which is not theirs to give. On the more crucial question of "the Third Intifada," we need no longer wait to see how Palestinians will respond, or whether it is in the offing or not. The Third Intifada has already happened. It is called the Arab Spring.

The Arab Spring, now having endured its summer and entering the maturity of its fall and winter, is the commencement of the Third Intifada on a transnational, pan-Arab, and pan-Muslim scale.

The thick colonial walls that have hitherto separated Palestinians from their masses of millions of supporters around the globe have crumbled under the mighty weight of the Arab Spring. It is impossible to exaggerate the significance of the Palestinian struggle for Arabs and Muslims around the globe. Netanyahu is a fool to think that he can divide the Arab and Muslim world by propping up Israel-friendly regimes, isolate the Palestinians, and thus be able to continue to steal their homeland with impunity. The Third Intifada of which he and his Zionist cabal were afraid has just erupted and spread far beyond the Palestinian borders, far beyond the ability of the Israeli army to repress.

In his unabashedly racist and condescending comments on the Arab Spring, precisely at the moment when he admonished the UN for having rightly denounced Zionism as racism, Netanyahu (just like Ahmadinejad) tried to divide the revolutionary uprisings into various parts to appropriate or dismiss them to his liking.

"Can you imagine that man who ranted here yesterday," he said, referring to Ahmadinejad,

> can you imagine him armed with nuclear weapons? The international community must stop Iran before it's too late. If Iran is not stopped, we will all face the specter of nuclear terrorism, and the Arab Spring could soon become an Iranian winter. That would be a tragedy. Millions of Arabs have taken to the streets to replace tyranny with liberty, and no one would benefit more than Israel if those committed to freedom and peace would prevail.

This from the man who sits atop a deadly stockpile of un-declared nuclear weapons, who refuses to sign the NPT. No one dares to challenge *his* madness, which involves stealing an entire country from its people.

For decades Israel has perpetrated "nuclear terrorism" on Arabs and Muslims in and out of Palestine with full US support. Among those "millions of Arabs" taking to the streets were Egyptians and Jordanians who lowered the Israeli flag, raised the Palestinian flag, and forced Israeli envoys to run back to Tel Aviv. Is the man delusional or just a plain hypocrite?

Stupidity and spite

Netanyahu's Iranian counterpart, Ahmadinejad, competed in hypocrisy with his Israeli nemesis. He once again denied the Holocaust, and joined the conspiracy theorists on the events of 9/11. But these were just warm-ups to give the world body a lecture on the proper manner of running the world and ad-dressing its miseries.

This from a man who represents a regime that has just brutally repressed a massive civil rights movement, whose two principal presidential rivals have been under house arrest and incommunicado for months, whose dungeons are filled with political dissidents, journalists, lawyers, filmmakers, and academics. Millions of citizens in his country are denied their basic civil liberties, among them a young woman blogger, Somayeh Tohidlu, who has just been lashed fifty times for having criticized Ahmadinejad in her blog. His administration is currently under investigation by a parliamentary commission for the largest case of bank fraud in Iranian history.

Stupidity and spite have a strange rendezvous in Netanyahu and Ahmadinejad – each cherry-picking what part of the Arab

Spring to endorse and what part to dismiss, both blinded to the fact that the Arab Spring is the Third Palestinian Intifada writ large, no longer at the mercy of the Israeli army or the propaganda machine of the Islamic Republic.

The Third Intifada has now broken out, on a scale that neither Netanyahu, nor the errant US president, nor the Saudi potentates, nor the Egyptian generals, nor the ruling clerics in Iran can appropriate. This is much bigger than their limited imaginations can fathom.

What depth of cowardice or blindness could have befallen a man to have seen the revolutions in Tunisia and Egypt, to have witnessed the millions at Tahrir, to have observed those heroic Syrians marching towards their freedom, to have had an inkling of the Arab Spring, and before it the Green Movement, and yet to have delivered that utterly inane speech that Obama delivered at the UN about Palestine?

After that speech, the mayoral election in Izmir is far more exciting and consequential than the presidential election in the United States. Who could care any longer if Obama wins the next election, or if Jack or Jane the Ripper of the Tea Party win instead?

Domestically, Obama saves corporate ballrooms and banking executives, while the indignity of jobless Americans intensifies. This state of affairs is now spiralling into a national uprising centered on the Occupy Wall Street Movement. Globally, all Obama can say to Netanyahu's "Jump!" is "How high?"

Obama entered the White House banking on the legitimate sentiments of millions of Americans wishing to see the centuries of injustice against African Americans come to a symbolic end. That was, and it remains, a noble moment in the history of the nation. But what of that history of slavery when Obama in effect told Palestinians to go and sit in the back of the bus, to drink from a different fountain, and to designate them as the wretched of this earth?

W.E.B. DuBois, Martin Luther King, Malcolm X, and generations of other African-American revolutionaries and civil rights activists must be turning in their graves watching Obama. He will go down in history for systemic mendacity in American politics, hostage to a sheer inanity called AIPAC, called Israel, called Zionism.

The first Jewish president: there is no way that the dignity of an entire people, the sanctity of a world religion, are to be wasted on this ignominy. Obama is Zionist, not Jewish. He is not the first or the last Zionist president that the United States will see. It has had all sorts of Zionist presidents, and a whole slew of Zionist would-be presidents are waiting to succeed Obama. However, the world – now from one end to the other, revolting against the indignities of this politics of despair – no longer cares. The world, shoulder to shoulder with Palestinians, is charting a different future for itself – and the calamity code-named "the West" cannot stop it.

False friends, fake enemies

The Arab Spring cum the Third Intifada has changed the moral map of what colonial officers had termed "the Middle East," and brought the United States and the Islamic Republic much closer to each other in terms of their shared fears than they might think. Saudi Arabia and Israel are the sidekicks of the self-assigned "superpower."

That "superpower" cannot bring anything to the world except death and destruction. Yet, precisely because the Arab Spring/Third Intifada is constitutionally non-violent, the vulgar violence embedded in the US–Israeli alliance is rendered useless and abhorrent. And the US and Israel are not the only losers in the configuration of this new realpolitik; Saudi Arabia and Iran are too. Consider the two consecutive, typically gaudy, conferences in Tehran, one on "Islamic Awakening" and the other on the "Palestinian Intifada," marking the Islamic Republic's futile attempt to appropriate the Palestinian cause and the Arab Spring to its own increasingly jeopardized regional position.

One must view these two conferences in the context of the increasingly evident fact that the Islamic Republic looks singularly inept and irrelevant within the region, particularly in light of the principled rise of Turkey as a major force. Only the United States and Israel look as absurd and confused as the Islamic Republic and Saudi Arabia in their responses to the Arab Spring, which has caught them all off guard and exposed their outdated and flatfooted hypocrisy.

Referring to Palestine (in Persian) as an "Islamic country" that has been taken away from its people and given to foreigners, Ali Khamenei, "the Supreme Leader," tried to hit two birds with one stone: to both defend the cause of Palestine for his own internal and regional reasons, and categorically Islamize it too.

Palestinians, of course, are not all Muslims. From the combined traces of Palestinian Muslims, Christians, Druze, Samaritans, Jews, Baha'is, and agnostics, a bona fide civil religion has emerged that incorporates the symbols and rituals of all Palestinian people. In other words, the Palestine of Ayatollah Khamenei's imagination has no room for Edward Said, Joseph Massad, Elia Suleiman, or millions of other non-Muslim Palestinians.

But even if Palestinians were all Muslims, this would not mean that they wished to create an "Islamic Republic of Palestine" after sixty years of dealing with the Jewish State of

Israel. The fact of one Islamic Republic, next to a Jewish state, presided over by a Christian empire, in the vicinity of Hindu fundamentalism, is calamitous enough for the whole world. The question for those among "the Arab left" (or what is left of it) who think of the Islamic Republic as an ally is whether or not they are really struggling for an "Islamic Republic of Palestine," with a "Supreme Leader" as their sultan. The answer is of course not. As a leading Palestinian public intellectual remarked to me recently: "Every time Ahmadinejad opens his mouth he pushes the cause of Palestine back by a decade."

Falsely Islamizing the Palestinian cause

So Palestinians should not wish upon Iranians what they don't want to happen to Palestine. The case is reversed for former and current Iranian employees of WINEP (the Washington Institute for Near Eastern Policy – the intelligence arm of the pro-Israel lobby in the United States). Disguising themselves as supporters of the Green Movement, they planted the nativist slogan "Neither Gaza nor Lebanon" from Voice of America in the midst of demonstrations in Iran. The problem for both sides – segments of the Arab left and platoons of the Iranian right – is that they are both out to lunch when it comes to the emerging geopolitics of the region.

It is not only the ruling clerics of the Islamic Republic who are falsely Islamizing the Palestinian national liberation movement. So is the Iranian opposition. Seyyed Mohammad Sadr, a deputy foreign minister in the cabinet of former president Mohammad Khatami, called the Syrian insurgency "the most Islamic uprising in the region." But according to what authority?

The reformist opposition, in branding the Arab Spring "an Islamic wakening," wishes to expose the hypocrisy of the ruling faction in disregarding the Syrian uprising. But its action instead serves to bring the two factions together, thereby extending the banality of the Islamic Republic into the region at large.

There is no doubt that Syrians, as Muslims, have every right to define their political future in line with who and what they are. But so do generations of Syrian political thinkers, artists, journalists, intellectuals, and scholars, who are not on record as having wished for an "Islamic Republic of Syria" on the model of "the Islamic Republic of Iran" – built as it has been on mass graves, numerous university purges, ruinous cultural revolutions, the forced exile of entire generations of dissenters, and the maiming and murder of ideological opponents. Binyamin Netanyahu, of course, loves nothing more than a provocative statement from Khamenei or Ahmadinejad to distract attention from his government's continued armed robbery of Palestine.

According to Al Jazeera,

> Binyamin Netanyahu ... reacted angrily to Khamenei's speech. "The declarations of hatred from the ayatollah regime on the intention to destroy the state of Israel reinforces the government's steadfast position for the security needs of Israel's citizens and the demand for recognition of Israel as the Jewish state", Netanyahu said.

Logic and consistency be damned: two times two equals "we need a Jewish Republic of Israel." Contrary to their protestations, Israel and the Islamic Republic are two sides of the same outdated coin.

The Arab Spring as a transnational intifada spreading the Palestinian cause region-wide puts both sides of this hypocrisy out of business. And that is precisely the reason why both want to push back the current uprisings to the status quo ante, to assume a ludicrous warring posture and rob Arabs and Muslims of their world-historic uprisings against remnants of European colonialism (Israel), domestic tyranny (Islamic Republic, Saudi Arabia, Syria, etc.), and globalized imperialism (the US, the EU, and their NATO) at one and the same time.

Israel and the Islamic Republic (joined by Syria and Hezbollah) are integral to the combined effects of domestic tyranny and Euro-American imperialism, not the cure. What the subservient Iranian press and Binyamin Netanyahu and his government both fail to consider is that at the very same conference in Tehran, Khaled Meshaal, the Hamas leader, in fact defended Mahmoud Abbas's UN move and praised it as courageous and a symbolic triumph for Palestinians.

This position is a triumph for both Hamas and the Palestinian national liberation movement, which increasingly are able to dissociate themselves from the discredited ruling regimes in the Islamic Republic and Syria. The Israeli colonial settlement would have never imagined this drastic change of events when in 1997, under direct instruction from Binyamin Netanyahu, Khaled Meshaal was the target of an unsuccessful assassination attempt by Israeli assassins.

Third Intifada writ large

If Khaled Meshaal, or any other Palestinian leader, does not dissociate himself quickly enough from both Syria and the Islamic Republic, he will have forfeited his claim on the Arab Spring cum the Third Intifada.

The Arab Spring clearly *is* the Third Intifada.

There is no cause of liberty so constitutionally definitive to the Arab and Muslim world, or as poignant in moral and imaginative terms, as that of the Palestinians. It is the gushing wound of the last remnant of European colonialism, having hooked itself to American imperialism. Irreducible to Islamism, socialism, or nationalism, the Palestinian cause is a microcosm of the Arab and Muslim world's struggles for dignity, justice, and democratic governance. Neither a Jewish state nor an Islamic Republic can be the blueprint for that future. Liberation of Palestine is the first and final liberation of that world held hostage by European colonialism, American imperialism, and the mini-tyrants who either collaborate or else feign opposition to them – having produced and conditioned domestic tyrannies from one end of Africa to another in Asia.

We as a people deserve, and will do, better.

Israel, the United States, the Islamic Republic, Saudi Arabia, along with the other Arab and Muslim tyrants strangling their nations under the false pretense of resisting imperialism are equal losers in this transnational eruption of the Palestinian intifada as the Arab Spring. Each, in its own hypocritical way, tries to thwart and distort this uprising – but in vain.

Originally published on Al Jazeera in October 2011

Slavoj Žižek and *Harum Scarum*

In Gene Nelson's *Harum Scarum* (1965), featuring Elvis Presley as the Hollywood heartthrob Johnny Tyronne, we meet the action movie star traveling through the Orient while promoting his new film, *Sands of the Desert*. Upon arrival, however, Elvis Presley/Johnny Tyronne is kidnapped by a gang of assassins led by a temptress "Oriental" named Aishah, who wish to hire him to carry out an assassination. Emboldened by proper "Western virtues," Elvis will do no such thing and manages to sing and dance his way out of the company of the conniving "Orientals."

In an interview with Al Jazeera, the Slovenian philosopher Slavoj Žižek made a rather abrupt staccato observation – a hit-and-run strike worthy of an action hero – very much reminiscent of the fate of Elvis Presley and his Oriental sojourn:

> I think today the world is asking for a real alternative. Would you like to live in a world where the only alternative is either Anglo-Saxon neoliberalism or Chinese–Singaporean capitalism with Asian values? I claim if we do nothing we will gradually approach a kind of a new type of authoritarian society. Here I see the world historical importance of what is happening today in China. Until now there was one good argument for capitalism: sooner or later it brought a demand for democracy … What I'm afraid of is, with this capitalism with Asian values, we get a capitalism much more efficient and dynamic than our Western capitalism. But I don't share the hope of my liberal friends – give them ten years [and there will be] another Tiananmen Square demonstration – no, the marriage between capitalism and democracy is over.

What precisely are these "Asian values" when uttered by an Eastern European, we Asians of one sort or another may wonder? Did capitalism really have to travel all the way to China and Singapore (as Elvis did to the Orient) to lose all its proper Western virtues (whatever exactly they might be) and become corrupted (or indeed carry its destructive forces to their logical conclusion)? So, are we to believe, when it flourishes in "the West," capitalism flowers in democracy and when it assumes "Asian values" it divorces that virtue and becomes a promiscuous monster? Elvis Presley indeed. Let us rescue capitalism from that treacherous Aishah and her Asian values and have it go back to his Western virtues.

What Žižek warns the world against is capitalism with its newly acquired "Asian values," as distinct from what he calls "our [i.e. his] Western capitalism," obviously adorned with

"Western virtues" – which promiscuity has already resulted in decoupling of the happy-ever-after marriage of capitalism and democracy. In other words, capitalism "Western style" brought the world the fruit of *democracy*, while capitalism with "Asian values" is obviously not democratic, but instead is driven to extreme ends – totalitarianism; fascism; coldblooded, cutthroat capitalism – none of which, evidently, was in sight in the birthplace of capitalism and democracy, "the West." The proposition becomes "curiouser and curiouser," as Alice would say. Is that perhaps Buddhism, Hinduism, Islam, Taoism, anticolonial nationalism, Third World socialism, Satyajit Ray's realism, or that of Akira Kurosawa, or Abbas Kiarostami, whose "Asian values" have replaced the proper Protestant ethic and corrupted the good old spirit of capitalism? We Asian followers of Al Jazeera and its featured interviews are at a loss here.

Why is it that the marriage of capitalism to "Asian values" – whatever they may be – results in calamity, while when it was happily married to "the West" it gave the world the gift of democracy? Should we think of these "Asian values" as a treacherous harlot, or perhaps a harem full of temptresses (Aishahs to Žižek's Elvis Presley) who have seduced poor old capitalism and led him to divorce his pious spouse "the West" and abandon their beloved child, democracy? The metaphor is quite amusing – were it not that not only Elvis Presley wished to sing in this particular desert.

Žižek's pedigree

The notion that "Asian values" (we are on a blind date here, for we have no clue what they are) should bring out the worst in capitalism – and thus the "Orientals" who gave birth to such values lack any decent, emancipatory, liberating thoughts or dreams – is not the invention of Žižek. It is deeply rooted in European philosophy.

On more than one occasion the distinguished Lithuanian phenomenologist Emmanuel Levinas (1906–1995) – who was no Elvis Presley and whose thought and manner lacked all theatricality – went out of his way to dismiss the non-European as non-human: "When I speak of Europe," he wrote, "I think about the gathering of humanity. Only in the European sense can the world be gathered together ... in this sense Buddhism can be said just as well in Greek."

The problem is that if humanity were to follow Levinas's decree and gather in Europe to become human they would not be welcomed there – and would first have to shave their beard, take off certain items of clothing, change the color of their skin, chop off part of their nose, alter the pigmentation of their eyes, and Almighty only knows what else to become human. Staying what and who they are, how they were born, they are no human – in the eye of the ethical philosopher who famously sought the sight of the (European) knowing subject in an encounter with "the face of the other."

"I often say," Levinas said (not once or twice, but "often"), "although it is a dangerous thing to say publicly, that humanity consists of the Bible and the Greeks. All the rest can be translated: all the rest – all the exotic – is dance."

So these "Asian values" that Žižek has in mind might perhaps have something to do with our habitual Asian dancing moves – as his European predecessor characterized all we have ever thought or done. Though one may be baffled as to why this "is a dangerous thing to say publicly" given that it was Levinas's wont to say it frequently. After all, on another occasion, he reassures the reader that "There is no racism intended."

Of course no racism was intended – and no racism was understood, sir. It is simply a pure phenomenological truth that we Asians like to dance a lot and become human only to the degree that are close to the Bible and the Greeks. But the question remains: do we, sir, stop dancing when we pick up your Bible and befriend the Greeks? Can we manage to sit still and perhaps learn a thing or two to correct our Asian ways?

Geography and history be damned – the Bible came into being in Asia; the Greeks and their philosophies were known in Asia centuries before "Europe" was invented as a civilizational category. In the mind of the ethical philosopher, we poor Asian folks become alienated from what we have in fact produced and what we have known.

Why, we might wonder – caught up as we are in our "Asian values" – would a philosopher single out and denounce non-European thinking as not just irrelevant, but non-human? Why privilege the Europeans (and their take on the Bible) as the only thing that matters – as the only thing that is human?

There is now an entire industry dedicated to dissecting Heidegger's philosophy not as incidental but as definitive of Nazism – and rightly so. But is Levinas any less integral to Zionism than Heidegger was to Nazism? Is it strange, with that kind of philosophical imprimatur from probably the most prominent Jewish philosopher of the twentieth century, that Israelis do not consider Palestinians human? Even after the horrors of the Sabra and Shatila massacres, Levinas, in an acclaimed radio interview, refused even to acknowledge Palestinians as human enough to be his "other." He said his definition of the other was "completely different," and concluded that "There are people who are wrong." In his thinking Levinas looked at Palestinians, and with them Arabs, Muslims, and the whole world outside of Europe, along with their take on the Hebrew Bible, through the gun sights of an Israeli soldier: as a moving target, a dancing duck.

From Žižek to Levinas to Kant

Arguably Levinas should not be singled out, as the origin of this illustrious record of dislodging humanity at large from the fold of "the West" as the single site of what it means to be human. "What trifling grotesqueries do the verbose and studied compliments of the Chinese contain!" That is Immanuel Kant (1724–1804), the father of the European Enlightenment. Kant insists that

> Even their [that is, Chinese] paintings are grotesque and portray strange and unnatural figures such as are encountered nowhere in the world. They also have the venerable grotesqueries because they are of very ancient custom, and no nation in the world has more of these than this one.

When Žižek asserts that capitalism is now corrupted with "Asian values" and is no longer conducive to democracy the way "our Western capitalism" is, perhaps he had these "grotesqueries" of Kantian vintage in mind. One may never know.

Kant was not particular about the Chinese, to be sure. He was quite ecumenical and cosmopolitan in this regard. For example, here he is discussing Native Americans:

> All these savages have little feeling for the beautiful in moral understanding, and the generous forgiveness of an injury, which is at once noble and beautiful, is completely unknown as a virtue among the savages, but rather is disdained as a miserable cowardice.

Similar sentiments are also applicable to Indians and the rest of humanity – though not in Africa: people of that particular continent have an exclusive claim on stupidity for Kant. Regarding an African who might have said something worthy of Kant's attention, the father of the European Enlightenment avers: "And it might be that there were something in this which perhaps deserved to be considered; but in short, this fellow was quite black from head to foot, a clear proof that what he said was stupid."

The only way that certain "Orientals" were to approximate humanity was if they were to become like Europeans – for which Kant volunteered Arabs as Spaniards, Persians as French, and Japanese as Englishmen.

The point here is not to cite a litany of colorful skeletons hiding in the closets of European philosophy, or to reduce that multifaceted philosophical tradition to these unsavory revelations, or indeed to dismiss the entirety of a philosophical heritage based on scattered comments. European philosophy, like any other philosophy the world over, issued from the vantage point of power and hubris (including the philosophical heritage of empires of Arabs, Iranians, Muslims, Chinese, Indians, etc.), ranges from the sublime to the ridiculous. Nor is the point to cater to a vulgar nativism, which has been one particularly unfortunate by-product of Edward Said's *Orientalism*. From within European philosophy itself, many critical and emancipatory reactions to such racist proclivities have been widely discernible. The point, rather, is to mark the historical enabling of any philosophical legacy by the imperial power of denying it to others. What unites Kant, Levinas, and Žižek (among many others) is that their self-universalizing philosophies are invariably predicated on denying others the capacity to think critically or creatively by way of enabling, authorizing, and empowering themselves to think for the world.

That world, however, is coming to an end – and folks like Žižek have no clue how to read the change. One day they write a piece for the *London Review of Books* denouncing anything from the Arab Spring to European uprisings in Spain and Greece as pointless, and the next day they pop up in Zuccotti Park in Wall Street reading a silly story about a Walt Disney cat falling off a precipice and not noticing it – that cat is clearly Žižek himself and his brand of philosophy. All the cat has to do is look down and it is no more.

Can Arabs think?

The notion that when capitalism was with "the West" it begat democracy and when it went wayward with "Asian values" it became positively promiscuous is predicated on the idea that "Orientals" (à la Kant's and Levinas's reading of them) are incapable of thinking on their own (for they are black and too busy dancing) and producing rebellious, principled, and defiant ideas – a view that has now found its way from the hidden pages of European philosophy to leading articles in North American newspapers. The *New York Times*, for example, believes that – contrary to the evidence of all other revolutions – there are no thinkers within the Arab Spring:

> It has not yet yielded any clear political or economic project, or any intellectual standard-bearers of the kind who shaped almost every modern revolution from 1776 onward. In those revolts, thinkers or ideologues – from Thomas Paine to Lenin to Mao to Vaclav Havel – helped provide a unifying vision or became symbols of a people's aspirations.

What might immediately strike a groovy "Oriental" is a sense of wonder: we have now had an even longer period of uprisings in Europe, from workers in Greece to the Indignados in Spain to students and looters in the UK – a pattern that in fact pre-dates the Arab Spring. And who exactly, prithee, are the leading "intellectual standard-bearers of the kind who shaped almost every modern revolution from 1776 onward"? Do they include Žižek? And what about in the US – people were revolting against the bailing out of banks long before the Occupy Wall Street action began in fall 2011. Exactly which prominent US intellectual does the *New York Times* have in mind that Arabs have failed to measure up to? Michael Moore? He and Žižek are perfectly worthy activists who can appear on Al Jazeera or the *Keith Olbermann Show* and express solidarity with a social uprising. But in what way have the Arabs failed to match them or any other thinker, activist or public intellectual?

What the *New York Times* sees as an absence of leading Arab intellectuals deeply engaged with their revolutions is not just an expression of ignorance. It is a confusion of the order of things. There is nothing wrong with the Arab Spring – or with the European Summer or the American Fall for that matter. This is a winter of global discontent that the *New York Times* fails to read. Thus it asks flawed questions, putting the proverbial cart of these revolts before the horse.

Like all other revolutionary uprisings, the Arab Spring is generating its own thinkers. Marx did not engender the revolutions of 1848; they created Marx; likewise, in this sense, the American Revolution created Thomas Paine, the Russian Revolution created Lenin, and so on. The hands of the *New York Times* are too far away even from Zuccotti Park, under its nose, let alone from the pulse of the Arab Spring in Tahrir Square to know where the latter's thinking takes place. In the same way, Žižek pathologizes "Asian values," perceiving them as having exacerbated the disease of capitalism – so that *his* body-philosophy can be cleansed for renewed thinking, having first disqualified "Asians" from holding any emancipatory ideas – being not in opposition to the delusion of "the West," but in apposition to the emerging world they are helping shape.

Overthrowing the regime of knowledge

When people from one end of the Arab and Muslim world to the other cry "People demand the overthrow of the regime," they mean more than just their political regime. They also mean the *regime of knowledge* that fails to see that pogroms and the Holocaust too have been embedded in "Western values." Nazism in Germany, Fascism in Italy and Spain, totalitarianism in Russia and the rest of Eastern Europe (Žižek's own backyard), currents of racism down through European history, along with other forms of disease spreading from one end of the continent to the other – these developments have been coterminous with capitalism during its marriage to the West. Žižek cherry-picks *democracy* as the only offspring of Western capitalism. As *aterritorial* capitalism wreaks havoc around the globe like bubonic plague, he identifies a flu strain he calls "Asian values." Orientalizing capitalism retroactively Westernizes an authenticity, for the move is entirely antithetical to the system's globalizing proclivity. Žižek's seeing capitalism's demise in its Orientalization reflects back on Max Weber's attempt to seek its origin in the Protestant ethic, a lineage that misses entirely the aterritorial disposition of capitalism since its inception.

Far more important than any ethnicization of the global calamity called capitalism is the vista of liberatory ideas that accompany – not lead – these uprisings in successive seasons of our discontent. Here, fortunately, East and West, and being Asian, African, Latin American, European, or American, no longer make any difference. The divisive world of "the West and the rest" no longer exists. We are on the verge of a new dispensation, *a new world* we are about to discover. In the making of that future, we, ordinary folks the world over, may occasionally look back at these prominent European philosophers – from Kant to Levinas to Žižek – without any rancor or jest and simply ask ourselves if, with that depth of dismissal and denigration, categorically pathologizing humanity at large outside their European tunnel vision, they have anything to say about the liberating vistas of the emerging world. As a philosopher Žižek represents the very last whimper of that phenomenon called "the West," which for so long had frightened the world out of developing the necessary confidence to generate ideas never dreamt of by its own philosophers. For to them whatever we say is "grotesquery," whatever we do is "dancing," for we are (and in this emancipatory acclamation Žižek is welcome to join us) "quite black from head to foot, a clear proof that what we say is stupid."

Originally published on Al Jazeera in November 2011

Fifth Column of the Postmodern Kind

The term "fifth column" is believed to have been coined in 1936 by Emilio Mola y Vidal (1887–1937), a nationalist general during the Spanish Civil War (1936–39). As his army of four columns was approaching Madrid, he said that a "Fifth Column" would join them from within the city. Ernest Hemingway's *The Fifth Column and the First Forty-Nine Stories* (1938) is a homage to that coinage. The expression has developed to mean the militant supporters of an approaching enemy, who would aid and abet them – or give them "aid and comfort," as Article III Section 3 of the US Constitution defines "treason" – once they enter their target destination.

In the age of globalized imperialism and the chimerical creature called "humanitarian intervention," we now seem to have chanced upon a renewed conception of the "fifth column" that one might venture to call "postmodern." The question the term now raises is this: where precisely does noble opposition to a tyrannical regime end, and treacherous collaboration with belligerent warmongering against one's own people begin?

Three consecutive and dramatic events have come together to produce the "postmodern fifth column" that is now winking and elbowing in order to encourage the US and Israel to invade Iran: the NATO military intervention that led to the downfall of Colonel Gaddafi; renewed bellicose Israeli warmongering against the Islamic Republic; and the spin that the US and Israel have put on the IAEA report on the Iranian nuclear programme.

This emerging band of Iranian fifth columnists took one obvious cue from two back-to-back interviews that US Secretary of State Hillary Clinton gave to Voice of America and BBC Persian programmes in October 2011, in which she said the US would have helped the Green Movement if they had been asked to do so. Their palates primed since the NATO military intervention in Libya, these fifth columnists became positively voracious at the idea and soon got to work on the project.

Some of the most brazen and hypocritical among them have openly asked for the US to invade Iran (one claiming that the annual statistics for road and cancer deaths in Iran would be higher than that for casualties in a potential war, another using creative accounting to register a low number of civilian casualties in Libya), while others use convoluted Orwellian newspeak of the crudest kind in a bid to camouflage their treachery. Those who have openly asked for a military strike (aka "humanitarian intervention") à la Libya against their own homeland are beyond redemption. I have very little to say about them, for history itself is a harsh and unforgiving judge. It is the latter group – those who practice Orwellian newspeak – that I refer to as "postmodern fifth columnists."

Confusing the concepts

In order to accomplish their mission, these postmodern fifth columnists have started to loosen the solid foundations of certain key concepts, threby rendering them less trustworthy and reliable. They aim to create confusion and chaos in the minds of those they target in order to pave the way for a military strike against Iran, presenting this as something positive and liberating: not a military invasion, but "a humanitarian intervention." First in Libya, they say, then in Syria, and then ("perhaps, no I did not quite say that, did I, but should the circumstances demand, then yes, why not?") in Iran. Their manner of speech is in fact pre-Orwellian, akin rather to Lord Polonius instructing Reynaldo as to how to spy on his son Laertes without appearing to do so: "See you now; / Your bait of falsehood takes this carp of truth: / And thus do we of wisdom and of reach, / With windlasses and with assays of bias, / By indirections find directions out." If one overlooks the crudity of their diction and bears with their pedestrian prose and politics, what they do and say rehearses the Orwellian nightmare: they issue a statement "against war," which in fact paves the way for war. Or, in Orwell's prophet words, "war is peace, freedom is slavery, ignorance is strength."

Such Orwellian newspeak puts a new spin on reality. In statements against war they say that the threat of war is not that serious, and that even warning against it is perilous to the cause of liberty in Iran. And they do so with a straight face. As Syme would say: "It's a beautiful thing, the destruction of words."

Their verbiage, doublespeak and talking from both sides of their mouth is of course not lost on careful readers, who (in Persian) have dissected their position and exposed their hypocrisy point by point. They recite the mantra that Iran is a threat to world peace, the single line of the Israeli propaganda machine, as if Israel were the sole advocate of peace and serenity in the world. Meanwhile, they beat the drum of war against Iran, all the while glossing their statement as being "against war." The newspeak is no longer merely immoral; it is unhinged.

Another key example is that these postmodern fifth columnists have started playing footsie with the idea of imperialism. There is no longer any imperialism, they insist; this is "an old discourse" (they love the Persian word coined for "discourse" – *gofteman* – so much that they keep using and abusing it). Imperialism was something in the past; it is only retarded leftists who insist the term retains currency. (One notes that some of these fifth columnists used to be militant Stalinists in their youth.)

But now they have moved from Tehran to Tehrangeles, imperialism looks *démodé*, out of fashion: the US army is out vacationing in Afghanistan, Iraq, Pakistan, Yemen, Libya, Somalia, all around the globe. The US has upwards of 700 military bases around the globe, as the late Chalmers Johnson so painstakingly documented, including 234 military golf courses for entertainment. The hundreds of books and articles published that detail the specific contours of US imperialism – most recently Johnson's *Blowback* trilogy – are clearly fictitious, for "ignorance is strength."

Accompanying this cavalier dismissal of imperialism as a global phenomenon is the insistence that "national sovereignty" and "independence" no longer mean anything. Wake up and smell the globalized postmodern roses, they say. A country like Iran (or Iraq, Afghanistan, Libya) no longer has any claim to territorial integrity as a site of potential resistance to predatory capitalism. Nationalism is merely tribalism, they asssert, which has set about portraying "the West" as a monster.

While rebelling against homegrown tyrants, the poor inhabitants of these countries have also (entirely unbeknownst to themselves, but decreed by the postmodernists in Tehrangeles) forfeited any claim of sovereignty over their homeland. "I am sorry, then," they say along with Burgundy to the poor Cordelia of these unfortunate nations. "You have so lost a father / That you must lose a husband." If they lack the kind of democracy approved by the US National Endowment for Democracy (NED), then they relinquish the claim to national sovereignty.

Some create a bogeyman out of "colonialism," a word which these expat professors navigating their SUVs between one college campus in California and another always like to put into scare quotes. So, no, colonialism does not exist. Palestinians are just having fun with the humanitarian intervention of Zionism in their living rooms. No sir, from Fanon to Said to Spivak, from José Martí to W.E.B. DuBois to Malcolm X, from Mahatma Gandhi to Aimé Césaire and Léopold Sédar Senghor: all were bogeymen frightening folks out of their wits. "Ignorance is strength"? No sir, ignorance is bliss.

There is no colonialism, no imperialism, no national sovereignty – these are all fictions that "old lefties" have made up.

Hooray for humanitarian intervention

To crown their grand design, these postmodern fifth columnists celebrate the idea of "humanitarian intervention." No, they insist, this is not a military strike; nor is it imperialism. It is "humanitarian intervention" – just as the US and NATO say it is, from which sources these good folks take their cues.

The link between knowledge and power could not be more pointedly manifest. Not that these folks care to read much beyond their own statements. In *Reading Humanitarian Intervention: Human Rights and the Use of Force in International Law* (2007), Anne Orford goes back to the 1990s, almost two decades before the Libyan uprising, when "humanitarian intervention" was first posited as a move beyond imperialism and national sovereignty. She demonstrates in exquisite detail how the concept "humanitarian intervention" was in fact a ruse: old-fashioned imperial designs expressed in a new register. Bringing together feminist, postcolonial, legal, and psychoanalytic theory, Orford takes the bogus notion of "humanitarian intervention" to task on legal and political grounds.

In *Saviors and Survivors: Darfur, Politics, and the War on Terror* (2009), Mahmood Mamdani, for his part, analyzed the crisis in Darfur within the historical context of Sudan, where the conflict began as a civil war (1987–89) between nomadic and peasant tribes, triggered by a severe drought that had expanded the Sahara Desert. Mamdani links the conflict to the way in which British colonial officials had artificially tribalized Darfur, dividing its population into "native" and "settler" tribes – very much on the model that Nicholas Dirks demonstrates in his *Caste of Mind*, which shows how the British reordered the caste system for their own colonial interests. The Cold War then exacerbated the civil war in neighboring Chad, creating a confrontation between Gaddafi and the Soviet Union, on one side, and the Reagan administration, allied with France and Israel, on the other, moving into Darfur and violently aggravating the conflict. The involvement of the Sudanese opposition parties gave rise in 2003 to two rebel movements, leading to a brutal insurgency and counterinsurgency.

By 2003, as Mamdani demonstrates, the war involved national, regional, and global forces, including the US and Europe, who now viewed the conflict as part of "the War on Terror" and called for a military invasion dressed up as "humanitarian intervention." All the historical facts on the ground were categorically whitewashed under the jazzed-up urgency of the maneuver. Stanley Motss/Dustin Hoffman of *Wag the Dog* (1997) could not have produced a more lavish scenario.

When making a case for the military strike against Libya, even President Obama saw the hypocrisy at the heart of the operation when Bahrain and Yemen (as the most glaring examples) were so loudly calling for comparison. He sought to explain the cherry-picking in terms of the coincidence of American "values" and American "interests." The Iranian "humanitarian interventionists" are even more audacious than the American president in registering no innate contradiction in their hypocritical actions.

If one takes a New York bus these days, one can see though the window that New York cabs have taken to sporting advertisements for "New York dolls" available at "gentlemen's clubs." It must be something in the air. Why call bordellos by their name when you can call them "gentlemen's clubs"? Likewise, why call imperialism by its name when you can call it "humanitarian intervention"? Bordellos and imperialism belong to old and clichéd discourses. The newspeak that prefers "gentlemen's club" and "humanitarian intervention" is far gentler and kinder.

From Iran to Islamic Republic

Another ruse of these postmodern fifth columnists is to try to silence their opposition by accusing them of being agents of the Islamic Republic – not a very imaginative trick, you may think, but nevertheless seemingly effective in the infested pool of exile communities. If one were ever to dare to utter a word against these inanities that they weave together, then you must obviously be a paid agent of the Islamic Republic.

That people who object to such inanities have repeatedly served jail terms in the dungeons of the Islamic Republic, have gone to the point of death and returned during their hunger strikes, have petitioned Khamenei and the Islamic Republic while in Evin prison, and that there are people opposed to their warmongering who have barely escaped the firing squad, and others whose parents have been butchered by agents of the state, makes no difference to these valiant motorists daring to navigate the DuPont Circle and Los Angeles highways.

"Some of these people have never been as much as slapped once in their lives," said Akbar Ganji recently in an interview. "And they call people like me agents of the Islamic Republic." After his youthful attraction to Muslim revolutionaries in the late 1970s, Ganji emerged as one of the most courageous investigative journalists and human rights activists of his generation, exposing the criminal atrocities of the Islamic Republic, a feat that has twice landed him in the dungeons of the theocracy, for more than six years, and almost led to his death after a prolonged hunger strike. He and his family continue to pay dearly.

What representational legitimacy the pro-war (aka pro-"humanitarian intervention") advocates lacked, the *Wall Street Journal* was happy to manufacture for them in a quick fix by implicating the dissident voices inside Iran – a ruse that was revealed as such when Akbar Ganji gave chapter and verse from the positions of major oppositional voices inside Iran (some inside the notorious Evin prison) opposed to military intervention. Even before Ganji, the former Iranian president Mohammad Khatami had very specifically said that in the event of a military strike the reformists and non-reformists would be united against any harm coming Iran's way – a fact that even *Haaretz* reported to its Israeli readers, even if it escaped the attention of the warmongers.

There is a vast and insurmountable difference between being opposed to the criminal atrocities of the Islamic Republic and becoming the fifth column of an US/Israeli design on Iran. The postmodern fifth columnists have confused the two, and have from the nobility of one now degenerated into the treachery of the other.

Massive crackdowns on the opposition, belligerent Sultanism, and many other factors indicate that this ghastly regime is headed for the dustbin of history. And yet when the first bomb is dropped on Iran, the entire nation will be united, precisely as the postmodern fifth columnists from Washington DC to Los Angeles jump in their SUVs, hit the nearest highway and head for cover. Who now remembers Kanan Makiya, Ahmad Chalabi or Fouad Ajami? Their ignoble names, which incited violence against Iraq, are now forgotten for good reason.

Perhaps the most magnificent response to one such "humanitarian interventionist" has come from a courageous oppositional figure named Abed Tavancheh, barely out of the dungeons of the Islamic Republic, responding in an interview while in the city of Arak in Iran, just after having read that Washington DC-based Iranian warmongers are enticed by the events in Libya:

I want to live – and if I am to die for something I wish to die voluntarily and for my own ideals, and I wish to emphasize that I can only decide for my own life, and not for 25 out of every 1,000 Iranians [an estimate of how many will perish in a military strike]. I wish to know for what and for whom I die. Neither the US, nor NATO, nor indeed any other coalition with no matter how many flags on top of it, authorized by I could not care what organization, has the right to impose on me as an Iranian living in Iran any "humanitarian intervention." I could not care any less if these bombs were guided by laser or by God Almighty Himself. I refuse to accept the risk of being among 25 in each 1,000 who shall die, and you sir [addressing a militant military interventionist heralding from NED] so long as the chance of your being among these 25 is zero – because you live in Washington DC and from each side of your location you are safely distanced from here by an ocean and a couple of continents – please keep your opinion to yourself about me and people like me who live in Iran, and kindly do not add any more fuel to the fire of foreign invasion. That is all.

Shedding skin

The rise of these postmodern fifth columnists is actually a positive development for the future of democracy in Iran. For the delusions of a false solidarity among the dissidents in and outide Iran is dissipating and clearer bifurcations are emerging. Illustrious figures identified with the Washington Institute for Near East Policy, the Bush Institute, and the National Endowment for Democracy are now championing a solid alliance with the Zionist/neoconservative forces in the United States, to the point of persuading them to attack Iran to liberate it for them.

We have (dare I dream) a solid foundation for the emergence of a new left from the ashes of the reform movement of the 1990s, from which a few progressive forces have been salvaged. The rest have either returned to their mysticism, joined the fifth columnists, or dropped their protestations and joined ranks with the emerging left. These divisions will not weaken dissident voices. Rather, they will strengthen the democratic future of the republic that is set, willy-nilly, to succeed this belligerent theocracy. Iranian political culture is molting.

My only recommendation to active members of this fifth column brigade is to consider the fate of Kanan Makiya (aka Samir al-Khalil), who was equally, if not more, adamant in encouraging the US to invade Iraq to liberate it. Half a decade later, in 2007, his homeland in ruins, hundreds of thousands of his fellow Iraqis dead, Makiya was in an agony of remorse, acknowledging the horror of his mistake, when the *New York Times* had him reflect on his cheerleading of the US-led invasion of Iraq:

> In the buildup to the Iraq war, Makiya, more than any single figure, made the case for invading because it was the right thing to do – to destroy an evil regime and rescue a people from their nightmare of terror and suffering.

Even though in 2007 the full scale of the Iraqi carnage was yet to unfold, the *New York Times* had concluded:

> Now, of course, those dreams are gone, carried away on a tide of blood. The catastrophe in Iraq has thoroughly undermined the idea of democratic change in the Middle East. It has undercut the notion ... that American military power can achieve humanitarian ends. And it has made Makiya and the others who justified the invasion look reckless and naïve.

Others may, of course, prefer more telling adjectives than "reckless and naïve." For now, I have generously opted for the phrase "postmodern fifth columnists" to characterize Iranian variants of Kanan Makiya.

Faring well

Having said all of this, it would be inaccurate and unfair to dismiss all those who have signed up to the business of "humanitarian intervention" as heartless warmongers who care nothing for their homeland. More than three decades of a terrorizing and criminal theocracy with no regard for human decency have driven many Iranians to desperate measures. Thousands of Iranians have been cold-bloodedly murdered in the dungeons of the Islamic Republic; hundreds of thousands perished in a prolonged and wasteful war; millions have been forced to leave their homeland and endure the indignity of exile; and an entire nation is terrorized into submission to a vicious, corrupt, and subhuman tyranny.

Two years ago millions of Iranians poured into their streets demanding civil liberties – to be met with vicious and wanton disregard for human decency. Millions of Iranians around the globe, proud of who and what they are, wish to go back to their homeland, join their families inside Iran and build a better future for their children, and yet the plague called "Islamic Republic" grips that nation with wicked tenacity.

It is precisely for these reasons that rushing into the military option code-named "humanitarian intervention," over which these exiled Iranians have absolutely no control, is not the answer, because it would have catastrophic consequences of every conceivable kind. Libya is Libya; Iran is Iran. These two countries will continue to struggle for their liberties in a manner that is at once common and yet rooted in distinct histories. No country can be a model for another.

But if war is not the answer – then what is? The answer is not to be found in the wooden box of any apothecary. It is in the emerging spirit of liberation now sweeping the globe, which in one way or another will come to Iran. In social and revolutionary

uprisings, activists do not have the luxury of picking and choosing their model – say the Libyan over the Tunisian. The logic of
social movements is embedded in their historical roots. Thus,
an employee of NED, or WINEP, or the Bush Institute, or an
obscure college professor in California is not in a position to
pick and choose the model for a democratic uprising halfway
across the globe. Not even those closest to the social uprisings,
suffering in the dungeons of the Islamic Republic – not even
Karroubi and Mousavi, who are on record as having garnered
millions of Iranian votes – can determine in what direction the
Iranian democratic uprising will go.

That democratic uprising – rooted, real, enduring, and determined to succeed – will find its own way. Our task is not to
impose a method on it, but to discover and encourage its inner
logic. Lasting ignominy – indeed shame – will be the lot of
those who fail to observe and learn that logic, and who instead
seek to impose their own desires, whether noble or treacherous.

Neither the Islamic Republic nor any other tyrannical – nor
even democratic – state has the right to develop weapons of
mass destruction, at the mercy of which our fragile globe lives
in fear and trembling. Yet the current configuration of regional
and global power has no moral authority whatsoever to tell
the Islamic Republic not to develop nuclear arms. In one way
or another the Islamic Republic will develop nuclear weapon
capability; and there is little that the apartheid Israeli garrison
state sitting on hundreds of nuclear bombs and refusing even
to sign the Nuclear Non-Proliferation Treaty can do about the
matter. Whatever Israel and its US and European allies do will
make no difference. If they leave the Islamic Republic alone, it
will move closer to that capability. If, on the other hand, they
attack it – and indications are that in terms of cyber warfare they

have already done so – this will also serve to push the project forward. This paradox can only be resolved by bringing to an end the supreme hypocrisy of Israel and the US finger-pointing at the Islamic Republic about its nuclear program. The Islamic Republic and the Jewish state are now staring each other down like two thuggish cowboys – and the fate of one has become contingent on the other. Israeli defence minister Ehud Barak fancies Israel "a villa in a jungle" (the racist implications of his favorite metaphor being self-evident). But from the vantage point of the natives of that "jungle," both the Jewish state and the Islamic Republic appear as two garrisons destined to dismantle each other – to the benefit of Iranians and Israelis, Palestinians and Arabs, Muslims and humanity at large.

Whether or not this paradox is resolved, neither the Jewish state, nor the Islamic Republic, nor indeed the Christian empire presiding over them both, will escape the force of history coming their way. We may call it intifada in Palestine, "tent revolt" in Israel, the Green Movement in Iran, the Arab Spring in the Arab world, Indignados in Europe, or Occupy Wall Street in the US and around the globe, but what is certain is that against that force all hypocrisies and all paradoxes will sooner or later dissolve.

The natural habitat of ordinary people revolting against injustice and tyranny is a moral and not a military position. Those who encourage war by way of offering political justification for it have categorically abandoned that moral position. They have aided and abetted acts of violence, at the receiving end of which are millions of innocent and helpless human beings, who have no control over them, who have no protection against them, and yet who must imagine and achieve a better and more just world beyond them.

Originally published on Al Jazeera in November 2011

Merci, Monsieur Badiou

In a powerful essay for *Le Monde*, Alain Badiou, arguably the greatest living French philosopher, pinpoints the principal culprit in the success of the far right in the recent French presidential election that put François Hollande in the Elysée Palace.

At issue is the evidently not-so-surprising success of the French far-right, anti-immigration, Islamophobe nationalist politician Marine Le Pen – to whom the French electorate handed a handsome 20 per cent and third-place prestige.

As Neni Panourgia has recently warned, "the phenomenon of Golden Dawn (Chrysi Avgi in Greek), the neo-Nazi organization that received almost 7 per cent of the vote in the Greek elections of May 6" is a clear indication that the rise of the right is not limited to France. The gruesome mass murder committed by Anders Breivik signalled from Northern Europe a common specter that haunts the whole continent – marked most recently by the trial of the Bosnian Serb General Ratko Mladic, accused of eleven counts of war crimes and of crimes against humanity, including orchestrating the week-long massacre of more than 7,000 Muslim boys and men at Srebrenica in 1995 during the Bosnian war.

As Refik Hodzic, a justice activist from Bosnia and Herzegovina puts it, the implications of that murderous incident are not to be missed:

> The statement that will haunt the consciousness of Bosnians, Serbs and the world for decades to come was recorded in the immediate aftermath of the fall of Srebrenica, a UN-protected enclave in eastern Bosnia: "On this day I give Srebrenica to the Serb people," he announced into a TV camera. "The time has finally come for revenge against Turks [Bosnian Muslims] who live in this area." These chilling words were the prelude to a

systematic execution of some 7,000 Bosnian Muslim men and boys who had sought refuge with the Dutch UN battalion or tried to reach safety through the woods surrounding Srebrenica. Years later, the International Criminal Tribunal for the Former Yugoslavia (ICTY) and the International Court of Justice would judge the massacre, directed by Mladic and carried out by his subordinates, to be the first act of genocide committed on European soil after World War II.

Who is responsible?

In this poignant and timely essay, Alain Badiou dismisses the pop sociology of blaming the rise of the right on the poor and disenfranchised French, supposedly fearful of globalization. He denounces the blaming of the French poor by the educated elite for all its ills, and offers instead a far more sensible view and factual evidence for what seems to be the matter with the French – and, by extension, other Europeans.

Blaming the poor, Alain Badiou retorts, is reminiscent of Bertolt Brecht's famous sarcasm that the French government evidently does not have the people it richly deserves. Turning the tables on French politicians and intellectuals, Badiou blames them directly for the rise of the right. He lists the most recent anti-labour and anti-immigrant statements uttered by Socialist politicians and charges them with responsibility for the rise of the right.

"The succession of restrictive laws, attacking, on the pretext of being foreigners, the freedom and equality of millions of people who live and work here, is not the work of unrestricted 'populists'." He accuses Nicolas Sarkozy and his gang of "cultural racism," of "raising high the banner of 'superiority' of Western civilization" and of "an endless succession of discriminatory laws."

But Badiou does not spare the left, and accuses them of complacency: "We did not see the left rise forcefully to oppose ... such reactionary" laws. Quite to the contrary, this segment of the left maintained that it understood the demand for "security," and had no qualms about the public space being cleansed of women who opted to veil themselves.

Badiou accuses French intellectuals of having fomented Islamophobia, and successive French governments of having been "unable to build a civil society of peace and justice," and for having abused Arabs and Muslims as the bogeymen of French politics.

But this is not just a French thing

The malady that Alain Badiou has diagnosed is not limited to the French, or even to Europeans. It is crucial to keep in mind that there are those among expatriate Iranian, Arab, and South Asian intellectuals in Europe who express an identical Islamophobic racism against Muslims. A significant segment of these expat intellectuals, clumsily wearing white masks over their brown skin, are integral to secular fundamentalists' disdain for Islam and Muslims.

The current Islamophobia in Europe is a disease – a slightly updated gestation of old-fashioned European anti-Semitism. The disease is widespread in North America too. In the US, the selfsame malady is now evident in the fact that US military officers have for years been indoctrinated by a viciously anti-Muslim pedagogy that teaches US military personnel that Muslims "hate everything you stand for and will never coexist with you, unless you submit."

They go further, asserting that the war against Muslims is so vicious that "the Geneva conventions that set standards of armed conflict are no longer relevant," which "would leave open the option once again of taking war to a civilian population wherever necessary"; that "Saudi Arabia [ought to be] threatened with starvation ... Islam reduced to cult status"; and that the US must "wage near total war" against 1.3 billion-plus Muslims.

And what exactly do the white-masked/brown-skinned among these expat intellectuals have to say about that? When the Danish cartoon row engulfed Europe, Salman Rushdie and his ilk – the talented Ms Ayaan Hirsi Ali, Ibn Warraq, Taslima Nasreen and a few other comprador intellectuals like them, keeping good company with none other than the one and only Bernard-Henri Lévy – were up in arms charging that after "fascism, Nazism and Stalinism" the world now faced "a new global threat" in what they called "Islamism."

Yet they become completely dumb, deaf, and blind when a mass murderer such as Breivik goes on a rampage killing scores of innocent people due to his pathological loathing of Muslims and Marxists. They are also blind to the fact that military officers of the most brutal killing machine on Planet Earth are being indoctrinated with such criminally insane thoughts as those taught to US military personnel. Neither do they care when copies of the Quran, the holy book of Muslims, are flushed down the toilets in Abu Ghraib, or burned in military bases in Afghanistan.

The new moral imperative

The ailment that Badiou diagnoses is not limited to French or even European intellectuals, or American Christian fundamentalist Quran-burning pastors, or what passes for comedians in the United States (does anyone outside the United States care to know who Bill Maher is?). It extends well into fanatical secular fundamentalists among expat Arab, Iranian, and South Asian intellectuals, whose pathological loathing of Islam and Muslims has even led some of them to form what they call a "Council of Ex-Muslims," while another group that calls itself "Communist" unabashedly hold its anti-Muslim rallies shoulder to shoulder with neo-Nazis. Still others among "ex-Muslims" are as vicious and brutal in ridiculing, denigrating, and even physically assaulting a veiled woman who comes from their own country on a short visit to Europe.

The disease that Badiou has judiciously diagnosed is fairly contagious and has metastasized far wider than he may care to know. It is now the most recent affliction of the brown-skinned who wear white masks, wishing themselves white: comprador intellectuals who aid and abet European and US racists in demonizing their own people. A very thin line separates these self-loathing "ex-Muslims" from Anders Breivik – except that the Norwegian mass murderer hates their brown skin too, white masks notwithstanding.

What these "ex-Muslims" and their Euro-American counterparts share is a pathological essentialism concerning "Islam" and "Muslims." They are blind to the fact that there is a factual and existential difference between the "Islam" of a rich Kuwaiti sheikh negotiating his fat belly around the table and fearfully watching his cholesterol in a fancy restaurant on the Champs-Elysées and the "Islam" of a an illegal Algerian busboy washing the dishes in the basement of the same restaurant.

That existential difference is the moral imperative of a new intuition of transcendence that escapes all these buffooneries and requires a new vision of what must be the highest moral imperative of a fragile world.

Of course the rest of the world's Muslim population is implicated in the acts of other members of their religion; the retort
"that's not the real Islam" is not a sufficient excuse. But by
what stretch of the imagination, and on what authority, can a
pharmacist or an electrical engineer or a retired journalist, or
a "religious intellectual" tell the bearded ayatollahs and Hojjat
al-Islams in Iran, or Ayman al-Zawahiri or Mullah Omar in
Afghanistan, that they are not real Muslims?

Of course Ayatollah Khamenei is a Muslim, as was Ayatollah
Khomeini, as is the entire ruling elite of the Islamic Republic
with their zero tolerance of dissent. Ayatollah Khomeini was
never a fuller figure of Muslim authority than the instance
when with one stroke of his pen he ordered the mass execution
of political prisoners in Iran. Of course every single "religious
intellectual" (as they call themselves) – must feel accountable
for the vicious tortures at Kahrizak and other torture chambers
of the Islamic Republic.

The same Islam that has created Muslim mass murderers in
Mumbai, Madrid and New York is perfectly capable of producing – and having given dignity, purpose and solace to – millions
of other Muslims leading an infinitely more dignified life,
located in a far more worldly relation to the moral mandates
of their time. The moral and intellectual incapacity of these
"ex-Muslims" to distinguish between the criminal theocracy
that rules over Iran and an Afghan or Somali migrant labourer
in Germany or France is where the visionary insight of Alain
Badiou establishes its demarcation.

The moral imperatives of our time

When a malady thus unites the right and the left, the European
and the ex-Muslim, mass murders and expatriate intellectuals,

then the common disease also necessitates a new definition of "the public intellectual" that focuses closely on the ravages of capitalism – and particularly on the fact of labor migration – entirely irrespective of the varied cultures that capitalism promiscuously engages.

There is a structural link between the neoliberal economics of the Muslim Brotherhood and the ruling regime in Iran, extending all the way to its morally and intellectually bankrupt "opposition" headquartered in California and Washington DC – the fifth columnists who wish the US to invade and "liberate" Iran so they can go back and rule it. There is no difference between the neoliberalism of the Muslim Brotherhood and that of Hosni Mubarak, or the neoliberalism of the reformists in Iran and that of their "opposition" in California – they are made of the same cloth, and that's why they hate each other.

Confronting them is the necessity of a renewed pact with a principled moral position that crosses over fake cultural bifurcations between "Islam and the West" or "the religious and the secular." The moral imperatives that our exceedingly fragile and vulnerable world now faces require a radical reconfiguration of ethical principals far beyond sectarian alignments or denominational identification.

Humanity needs new visionaries to shape its highest aspirations. The principal facts on the ground – acting as a beacon to those visionaries – are the wretched of the earth, the millions of human beings roaming the globe in search of the most basic necessities of life and liberty or else in fear of persecution. Muslims and Africans face the same ghastly discrimination in Europe as Latin American illegal immigrants do in the United States, as Afghan refugees do in Iran, as Palestinians (now joined by Africans) do in Israel, and as Filipino and Sri Lankan laborers do in the Arab world.

That fact is the ground zero of principled moral positions. The morally blinded who hide their xenophobia or political bankruptcy behind a callous "secular" fanaticism and who are indifferent to the terrors that an Afghan or an Iraqi or a Somali migrant laborer faces – just because she wears a scarf or because he sports a beard – must be exposed for the indecency of their position, and thus new alliances cultivated far beyond and above the tired old cliches of "Islam and the West."

The moral imperative of our time demands sublimation of our inherited faith into something with a more worldly grounding. Is Badiou a Christian, a Jew, an atheist, an agnostic, a Marxist, so be he a grace to all Muslims? Is Badiou a French-man, a European, or a Martian, so be he a gift to all humanity?

For now a simple thank you will do: Merci, Monsieur Badiou!

Originally published on Al Jazeera in May 2012

CONCLUSION

The Continued Regime of Knowledge

As the Israeli slaughter of Palestinians – men, women, and children – was unfolding apace and in broad daylight for seven solid weeks in July–August 2014, and as the whole world (in Asia, Africa, Latin America, even sizeable populations in the US and Europe) was aghast at the wicked brutality of what the eminent Israeli historian Ilan Pappé has rightly termed the "incremental genocide" of Palestinians,[1] the equally eminent neuroscientist turned militant Jewish atheist Sam Harris wrote a piece in which he responded to the unsettling question, "Why Don't I Criticize Israel?" The response to this question was as lame as the question itself, as might be expected from someone obviously committed to the wellbeing of a European colonial settlement in Palestine, to the systematic theft of another people's homeland, and to the periodic slaughter of its inhabitants. At one point in his excuse for not condemning the

---

1. See Ilan Pappé, "Israel's Incremental Genocide in the Gaza Ghetto," *Electronic Intifada*, July 13, 2014, http://electronicintifada.net/content/israels-incremental-genocide-gaza-ghetto/13562.

"incremental genocide" in progress, Harris seeks to defend this indefensible position with the following:

> So, when we're talking about the consequences of irrational beliefs based on scripture, the Jews are the least of the least offenders. But I have said many critical things about Judaism. Let me remind you that parts of Hebrew Bible – books like Leviticus and Exodus and Deuteronomy – are the most repellent, the most sickeningly unethical documents to be found in any religion. They're worse than the Koran. They're worse than any part of the New Testament. But the truth is, most Jews recognize this and don't take these texts seriously. It's simply a fact that most Jews and most Israelis are not guided by scripture – and that's a very good thing.[2]

The issue when reading these kinds of lame excuses for evading the moral and ethical responsibility to condemn the slaughter of innocent people – whether in Auschwitz or in Gaza – is not the startlingly bigoted proposition that whereas among Jews and Israelis "books like Leviticus and Exodus and Deuteronomy" are not really taken seriously, Muslims for their part are guided much more closely by the Quran – which, according to Harris's atheism, means that Muslims en masse are a far bigger danger in this world than Jews or Christians.

Sam Harris's categorical, psychopathological fear of Islam and Muslims (commonly called "Islamophobia"), in tandem with his inability to criticize Israel, even (or particularly) when it goes on a rampage slaughtering Muslims, or "mowing the lawn,"[3] ultimately narrows down to that subordinate phrase "worse than

---

2. See Sam Harris, "Why Don't I Criticize Israel?" July 27, 2014, www.samharris.org/blog/item/why-dont-i-criticize-israel (accessed October 10, 2014).

3. "This is the fourth war in Gaza in a decade," wrote Paul Vallely for the *Independent*; "Israeli military strategists talk, chillingly, of "mowing the lawn." See Paul Vallely,"Israel's Mowing of Gaza's Lawn is an Unjust War," www.independent.co.uk/voices/comment/israelgaza-conflict-israels-mowing-of-gazas-lawn-is-an-unjust-war-9659364.html (accessed October 12, 2014).

the Koran," for here he exposes his inner anxiety and conviction that Islam and thus Muslims are the fundamental measure of barbarity. To the degree that the Hebrew Bible might share some such traits, he is convinced that Jews and Israelis do not believe in them. Meanwhile, his extensive knowledge of and research on Islam (for which there is no public substantiation) convinces him that the first thing 1.5 billion Muslims do when they get up in the morning, before breakfast, is to find a woman to stone to death or else at least locate an infidel and chop off his head.

The case of one or two, or even a dozen or more, militantly vocal Islamophobes in the US and Europe matters little unless it points to a far more serious form of knowledge production conducive to murderous modes of regional and global domination, against which Muslims and non-Muslims alike have revolted in successive and simultaneous uprisings. These bellicose ideologues see such revolts (which they perceive to be on the model of the Palestinian intifada that they fear like the plague) as detrimental to their class and racialized interests. Today there is little doubt that militant atheism of the Jewish (Sam Harris), Christian (Christopher Hitchens), or Muslim (Salman Rushdie) vintage is in fact rooted in the common denominator of their rabid Islamophobia. There is a structural link between their Islamophobia and their atheism – or, rather, a professed atheism that amounts to little more than an irrational, illogical, unethical, and thus bigoted hatred of Muslims. Occasioned by their Islamophobia, their atheism feigns an equally critical stance towards Judaism or Christianity, only to hit harder at Muslims and their ancestral faith.

This Islamophobia-cum-new atheism I believe to be instrumental now in the American and European "War on Terror," and therefore definitive of the American (and by extension

European, Australian, Canadian) racist imperial ideology that seeks to control and dominate the (Muslim) world.[4] The Islamophobia that now camouflages itself as the "new atheism" and provides a solid neoliberal foundation for Euro-American (US/ Israeli) militarism locates and places the moment in history we are now living through on a critical path. The public sphere at the disposal of propagandists like Harris, Hitchens, and Rushdie generates and sustains a regime of knowledge that seeks to gloss over a vast history and a multifaceted culture of which they are frightfully ignorant, connects their decidedly vested interests to the ideological priorities of the time, and seeks to keep the formal structure of power that privileges them intact.

This volume and my two earlier books for Zed Books are among the preliminary steps I have taken to alter the texture, disposition, and timbre of our thinking against the grain of that neoliberal ideology that systematically sustains American imperialism and its regional allies and global beneficiaries. I have done so not by taking issue with the power and mood of representation just on the imperial site from which neoliberal choirboys like Harris, Hitchens, and Rushdie sing their banal songs, but from the actual location of world-historic events that have frightened them into peddling their nonsense. What I have written here is thus not just contrary to that dominant ideology, but is deliberately geared towards an alternative, repressed, and hidden world – the vast imperial cosmopolitanism that has been constitutive of the Muslim world over the last fourteen hundred years, only to be left in ruins under the mighty but mendacious force of globalized imperialism. That

---

4. Terry Eagleton, in his talk on "The New Atheism and the War on Terror" at Columbia University in November 2010, addressed the capitalist infrastructural roots of this very issue. Watch the talk at: http://vimeo.com/16769197. Equally significant is Terry Eagleton's *Reason, Faith, and Revolution: Reflections on the God Debate* (2010).

imperialism no longer has a center. Indeed the whole topography of domination and resistance is changing in what in my *Arab Spring* I call "liberation geography."

The problem with the new atheists and their Islamophobia is that what little they know or care to learn about Islam is assimilated backwards to whatever it is they have known about their Judaism or Christianity. Islam shares a fundamental monotheism with Judaism but it is vastly different from it by virtue of its prolonged imperial heritage. Since the Babylonian conquest of Palestine (6th century BCE) and later the Roman destruction of the Second Temple (70 CE) and the subsequent emergence of the Jewish Diaspora, Judaism has been, until very recently, a decidedly *communal* faith, the gathering lore of scattered diasporic enclaves within a non-Jewish political spectrum, including Islamic and Christian empires, and in that sense radically different in terms of its historical experience to Islam, for which imperial globality was definitive to its historical unfolding. In this respect Islam and Christianity have much more in common, although in their imperial expansionism Muslims lost out to Christianity in the fateful encounter with the New World conquest and colonialism.

Successive epic imperial contexts – from the Abbasids in the eighth century through the Seljuqids in the eleventh century down to the Ottomans in the sixteenth century and after – have been definitive of the production of knowledge in Islam, what it means in the plurality of its significance, and thus the constitution of Muslims as knowing subjects. Major cosmopolitan metropolises like Baghdad under the Abbasids, Isfahan under the Safavids, and Istanbul under the Ottomans have been the *loci classici* of (self-)knowledge production in Islam and have sustained Muslims with a multicultural, multilingual, and polyfocal variety of multiple discourses – ranging from law and theology to philosophy and mysticism.[5] Without a preliminary understanding of that dynamic it is impossible to attribute to Islam one thing or another. In the aftermath of the collapse of the last Muslim empires – the Ottomans, the Safavids, and the Mughals – and in the fateful encounter of Muslims with European imperialism we have witnessed a radically different form of cosmopolitanism in Muslim societies. Militant atheist Islamophobes are blissfully ignorant of this development.

This book is a sustained course of reflection on the epistemic retrieval of Muslim worldliness above and beyond its imperial pedigree. It thereby avails itself of the possibility of thinking outside but adjacent to the mighty received European intellectual traditions, which in and of themselves enable dissent and defiance. Thinkers like Edward Said, Aijaz Ahmad, Pankaj Mishra, Walter Mignolo, Souleymane Bachir Diagne, Kojan Karatani, and countless others (regardless of their important differences) are neither beholden nor actively alien or hostile to that European tradition.[6] European modernity achieved a colonial resonance around the globe. That fact neither categorically discredits the project nor exhausts the alternative manners of subjection and agency for people across the world.[7] The impetus to engage with these and similar thinkers is no mere intellectual pastime but is occasioned by massive world-historic changes in our time, now widely affecting the Arab and Muslim world and that of non-Muslims alike. The rapid rise of a wicked

5. I have detailed this theory of Islamic knowledge production on many occasions, most recently in my *Being a Muslim in the World* (2013).

6. In *From the Ruins of Empire: The Revolt Against the West and the Remaking of Asia* (2013), Pankaj Mishra has examined the history of this dialectical thinking in the course of nineteenth-century European imperialism.

7. I have explored one such possibility of subjection and agency outside the purview of European modernity in *The World of Persian Literary Humanism* (2013).

Islamophobia in Europe and the US – whose chief proponents range from the Norwegian mass murderer Anders Breivik, to Dutch politician Geert Wilders, to Somali propagandist Ayaan Hirsi Ali, to the Indian novelist Salman Rushdie to the Zionist atheist Sam Harris – is only one aspect of this epistemic twist to the reigning regime of knowledge at the service of globalized imperialism and the madness of its late capitalist "logic." The Egyptian military junta led by General Sisi, the brutal Syrian regime headed by Bashar al-Assad, the murderous mercenary gang of Isis are all integral to this geopolitics of power and domination.

This book is also a document, a vindication – in the spirit of a battlefield between the ruling and the changing regimes of knowledge – of what we have inherited and what is emerging by virtue of the world historic changes to which we happen to be witness, as we read, write, recall and record them. What I have purposed as the necessity of "dismantling the regime of knowledge," predicated on "an open-ended revolution," is not on acccount of anyone in particular willing it, but by virtue of the historical fact of living it. In that spirit I have offered my writings – whether in the urgency of their immediate reactions to events as they unfold or here in the constellation of their point and purpose – as an act of solidarity with the hopes and aspirations of people around the globe and beyond any religious denomination. By way of seeking to reorient our reading of the world, whether we march in the streets or reflect upon them in the public privacy of our thoughts, we people of the pen cannot but fight shoulder to shoulder with the steadfast resilience of Palestinians in Gaza and Kurds in Kobani.

Index